AMERICAN HOPE

AMERICAN HOPE

What Pope Leo XIV Means for
the Church and the World

CHRISTOPHER LAMB

Copyright © Christopher Lamb 2026

The right of Christopher Lamb to be identified as the Author of the Work has been asserted by him in accordance with the Copyright, Designs and Patents Act 1988.

First published in 2026 by Headline Press
An imprint of Headline Publishing Group Limited

1

Apart from any use permitted under UK copyright law, this publication may only be reproduced, stored, or transmitted, in any form, or by any means, with prior permission in writing of the publishers or, in the case of reprographic production, in accordance with the terms of licences issued by the Copyright Licensing Agency.

Cataloguing in Publication Data is available from the British Library.

Hardback ISBN 978 1 0354 4057 3
Trade Paperback ISBN 978 1 0354 4058 0

Designed and typeset by EM&EN
Printed in the United States of America

Headline's policy is to use papers that are natural, renewable and recyclable products and made from wood grown in well-managed forests and other controlled sources. The logging and manufacturing processes are expected to conform to the environmental regulations of the country of origin.

Headline Publishing Group Limited
An Hachette UK Company
Carmelite House
50 Victoria Embankment
London EC4Y 0DZ

The authorized representative in the EEA is Hachette Ireland,
8 Castlecourt Centre, Dublin 15, D15 XTP3, Ireland (email: info@hbgi.ie)

www.headline.co.uk
www.hachette.co.uk

For Joseph, Martha, and Tom

Contents

Prologue: The Conclave *ix*

Introduction *1*

1: Listening Pope *19*

2: Spiritual Counterweight *65*

3: Unifying the Church? *111*

4: Quiet Reformer *143*

5: Balancing the Books *181*

Epilogue: Gen Z Catholicism *213*

Acknowledgments 231

Bibliography 233

Notes 235

PROLOGUE

The Conclave

On Saturday May 3, 2025, one week after the funeral of Pope Francis, President Donald Trump posted an AI-generated image of himself dressed in the white cassock and miter of a pope. The image appeared on his Truth Social platform and was re-shared by the White House's official X account. Within seconds it had gone viral. A few days earlier, when asked by reporters who he would like to see elected as Francis's successor, the president had quipped, "I'd like to be pope. That would be my number one choice."

The reaction from Catholics around the world varied from disquiet to outrage. The AI image, as is so often the case with Trump's posts, was both tongue-in-cheek and provocative. For Catholics, it was, at the very least, disrespectful. Nor did the image go unnoticed by the cardinals who had started gathering in Rome ahead of the conclave set for May 7—the election process that would decide the new pontiff. Cardinal Pablo Virgilio David—an outspoken Filipino prelate who had received death threats when he had criticized President Duterte's brutal drug war—replied to Trump on Facebook saying, "Not funny, sir," which he translated into ten different languages. Cardinal Timothy

Dolan of New York, who was known to be friendly with Trump, said the image "wasn't good," but when asked by Reuters if an apology was needed, replied, "Who knows?"

Trump's post only seemed to intensify the media interest in the papal election proceedings. More than 4,000 reporters were descending on the Vatican to cover the event and the cardinals found themselves mobbed as they walked to meetings. The public's interest, too, was unusually high because of the popularity of the 2024 movie *Conclave*, a thriller that depicted the worldy ambitions of men in vying to become pope.

During his pontificate, Francis had shaken up the College of Cardinals—the body that would appoint his successor. He had made its membership more international and diverse to reflect the fact that the Church was changing. For years its axis had been shifting away from Europe and the West to encompass the growing numbers of Catholics in Africa and Asia. As a result, the voting cardinals arriving for this conclave had traveled from seventy different countries. Since many of them barely knew each other, they wore name badges during their meetings.

The conventional wisdom had always been that the cardinals would not choose an American pope. Given the enormous power of the United States politically, culturally, and economically, the cardinals were unlikely to elect a pope from that country. But something had changed since the election and re-election of President Donald Trump on an America First agenda. There was a distinct sense that the role of the US in the world was shifting. A few days before the conclave started, I interviewed Cardinal Oswald Gracias, the retired archbishop of Bombay and a

The Conclave

hugely respected figure across the Church in Asia. Could there be an American pope, I asked? In the past, he said, this was "unthinkable." But then he paused and said, "There could be an American pope ... why not?"

There was in fact an American name on my shortlist of *papabili*, someone who could become pope: Cardinal Robert Prevost. I knew him as the leader of the Vatican's powerful office for the department for bishops, which played a crucial role in appointing bishops and in holding them to account. And I had recently been hearing his name mentioned. On April 17, Holy Thursday, I'd had dinner at Scarpone, a restaurant on Gianicolo Hill, with colleagues. Among them was Mark O'Connor, a Catholic journalist who works for the Diocese of Parramatta in Australia. "Cardinal Prevost," Mark said, shortly after sitting down at the table. "He could be pope." Mark had also heard Prevost's name spoken by others in the Vatican and had seen him recently. His words to me that evening had made me think more seriously that, yes, Prevost *could be pope*. I had met Prevost on one occasion in Rome. He had struck me as thoughtful and a good listener. A low-key figure who didn't give interviews, someone who seemed at peace with himself. And, intriguingly, although he had been born in Chicago, he had spent decades of his life working as a missionary and bishop in Peru. He was, you could say, "an unamerican American."

Francis had made Prevost a cardinal only in October 2023. Several months earlier he had selected him as prefect of the Vatican department for appointing bishops. The prefect position meant that he met almost weekly with the pope to discuss episcopal appointments and resolve problems. He had developed a reputation as an expert listener, a consensus builder, and a hard worker. Francis seemed to have noticed some of these leadership qualities back in 2014 when he had appointed him Bishop of Chiclayo, Peru. On February 6, 2025, just eight days before he was hospitalized, Francis promoted Prevost to Cardinal Bishop, the highest rank within the College of Cardinals. Prevost's rise had been fairly rapid but it had gone largely unnoticed. Few, if any, imagined that he would actually be the next pope.

As the cardinals prepared to enter the conclave in early May, the fierce criticisms some of them had had of Francis melted away. The focus now was on how the next pope could continue his predecessor's reforms and, crucially, exhibit a prophetic spirit which engaged with the world. "We need a voice!" Cardinal Charles Bo of Myanmar told me in an email before the conclave. "A voice that evangelizes the hardened hearts of those who threaten the very survival of humanity and nature. A voice that calls humanity back from the edge of destruction! The world urgently needs a new breath of hope—a synodal journey that chooses life over death, hope over despair. The next Pope must be that breath!"

Alongside their discussions, the cardinals had also been meeting privately for dinners in the restaurants of the Borgo Pio medieval quarter near the Vatican and at one another's apartments and residences in Rome. Any cardinal perceived to be campaigning overtly on his own behalf was immediately disqualified so the politics were subtle. Alongside the papal candidates, *papabili,* there was a group of influential and well-connected cardinals known

The Conclave

as "kingmakers" who sought to bring different electors together and canvass support. The "kingmakers," I was told, were not afraid to speak frankly in making known their objections or their support when asked their opinion on candidates.

At this point, the result of the election was anyone's guess, but there were known frontrunners, among them Cardinal Pietro Parolin, who was the Holy See Secretary of State and an experienced Church diplomat from Veneto, northern Italy. Parolin appeared to be the leading "unity" candidate: he would not row back on Francis's main reforms but might cautiously reorder priorities. For the "diversity" group, there was the charismatic Cardinal Luis Antonio Tagle from the Philippines, who ran the Vatican's evangelization office. He would represent strong continuity with the Francis agenda. Behind the scenes, however, Prevost had been quietly gathering support.

On May 7, the commencement of the conclave, Cardinal Giovanni Battista Re, the Dean of the College of Cardinals, presided at a Mass for the election of a new pope in St. Peter's Basilica. When the Mass ended, the 131 cardinal-electors walked in procession to the Sistine Chapel singing the ancient "Veni Creator Spiritus" ("Come Holy Spirit"). Once they were all inside, the traditional command was given: "*Extra omnes!*" ("Everybody out!"), meaning that anyone not part of the conclave had to leave. Now that the cardinals were behind closed doors there could be no outside lobbying or influence on the electors. The conclave had become, in effect, a spiritual retreat. The cardinals were shut off from the outside world; they had surrendered their iPhones and iPads and could not be reached. Their focus was solely on discerning the action of the Holy Spirit in casting their vote. The task was a grave one, since they had to declare, in front of Michelangelo's fresco of the Last Judgment, that "my vote is given to the one whom, according to God, I believe should be elected."

In the meantime, a huge crowd had gathered in St. Peter's Square and was already spilling down into the Via della Conciliazione as people waited to see if black or white smoke would billow from the Sistine Chapel's chimney—black meaning no outcome had been reached and that the voting would continue; white meaning that a pope had been chosen. It's an ancient tradition. For centuries the rising of smoke has been seen as a form of communication between the human and divine.

By the early evening the crowd had swelled to about 45,000, with all eyes watching for the smoke signal. The long wait set off fevered speculation. Was someone ill? Had a pope already been elected? Did they decide not to vote tonight? It turned out that the delay was partly caused by a lengthy spiritual reflection given to the electors by Cardinal Raniero Cantalamessa before voting could get underway. Finally, at 9 p.m., black smoke rose from the chimney. The voting had not yet produced a pope, and would continue the next day.

The following day, May 8, just after 6 p.m., I was sitting on a temporary broadcasting set with my back to St. Peter's Square. As CNN's Vatican correspondent, I'd spent the last several hours on "smoke watch," keeping my eye on the small chimney on top of the Sistine Chapel, which was frequently being visited by seagulls. Suddenly, a television monitor in front of me showed smoke starting

The Conclave

to billow from the chimney. It was white! Erin Burnett, CNN's anchor for the 2025 papal conclave, who was seated to my left, immediately announced live on air: "I think we can say this is white smoke. And they have selected a pope!" The atmosphere was suddenly electric. People started flooding back into St. Peter's Square as news of the papal election rippled across the Eternal City. But I didn't feel excited. On the contrary, I experienced a strange sinking feeling. The cardinals had been inside the Sistine Chapel for little more than twenty-four hours. Such a short space of time suggested to me that one of the frontrunners had been elected. My guess was that Cardinal Pietro Parolin, Holy See Secretary of State, had been chosen. To my right on CNN's set was Kim Daniels, a Catholic commentator from Georgetown University. She'd made the same prediction. Cardinal Parolin would surely have been a competent and able pope. I knew him as a mild-mannered, thoughtful figure who had led the Holy See's diplomatic rapprochement with China and the rebuilding of relations with Vietnam. But did he have the charisma to connect with people? The day after Pope Francis's funeral, Parolin had presided at a Mass with 200,000 young people in St. Peter's Square and delivered a homily that fell flat. By contrast, Francis was renowned for his off-the-cuff "back and forth" reflections and questions with big crowds of youngsters. After the twelve-year whirlwind of Francis's papacy the election of Parolin would feel like a deflation.

More importantly, with the election of Francis, the first pope from the global south, the papacy had moved away from Italy. The Argentine pontiff had insisted on a

Church that pitched its tent among the people, a Church that is "bruised, hurting, and dirty" because it's been out on the streets. He wanted Church leaders to have the "smell of the sheep." Parolin, however, had little grassroots experience. He had never led a local church—a diocese—and had hardly spent any time in a Catholic parish. Parolin was a figure of the Church bureaucracy. All these thoughts were going through my head as St. Peter's Square continued to fill. An hour passed between the rising of the white smoke and the announcement of the new pope. In that time my feelings of gloom only deepened. Selfishly I started to worry about how, as a Vatican correspondent, I'd be able to cover the Parolin papacy. Would people be interested in a pope who was a man of the institution and unlikely to command anything like the attention of Francis?

As Cardinal Dominique Mamberti appeared on the balcony of St. Peter's Basilica to make the announcement, I still thought it could be Parolin. "*Habemus papam!*" Mamberti proclaimed. "We have a pope!" I listened intently as he pronounced the Latin formula. Then my heart skipped a beat. I heard: "Robertum Franciscum." Could it be? And then: "Prevost!" I immediately jumped in, live on CNN. "The first American pope has been elected! Cardinal Prevost!" A stunning decision. My previous feelings of deflation turned into excitement. The new pope, Mamberti declared, had taken the name Leo XIV. This was a truly historic moment, a bold decision for a new era. As Francis's own election had shown, there was no going back for a papacy that had left Europe—at least for the foreseeable future.

The Conclave

The sun had dipped behind the basilica as Pope Leo XIV stepped onto the balcony dressed in the white cassock, red mozetta, and papal stole. After hours of tense anticipation, the cheers of the tens of thousands gathered in the square rose to a great roar of acclaim as they saw the new pope for the first time. Leo gulped back tears but maintained his composure as he looked out to the masses before him. "*La pace sia con tutti voi!*" he told them. "Peace be with you all!"

A new chapter for the Catholic Church had begun.

Introduction

Cardinal Francis George, a former archbishop of Chicago, famously expressed skepticism about the possibility of an American pope. George was a highly influential, politically astute prelate who died almost a decade before Leo XIV's election. A pope from the United States was unlikely, he argued, while the US continued to be the world's dominant power. "Look, until America goes into political decline, there won't be an American pope," he was reported to have said.

The notion that no cardinal from the US could ever be elected pope was ingrained into Church thinking, particularly in the Vatican. Just before the conclave, Robert Prevost had found a moment to drop a line to a friend. "I am sleeping well," he wrote, "relying on the belief that there will never be an American pope."

In fact, this notion had existed even before America became a great power. It was the new pope's namesake, Leo XIII, who in 1899 denounced what he saw as the errors of "Americanism." He had resisted what he saw as American particularism, and worried that America's focus on individual liberty was undermining respect for Church authority.

American Hope

That the next pope to call himself Leo would come from the US is a remarkable historical turnaround. This book is an exploration of what that extraordinary decision by the College of Cardinals means both for the world and the Catholic Church. It is about the impact of an American pope chosen at this moment in history, and how the contemporary papacy exercises its influences on global events. The first year of Leo XIV's papacy has shown that this naturally shy Chicago-born friar is becoming a global counterweight to the Trump administration. Before the white smoke went up on May 8, 2025, the most famous American in the world was President Donald Trump. This changed with the news that "Robertum Franciscum Prevost" had been elected the 266th Successor of St. Peter. The first American pope, although holding a totally different role, is the nearest equivalent to the US president when it comes to visibility on the world stage.

This book is not a biography of the pope. It begins with an examination of Leo XIV's style of leadership, his priorities, and some of the influences on his pontificate, before going on to discuss Leo's interaction with the Trump administration, his broader political message, and his hope of offering an antidote to the growing political and cultural polarization of our times.

Leo has adopted a style that is different from that of Pope Francis. It is certainly more low-key. Yet beneath what might seem a meek exterior lies a steely determination. Leo is a lion who knows when to roar, and the moment he decides something, it's final. Unlike the politicians who are full of bluff and bluster and can see no further than the next election, Leo is charting a course for the long term.

Introduction

Some in the Church, particularly those deeply opposed to the last pontiff, had hoped that Leo's more formal style would mean a break with his predecessor. Almost a year into this pontificate and they are disappointed. Pope Leo has largely continued, and built upon, the reforms begun by Francis. However, as this book sets out, in overseeing a renewal of the Catholic Church he faces a complex task. Among the most pressing issues are the greater inclusion of women and laypeople, and the continuing action he must take to tackle the Catholic Church's sexual abuse crisis. When it comes to reforms, Leo has been handed the architect's plans and a building site with the foundations laid. He must now start building. But, as I will explain, he does not need to rush. As a Church lawyer and mathematician, he likes to follow a process. And at just seventy years old, he is also the youngest Roman pontiff to have been elected in almost half a century. Time, for now, is on his side.

Papal influence

Popes are not simply religious figures. Their words and gestures have an impact on world events, and at pivotal moments in history they are turned to for moral leadership. The contemporary papacy exercises a soft-power influence on global affairs, which is sometimes the topic of intense historical debate.

One of the most hotly contested is the record of Pope Pius XII during World War II. Historians continue to pore over documents from the Vatican archives, examining his actions. Critics point to Pius's failure to condemn publicly the horrors of the Holocaust, a silence that seemed to echo the shameful history of antisemitism in Christian Europe. The Vatican under Pius remained neutral during the war. Before he became pope in 1939, Cardinal Pacelli, as Pius then was, had been the Vatican's ambassador to Hitler's Germany, seeking to broker peace behind the scenes. Once war broke out, however, Pius found himself in a precarious position: he was living in the Vatican while the Nazis occupied the rest of Rome. Pius's supporters point to the fact that he sheltered Jews and displaced people in the papal summer palace of Castel Gandolfo, and to his other discreet forms of help, which, they argue, saved thousands of lives. He did receive praise for his actions during the war from former Israeli prime ministers, including Golda Meir. It could also be argued that his speaking out during that time could have done more harm than good. Pope Francis's opening of the Vatican's secret archives from this period has shed more light on Pius. He emerges as a complex figure—neither a saint nor a villain but concerned with protecting the institutional Church. The Pius XII question still hangs over the Church. When should the pope speak out, and when should he remain silent? It's a question Leo will wrestle with during the turbulency of the Trump presidency. There is an expectation that he, as an American pope, will speak out, and, so far, he's shown some willingness to do so.

What influence does a pope actually exercise? While popes of the past controlled armies and large swathes of land, the contemporary papacy relies solely on soft power.

Introduction

The secular influence of the twenty-first-century papacy takes the form of a prophetic voice on the world stage. The pope is the most visible and prominent Christian leader on earth. His influence in secular politics is strongly linked to his authority within the Church. As pontiff, Leo leads a global family of faith over which he has "full, immediate, and supreme power." He appoints and can remove the world's more than 5,000 bishops; he personally selects cardinals, issues legal rulings, and has authority over the eastern churches in communion with Rome. As leader of the world's largest Christian denomination, the pope is much more than a figurehead. Heads of state and leaders of government see the necessity of engaging with him.

As pope, Leo is both sovereign of the smallest country in the world, the Vatican City State, and leader of the Holy See—the papal government, which, traditionally, "presides in charity" over the rest Church worldwide. The different layers of authority can be opaque and difficult to understand. One cardinal, commenting on the British government's confusion on this point, said: "People in the Foreign Office … didn't know if they were dealing with San Marino or China when it came to the Holy See." The truth lies somewhere in between.

The Holy See has diplomatic relations with 184 states, in addition to the European Union and the Order of Malta, an ancient Catholic organization. It has permanent observer status at the United Nations, which gives it access to the UN security council and general assembly sessions. The pope is represented across the world by specially trained diplomats working in papal embassies. For foreign diplomats, the Vatican is known as a good "listening post," a place to pick up intelligence from the Church's extensive network. This can include missionaries based on the front lines in dangerous war zones or in places long evacuated by diplomatic missions. Vatican diplomats never leave a country, even if bombs are falling on them.

The papacy's influence has changed dramatically over time. For centuries, it held worldly as well as spiritual power. From the eighth century until the unification of Italy in 1870, the Church had control over the papal states, which covered most of central Italy. It was not until the 1929 Lateran Treaty and the founding of Vatican City State that the papacy's relationship with the Italian state was finally resolved. The process of resolving it raised fundamental questions about the tensions between Church and state—tensions that went far beyond the situation in Italy.

More broadly, these questions touched upon the relationship between Christian faith and political power, a prevailing theme throughout the Church's 2,000-year history. For many, the pivotal moment had come with the conversion of the Roman emperor Constantine to Christianity in 312, after which the early network of underground Christian communities were no longer persecuted and martyred but became established as an institutional Church with the protection of a secular power. In the Middle Ages, Christianity became entwined with the kingdoms and powers of Europe, leading to the expansion of Christendom, a period in which Christian beliefs and values formed the bedrock of society and its governance. By the mid twentieth century, however, the Church had recognized that radical changes were needed, and these came with the Second Vatican Council of 1962–65, often

Introduction

referred to simply as Vatican II. This was a pivotal and epoch-defining gathering of the world's bishops in the Vatican, which produced a council teaching document that gave support to religious freedom for all individuals and accepted the validity of a secular, pluralistic state.

As I explore in this book, however, Leo leads the Church at time when, once again, the boundaries between Church and state are beginning to blur. The United States and parts of Europe are witnessing the rise of what might be termed Christian nationalism. Like his predecessor, Leo is wary of this phenomenon and has no desire to see the return of state-sponsored Christianity. His position is to render unto Caesar the things that are Caesar's, meaning to give the government what is due to the government, and to give God what is due to God. In other words: respect the Church–state divide. "Christendom no longer exists," is how Pope Francis put it in 2019, addressing senior Vatican officials. The last decades have also shown that the pope is no longer the *de facto* chaplain to the West. The Catholic Church is no longer Eurocentric, but has become multi-polar and hugely diverse, encompassing the emerging Catholic communities in Asia and the fast-growing communities in Africa.

It was Vatican II that saw the birth of a world Church, and the papacy as a global moral leader engaging with major political events. In the years after the council, the Church sought to develop its prophetic voice among the peoples it served. In Latin and Central America it committed to a "preferential option for the poor," a teaching that prioritized the needs of the poor and the vulnerable. This teaching is embodied by the figure of St. Oscar Romero, the Salvadorean archbishop who was shot dead at the altar while saying Mass because he had spoken out against injustices. The council fostered, as Leo says, a renewed image of "a Church more closely resembling her Lord than worldly powers and working to foster a concrete commitment on the part of all humanity to solving the immense problem of poverty in the world." This pope has been profoundly shaped by the Church articulated by Vatican II. During his years serving as a missionary in Peru, he witnessed with his own eyes the benefits the council's reforms were having in Latin America. It is this vision that informs his papacy.

The Polish pope

The magnitude of Leo's election as the first American pope can only be compared with the choice of Karol Wojtyla, who became Pope John Paul II in 1978—the first non-Italian pope in 450 years. The Polish cardinal was chosen at the height of the Cold War. His election thrust the papacy into the heart of world events and would go on to shape them profoundly.

In response to the growing power of the Soviet Union, the Vatican had adopted the policy known as *Ostpolitik*, a strategy of dialogue with the communist countries of Eastern Europe. The aim was to provide support for the local Catholic churches and ensure their survival under atheistic regimes. It also meant that the Vatican dialed down its public criticism of communist rule. In addition,

Introduction

the communist authorities were given a power of veto over local candidates the Vatican wished to appoint as bishops. It must be one of the great ironies of history that the Polish authorities did not initially regard Karol Wojtyla as a threat and so did not block his appointment as an auxiliary bishop in Kraków.

John Paul II did not reverse *Ostpolitik* but the policy's emphasis shifted dramatically as he became more and more outspoken on human rights. As one of his biographers George Weigel wrote, it was Wojtyla who ignited the "revolution of conscience" which fueled the revolutions of 1989 and led to the fall of communism.

John Paul's visit to Poland in 1979 was the catalyst that changed everything. His homecoming attracted crowds in their millions. He told them that their Christian faith was bound up with their national identity. He spoke of hope, truth, conscience, spiritual freedom, and human dignity, all of which were anathema to communist ideology. "Let your Spirit descend and renew the face of the earth, the face of this land," he told the crowd in Victory Square in Warsaw. Christ could not be excluded from the history of humanity, he said, and spontaneously the crowd began to chant: "We want God!" Tom Fenton, the CBS News correspondent covering the trip, put it this way: "I knew in a moment that everything had changed, that nothing would be the same again."

During the 1980s, John Paul developed a close bond with US President Ronald Reagan. Both shared a deep antipathy to communism and a desire to defend human rights. It was during the Reagan presidency, in 1984, that the Holy See and the US established full diplomatic ties for the first time since the nineteenth century. John Paul's warm relationship with Reagan, evident in their written correspondence, face-to-face meetings, and exchanges of gifts, was characteristic of the kind of behind-the-scenes diplomacy that the papacy continues to exert. John Paul's trips to his homeland, and his powerful public appeals combined with discreet diplomatic efforts, made him not only a highly transformative pope but a major figure of twentieth-century history.

Leo's predecessor also left his mark. Francis, the first Latin American pope, was down-to-earth, friendly, and had a great sense of humor, which gave him an extraordinary ability to connect the Church with the world. He used every diplomatic lever at his disposal to alleviate suffering and push for a more humane and peaceful world. His first trip outside of Rome was to the island of Lampedusa in southern Italy, where he comforted migrants who had risked their lives by crossing the Mediterranean on makeshift boats. It had been a-spur-of-the moment decision (Francis had even called up Alitalia to book his own flights before the Vatican intervened), but it was a decision that would shape his papacy. On another occasion, after a trip to the Greek island of Lesbos, he returned with twelve Muslim refugees on the papal plane. Leo has said that he, too, will visit Lampedusa and has spoken strongly and passionately about those who leave their homelands in search of a better life.

The Argentinian pope amplified the Church's prophetic voice. He wrote an encyclical, a major papal document, on the environment, telling Catholics that they had a moral duty to protect the natural world. He built bridges

Introduction

with Muslim leaders, signing a landmark agreement on inter-religious co-operation with the Grand Imam of Al-Azhar. He was the first pope to travel to Iraq and the Arabian Peninsula. From the south lawn of the White House, he called for action on climate change. He quoted Martin Luther King in his appeal for help for the excluded. And in the last months of his life, he described President Trump's planned deportation of migrants as a "disgrace." It is perhaps no surprise, then, that Francis was a frequent target of attacks from MAGA and other conservative Catholics.

Leo, as I set out in this book, is taking up many of Francis's themes. He is pope at a time when millions of people are crying out for global statesmanship. Increasingly, they are looking to the American pope for guidance, a light in dark times.

Trump paved the way

It would be wrong to argue that the cardinal electors made a purely political analysis before casting their vote for Cardinal Prevost. Nor, I'm sure, did they decide that the US was now in a state of permanent political decline. What could be deemed "decline" might, after all, be the birth of a new era. Cardinal George's remark could be read in another way: the idea of voting in a pope from the United States could only be considered a credible proposition if something dramatic happened on the American political scene.

The moment that paved the way for the election of the first US pope occurred around six months before the 2025 conclave, when President Donald Trump was re-elected for an historic, non-consecutive second term in office. For many cardinals, America's role on the world stage, as the primary guarantor of both the post-World War II consensus and the rules-based international order, was being called into doubt. In the February before the conclave, Pope Francis signaled the alarm in an explosive letter to the bishops of the United States in which he explicitly criticized Trump's immigration policy. Soon, another senior Vatican official, Cardinal Michael Czerny of Canada, was expressing his concern about the effects of cuts to the USAID program, while the Church's global charitable arm based in Rome was warning that millions would die as a result of this decision. Cardinals from the developing world, serving in countries reliant on aid programs funded by the US, were a significant presence among those processing into the Sistine Chapel to vote for Francis's successor.

The late pope chose around 70 per cent of the cardinals who would elect his successor. Among them was Charles Maung Bo, the first cardinal from Myanmar and a man deeply immersed in the suffering of his country. Myanmar was among the countries most hurt by the USAID cuts. The aid had been funding displaced communities and democracy programs. Following the election of Leo, Cardinal Bo told a reporter that the new American pope would "fight with Trump," before, it seemed, correcting himself and saying he meant that Leo could have a "conversation and dialogue with Trump." Several US cardinals have insisted that Pope Leo was not voted in as an "American pope," nor did Trump have any influence on the conclave.

Introduction

Cardinal Prevost was appointed, they said, because he is a citizen of the world, a gifted linguist, and a skilled leader.

But the conclave did not take place in a vacuum. One Church source in Rome told me: "At least two cardinals I spoke to said electing a US pope was only possible because of Trump." What had previously been unthinkable was made possible by the dramatic changes that had taken place in US and world politics over the previous years, changes that included previously unimaginable behavior from an American head of state.

So, back to that AI-generated image of Trump as pope, posted by Trump himself, just five days before the conclave.

Most of the cardinals remained, publicly at least, silent about the image. But they saw, on full display to billions of people, that the holder of the most powerful political office in the world was willing to make a joke about a profoundly serious, spiritual process. A joke may be harmless, of course, but Trump was not known for his magnanimity in humor. It was hard not to sense a touch of menace and scorn mixed in with the laughs. Choosing the successor of St. Peter, whom Catholics hold as the first pope, is the most solemn task a cardinal can undertake. And with the posting of that image President Trump had crossed a line.

A figure of hope

Leo is the first pope in centuries to have served as a missionary before his election. He would not be pope were it not for the years he served in Peru, a time which profoundly shaped him and which brought him to the attention of Pope Francis. It exposed him to communities experiencing extreme poverty, natural disasters, and violent political turmoil. Some of the migrants now facing deportation from the United States are people from a part of the world that Leo knew well.

If the election of Trump opened the possibility of an American pope, it was the past experiences of "Bob" Prevost which made it a reality. He had been noticed as an emerging leader thanks to his position in one of the Vatican's most influential and demanding roles: Prefect of the Dicastery, or department, for Bishops. In this position, he oversaw the appointments of bishops around the world, and handled disciplinary problems such as abuse cover-ups and disputes involving Church leaders. And, as I have mentioned, in February, just days before he was admitted to hospital, Francis quietly made Robert Prevost a Cardinal Bishop, the highest rank in the College of Cardinals and a sign of the trust Francis had in him.

During his two years running the bishops' office, Prevost developed a reputation as someone able to handle complex cases sensitively and competently, something that will only have bolstered the impression in the cardinals' minds that he was *papabile,* a candidate for the papacy. Crucially, he also maintained a low public profile, giving no sit-down media interviews to anyone other than to the Vatican's official news outlet. The lack of any sense of self-promotion is likely to have further helped his candidacy among cardinals.

Here, too, was an American papal candidate who was perhaps the "least American" of the cardinals, someone

Introduction

who holds Peruvian citizenship and has a deep knowledge and love of Latin America. He is a polyglot who speaks Spanish fluently, along with a high degree of proficiency in Italian and several other languages.

Pope Leo has the gift of being a unifier. Those who have met him say he puts people at their ease, and virtually everyone has noted his listening skills. The foundation stone for Robert Prevost's life, as I set out in this book, is his membership of the Order of St. Augustine, the religious order which bases itself on the ancient rule of St. Augustine. The defining features of this order—with its focus on community, contemplative prayer, and unity—is written into Leo's governing style. His time as leader of the Augustinians provided him with insights into the Church globally, as he had to travel frequently to visit their communities dotted around the world. It also gave him insights into the growing churches of Africa and Asia, and experience of leading a complex, international Catholic community.

The word "catholic" means "universal", and it is the catholicity of the Church—its broadness and universality—which this pope embodies. He has French and Italian ancestry on his father's side; his mother's side has Spanish roots. Genealogical research has established that the pope has Creole roots, too, from New Orleans: the pope's great-great-grandmother was the daughter of two free people of color. Archbishop Paul Gallagher, the Vatican's foreign minister, described Leo's "family tree of many nations" at a July 4 celebration in Rome. Leo, he said, was "quintessentially American." At a time of "America First," Leo's life and ministry asks what it truly means to be an American.

American Hope

This book is titled "American Hope" because Leo carries the hopes of many both inside and outside the Church. Those inside the Church hope that he can oversee the renewal of Catholicism but keep it united. Today, the Church in the US is deeply polarized, but Leo has shown that he is working to heal those divisions. The hope is that Leo XIV can follow his namesake, Leo XIII, whose long pontificate from 1878 to 1903 helped establish a Catholic Church for a new era. Leo XIII, who died aged ninety-three, had to grapple with the loss of the papal states and the upheaval of the industrial revolution. He made a decisive contribution to Catholic social thinking, the body of Church teaching that engages with politics and civic governance, while steering away from the extremes of unfettered capitalism and ideologically driven socialism. While he issued warnings about "Americanism," he praised the US Catholic community from which, more than a century later, his successor as Leo would emerge. The American pope says he chose the name Leo because the Church today can offer its treasury of social teaching in the face of "another industrial revolution"—that brought by artificial intelligence.

His choice of name also—crucially—shows that he is working to build on his successor's legacy. It is not the first time that a Leo has followed a Francis. St. Francis of Assisi—the Argentine pope's namesake—had a friar called "Brother Leo" who was his closest collaborator and favourite disciple.

While rooted in tradition, the Leo papacy offers hope for the future to those looking for credible, moral leadership at a time when it is in short supply. His influence in

Introduction

the United States is like no other pope in history. Some of this is because he speaks English as a mother tongue, the first pope to do so in almost 900 years. He can communicate with the English-speaking world. It is not just what Leo says, it is who he is. His gentle, reserved style stands in contrast to politicians looking to dominate the news cycle, while his willingness to listen before speaking, to spend time in reflection before making decisions, suggest a leadership looking to a longer, deeper renewal, rather than short-term political gain.

This book shows what Leo is quietly, shrewdly, some might even say stealthily, doing as he leads the Catholic Church. It lays bare the difficult internal power dynamics he is contending with but shows that by adopting a more formal, rules-based papacy he could move the ball of reform further down the road than Francis had ever managed.

His papacy stands in contrast to the prevailing political culture of the day. In a world of conflict, he stands for peace. In a world of division, he tries to build bridges. In a world so often focussed on "me," he says don't forget about "us." At a time of uncertainty, he offers a sense of hope. And, as I explain in the pages that follow, younger generations see in him a figure who communicates authenticity and a sense of spirituality. Leo is a pope for the changing era. The cardinals' decision to make history by electing the first American pope will have a lasting impact, not only on the Catholic Church but on the world.

1

Listening Pope

I first met the future Pope Leo XIV outside the Paul VI audience hall in the Vatican. It was October 2023 and he had been taking part in a Vatican assembly, a month-long gathering that was part of Pope Francis's ambitious, multi-year project to reform and renew the Catholic Church. Francis's project, known as the synod, was aimed at creating a culture of listening inside the Church. It had opened up discussion on a range of hot-button topics such as the role of women and the use of power in the Church, and the necessity for fostering greater inclusion. Francis had also overturned the traditional way in which these Church gatherings took place. Inside the large hall, overlooked by the striking sculpture of *The Resurrection* by Pericle Fazzini, participants from across the globe were seated at round tables. In the past they would be have been sitting in rows with cardinals at the front and the pope facing them. This time, Cardinal Robert Prevost and other cardinals from the Roman Curia, the Church's central administration, were seated at tables with a diversity of laypeople, including religious sisters from Latin America, and young Catholics such as Julia Oseka, a twenty-two-year-old student from St. Joseph's University, Philadelphia. Everyone, regardless of rank, had the same allotted time to speak, and no one was allowed to interrupt.

Cardinal Prevost, unlike some senior prelates, seemed at home in this environment. I spoke to him alongside another synod delegate Fr. James Martin, a Jesuit priest known for his ministry to LGBTQ people. What struck me most clearly about Cardinal Prevost during our discussion was his capacity for listening. In Rome it is normal for cardinals, at the end of a meeting, either to get into a car or to rush off to another appointment. Cardinal Prevost made the time to stop and give us his full attention. As pope, Leo XIV has committed himself to continuing the synod process, which has faced significant resistance from elements of the Church hierarchies, some of whom feel threatened by a reform which calls for a greater sharing of authority between bishops and laypeople.

Navigating these tensions will require a listening pope. Leo is not simply a big-picture leader, who sets a broad strategy for others to implement. According to people who know him well, he studies issues in detail, takes a methodical approach, and wants to learn all the facts before deciding on a course of action. His leadership style could not be more different from the early months of President Trump's second term, which began with chaotic flurry of executive orders and other changes. By contrast, Leo's instinct is for moderation. He opts for incremental reforms, which, over time, become codified in the Church's law and culture, and irreversible. And, crucially, he wants to strengthen the unity of the Church. His papal motto is: "In the one Christ, we are one." He describes the Church as "a small leaven of unity, communion and

Listening Pope

fraternity within the world." Being unified, he believes, is critically important for the Church's effectiveness in carrying out its mission.

The early part of his papacy has focussed on listening and getting to grips with the issues. It is the strategy frequently used by a priest appointed to lead a parish: spend the first months listening. Inside the Vatican, plenty of people want Leo's attention and his support for their projects. The list of topics he faces is endless, from personnel moves and Vatican finances to crises taking place inside the Church. Crucially, Leo must build a network of people around him whom he can trust. Isolation is a risk for a pope, and not receiving the most accurate information. "Sometimes there's the presentation of the issues and then there's the real issue behind it," a friend of Leo told me when discussing the pope's approach.

A few days after his election as pope, I met Leo again, at a meeting he gave for representatives of the media. In the early days of his papacy, he seemed at times a little overwhelmed. During some of his early meetings, he would apologize for being late, asking for people to be patient with him while he became accustomed to the role. "The Vatican scheduling system puts four audiences all at the same time," he lightheartedly told the National Italian American Foundation. "That way, unfortunately, you have to wait for me and not vice versa." At this audience with journalists, he asked one of his aides if he should distribute the rosary prayer beads as a memento of the meeting. No, he was told. "*Sto imparando*," Leo joked. I'm still learning. This was how he would approach the role throughout the months after his election. Listening and learning. Nevertheless, he indicated even in that early audience that he didn't want all the attention. When a journalist asked for a selfie with him, he refused, which was quite unlike Francis, who regularly posed for them.

One cardinal I spoke to said that Prevost's work ethic, something Chicagoans are known for, was one of the appealing aspects of his candidacy in the 2025 conclave. But even by a Chicago Southsider's standards, Prevost's workload during that October synod in 2023 and again in October 2024, was crushing. He was spending six hours a day at the synod meetings while continuing his day job as prefect of the bishops' office in the Vatican. Inside the synod, one observer noted that he seemed tense. Perhaps the same could be said during the first three months of Leo's pontificate. Along with meeting a broad section of people from inside the Church, a steady stream of world leaders came to visit him. "My priorities are Ukraine, Gaza, and Myanmar," Leo told a friend of his during a private audience. The change in Leo's life would have been a lot for anyone to handle. In a very short time he had been transformed from a relatively obscure Rome-based cardinal into a global moral leader whose every word is carefully parsed and assessed, and who is tasked with using the papacy's soft power to work for peace.

After those nervy first months, Leo seemed to relax into the role. He has retained his sense of humor. When I told him, jokingly, that I now supported the White Sox, his beloved Chicago baseball team, he roared with laughter. On board the papal plane for his first international trip, I witnessed Leo in a warm and cheerful mood: he came to see the reporters travelling with him, posing for a selfie with me and others. His first trip took place over Thanksgiving, and he began by wishing the Americans on board a "Happy Thanksgiving" and looked happy to receive homemade pumpkin pies from two journalists. He also joked that he had managed to complete the Wordle puzzle in three tries that morning. Those who have met with him privately describe him as genial and funny. He's also a sensitive person, aware of the awesome responsibility of his role. As a public figure, he communicates the peace of one who has a deep interior life, something he acquired over his years as a member of the Order of St. Augustine. To understand Leo and his leadership of the Catholic Church, it is essential to understand his background as an Augustinian, a religious order founded in the thirteenth century.

A son of St. Augustine

Robert Prevost is not only the first American pope; he is also the first Augustinian pope: he grew up in the order. From 1969 to 1973, he attended the St. Augustine Seminary High School in Michigan, an all-male boarding school. Rev. Bernie Scianna, an Augustinian priest based in the United States, told me in Rome how the pope's early formation has deeply rooted him in the rhythm of the Augustinian life. The boarding school was a "minor seminary," a school for boys who had shown signs of interest in ordination to the priesthood. Minor seminaries were set up by the Church as a way of educating future priests from an early age, particularly in places where standards of education and literacy were patchy. The minor seminary offered an intelligent young boy with signs of a vocation a good education paid for by the Church. But they weren't always easy places. The author John Cornwell recounted his experiences of a minor seminary at Cotton College in Staffordshire, UK, in his book *Seminary Boy*. He described a time of emotional and spiritual struggles in a cloistered environment, where the threat of clerical sexual abuse was never far away. It left a deep impression on him: the students shared a strong sense of camaraderie and he formed close friendships. In the English-speaking world, and in much of the West, minor seminaries have largely disappeared.

For the young Robert Prevost, however, the experience of junior seminary was a positive one. John, one of his brothers, said that although it meant that Bob spent long periods away from home, he played a full role in school life, developing his singing talent, and taking part in the debate and speech team and the school government. It also provided him with an early grounding in what it meant to live in a religious community according to the values of St. Augustine, something he has sought to do for most of his adult life.

The Augustinian order bases itself on the fifth-century rule of St. Augustine of Hippo. It is the earliest monastic rule in the western world. The short, eight-chapter document isn't a detailed list of regulations but rather a guide for living out the Christian faith in community life. Among the defining features of the order are the emphases on building a community, contemplative prayer, and unity—all things which Leo seeks to embody in his papal ministry.

Listening Pope

St. Augustine was one of the most influential figures in early Christianity, but the path of his life had not been straightforward, as he recorded in his famous work, *Confessions*. Augustine lived in Carthage, North Africa, which at the end of the fourth century was a cosmopolitan hub and an important city in the Roman empire. As a young man, Augustine enjoyed a hedonistic lifestyle and would boast to friends about his sexual exploits. He even had a thirteen-year affair with a woman with whom he had a child. Meanwhile his mother, Monica, a Christian, patiently prayed for him. Conversion to Christianity, Augustine realized, was a process. It did not happen all at once. "O Lord make me chaste," he said famously, "but not yet." His writings and spirituality reflect a restlessness, a searching for God. "You have made us for yourself, and our hear is restless until it rests in you," Pope Leo said in the homily at his inauguration Mass, quoting one of Augustine's famous lines. St. Augustine lived his Christian life largely in a community, first with his early followers and his son, Adeodatus, and later as a bishop.

The first Augustinian pope has himself lived most of his life in community. The Augustinian order is like a family to him. Augustinians have a daily routine of prayer. It involves community prayers and the celebration of Mass, but each friar must also cultivate his own personal prayer life and relationship with God. This will include private prayer, the daily practice of spending time in silence. Rather than using prayer simply to ask for things, this form of contemplation encourages the individual to open themselves to God and to listen to the voice of the Holy Spirit. Leo is using this practice as he ponders the big decisions he has to make. He follows a simple yet profound spirituality of putting his trust in God day-by-day, and Leo has cited a book, *The Practice of the Presence of God*, by a seventeeth-century Carmelite religious brother as key to understanding him. The book sets out how to remain conscious of God throughout each day. He drew on this discipline when it became clear he would be elected pope. "I took a deep breath," he told reporters at a press conference after his first foreign visit. "I said, 'Here we go, Lord, you're in charge and you lead the way.'"

While St. Augustine wrote his rule in the fifth century, the Augustinian order was not established until 1244, when a group of hermits in Tuscany asked the pope to unite them into a single group. In the early years, the order sought a life of prayer largely cut off from the outside world. But over time they became involved in evangelization work in cities and attended the newly established universities. The spirit of a contemplative person in action can clearly be discerned in the life of Leo XIV: he has a deep interior prayer life, but he has also spent years as a missionary and a bishop in Peru. Today, the order is a worldwide congregation with communities of friars and sisters in many countries. It undertakes missionary work in Africa, Latin America, Japan, China, and India. Augustinian missionaries were the first evangelizers of the Philippines, which today has the largest Catholic population in Asia.

The order's headquarters are located near the colonnades of St. Peter's Square, in a 1950s building. Inside are portraits of each leader (known as priors general), including one of "Robertus Prevost" dressed in a black habit and wearing a cross. He led the order from 2001 until 2013, having been elected to serve two terms. The choice of the friar from Chicago to lead a complex international religious order was an indication of the future pope's leadership skills and ability to build consensus. Members of religious orders usually have few qualms when it comes to voting out a superior with whom they are dissatisfied, but they elected him and re-elected him. The skills Prevost developed as a leader within the Augustinian order inform the way Leo approaches his role as pope, particularly when it comes to balancing competing priorities inside the Church, hot-button topics, and global diplomacy. His Augustinian background means that Leo always puts the community first, not the individuals who shout the loudest. "St. Augustine reminds us that before we speak, we must first listen," the pope told the Augustinian Province of St. Thomas of Villanova, a branch of the Augustinian order in the US. He added these words from Augustine: "Do not have your heart in your ears, but your ears in your heart." The idea of focussed listening is key to his leadership style, as is interior reflection and the restless search for truth.

"The rule emphasizes thirty plus times the [spiritual] movement 'within,' before you then go out in service; the two have to be mutual," Rev. Tony Banks, a senior Augustinian who knows Leo, told me. "By going within, and then by dialoguing with one another, you may find the essence of the [Holy] Spirit speaking to you within community, hopefully by the common consensus. By the gift of listening to one another, of dialogue, you will be able to pick up where the Holy Spirit is calling the group and yourself into further service, further work for the Lord. That's at the heart of our community."

Those who worked closely with Bob Prevost say he embodied the Augustinian rule, although Banks jokes that, as a character, he doesn't give off much of a sense of restlessness. "The fundamentals of going within, of seeking, through prayer and through the dialogue, the way that the [Holy] Spirit is calling us, that will be the way that he'll try to govern the Church." Leo's Augustinian leadership is countercultural. At a time when political leaders seek to dominate news agendas and social media feeds and frequently push narratives that divide and rule in the pursuit of power, the American pope offers a very different style. It is, Banks explains, rooted in the idea that religious life—one that is communal and purposely detached from the pursuit of money and power—should be prophetic. Communities such as the Augustinians should "challenge both the internal system and culture of the Church as well as the external culture." It's something that Leo, in his quiet, determined manner, is seeking to put into action.

Banks says that Leo offers the "second" part of a major reform begun by Francis: the synod process. This is an attempt to encourage greater listening and participation and to place topics such as the role of women up for discussion. The Argentinian pope called for a discernment—a reflection ahead of making decisions—about the Church's future. This was to take place before the 2023 and 2024 sessions of a single synod spread over two years. The discernment sought the input of all 1.4 billion members of the Catholic Church. It was, in effect, the biggest consultation in human history. After the discernment comes the dialogue and the decision-making. Leo's job will be to give the process concrete form. It could be said that Francis's pontificate drew up the plans and laid the foundations for building the Catholic Church's mission for the third millennium. Leo, who is seventy and could be in post for well over a decade, is tasked with getting the works off the ground and turning the building site into a habitable home.

"He was a builder of unity, builder of community," Banks says of Leo's time as leader of the Augustinian order. As prior general he held major meetings focussed on the order's development in Asia and Africa, the two areas of growth in the order, and in the Catholic Church worldwide. It was a role in which he traveled, many times over, to Augustinian communities in around fifty countries. "He has a different perspective, I would suggest, to any previous pope in that he is far more traveled than anybody who's ever been elected to that position," Banks points out. "He knows the strengths and the weaknesses of different places and different churches from his global experience, so he'll bring all of that into play."

That experience is vital for a pope leading what has become a worldwide Church. Today the Catholic Church is a multilingual community of believers. That the two most recent popes have come from outside of Europe further underlines the change. Banks emphasized the pope's moderate approach as that of a man who is at peace with himself.

"Only on very rare occasions have I ever seen him move from being absolutely placid to 'No, this is what happens,'" the Augustinian explains. "He's capable of that but that's not the general mode of operation." Most of all he is someone who focusses on "process" and who wants to build "process around him" in a way that brings people together.

Builder of unity

The old Italian saying goes: "After a fat pope, a thin one," which means that the cardinals tend to counterbalance the previous pope's approach with that of the subsequent one. In Leo, the cardinals did not choose a copy of Francis but someone with a distinct spirituality and leadership style. The Argentinian pontiff was a disruptor who shook up the Vatican and the clerical establishment. He offered biting critiques of "clericalism," by which he meant an attitude of superiority among clerics and a concentration of power among a certain ordained or lay elite. Francis would frequently use provocative and salty language to describe clericalism, which he saw as a "cancer" and a "scourge," and which he found evident in "machismo and dictatorial attitudes." More than anything, he saw clericalism as a perversion of what the Church needed to be: close to the people, serving the poorest.

But Francis's comments would often infuriate members of the clergy opposed to his pastoral agenda. The opposition to the pope was strongest in certain parts of the English-speaking Catholic world, particularly in the United States. The relentless attacks Francis faced were without precedent. They included a public challenge to his authority in the form of a release of *"dubia"* (doubts) by a group of cardinals who opposed giving communion to remarried divorcees and an extraordinary dossier from a retired papal ambassador to the US, Archbishop Carlo Maria Viganò, calling on him to resign. In August 2018, Viganò accused Francis of turning a blind eye to sexual misconduct by ex-cardinal Theodore McCarrick (the former Archbishop of Washington, DC), while providing a vitriolic description of "the homosexual network" in the Church, which Viganò blamed for the sexual abuse, and its cover-up by the pope. A detailed inquiry into McCarrick, commissioned by the late pope, found that the Vatican and some bishops had indeed been informed of allegations about McCarrick's behavior—which included the alleged of abuse of trainee priests—but the inquiry did not pin culpability on Francis, who removed McCarrick as a cardinal in 2018 following complaints that he had abused minors. Viganò later drifted into a world of conspiracy theories, accusing Francis of supporting what he called the "climate fraud," and criticizing the late pope for promoting "an inclusive, immigrationist, eco-sustainable, and gay-friendly" Church. The archbishop was later excommunicated.

Some of the opposition to Francis amounted, in effect, to a rejection of his teachings and ministry. Certain Catholics, who under previous papacies had demanded loyalty to the Roman Pontiff, turned their face against him. While the Viganò case was an extreme example, there was plenty of silent opposition and heavy criticism of Francis within the highest levels of the Church, including in the Roman Curia. Francis refused to follow the Vatican script. He frequently ad-libbed during his homilies, and gave freewheeling press conferences at the back of the papal plane. In the early years of his papacy, at 7 a.m. Mass each morning, Francis would give his reflections on the scripture readings of the day and these would frequently make news headlines. He gave more media interviews than any other pope and would often arrange them himself directly with reporters, consulting no one at all in the Vatican press office. Philip Pullela, the former Vatican reporter at Reuters, said that Francis had called him in June 2022 after receiving an interview request, saying: "I've got your note, let's do it!" before asking, "But are you going on vacation?" Pullela said he could then hear Francis leafing through his diary. "What about July 2 at 4 p.m?" the pope said.

All of this caused ecclesiastical heart palpitations in the Vatican. Soon after his election, Francis had a meeting with officials from the Roman Curia and, as he always did, asked them to pray for him at the end of the meeting. "Oh, we pray for you," one of them said. "Especially when you speak off the cuff!"

While there was shrill public opposition to Francis from a minority of Catholics, coupled with a quiet, silent resistance from a section of the Church's hierarchy, most ordinary Catholics strongly supported him. That support also came from Christians outside the Catholic Church and people of other faiths who appreciated Francis's bridge-building. Even Francis's opponents had a grudging respect for the pope's determination to stay in office until the end, serving the Church until his very last day. Most Church leaders held Francis in high regard for his bold pastoral

Listening Pope

ministry to the most marginalized groups in society, and for his indefatigable efforts to push for peace and fraternity. These qualities were on full display when he embraced a disfigured man in St. Peter's Square, when he kissed the feet of South Sudan's warring leaders, and when he washed the feet of female prisoners. To the outside world, he was a leader who embodied the message of the Christian gospel and was a model of servant-leadership.

As with every papacy, however, when it comes to an end the cardinals make their own evaluations. One was a desire that the next pope should be less of a headline-maker and disruptor, and not lead the news agenda every time he gave an interview or a press conference. Toward the end of the Francis pontificate, there were media firestorms when it was revealed that he had used the derogatory slur *"frociaggine"* (faggotry) in saying that there were too many gay men training for the priesthood. On another occasion, he suggested that Ukraine should have the courage to raise the white flag in the war against Russia. While Francis's bold statements frequently cut through, some felt that when it came to interviews and statements, less is more.

Even Francis's most loyal supporters pointed to the need for a papacy that would consult and collaborate more broadly. While Francis called for a synodal Church—one where the hierarchy collaborated and listened—he himself didn't always put that into practice. Part of this was due to his distrust of the system and his determination to ensure that his pastoral agenda and reforms were not stymied. "In the end," one cardinal told me "Francis found it increasingly difficult to effect reforms internally because he worked outside the system." While the pope instituted a council of cardinals to help him in his leadership of the Church, it was largely an advisory body. Francis kept his cards close to his chest and although he consulted, he made decisions alone.

Part of Francis's distrust of the Roman Curia was was due to some negative experiences he'd had in Argentina. In 1998, a network of powerful figures led by Esteban Caselli, the Argentine Ambassador to the Holy See, sought to prevent the appointment of Jorge Bergoglio (later Pope Francis) as Buenos Aires' archbishop. In addition, the same network was behind several appointments of bishops who were at odds with Bergoglio. In 2008, an advisor to Argentina's government even hatched an unsuccessful plot to remove Bergoglio as archbishop and have him transferred to Rome. And as archbishop, one of Bergoglio's own key appointments—that of priest-theologian Victor Manuel Fernández to lead the Catholic University of Argentina—was blocked by the Vatican's doctrine office. There followed an eighteen-month standoff before the appointment was confirmed. The Vatican's concerns centered on the orthodoxy of Fernández's scholarship, but it revealed the tension—some might say antagonism—between the Argentinian archbishop and the Church's central administration.

As pope, Francis made Fernández the prefect of the Vatican's doctrine office (The Dicastery for the Doctrine of the Faith) and named him a cardinal. It was a bold statement. "Ultimately he found those past experiences hard to shake off," one official told me. During his pontificate he would offer blistering critiques, famously accusing the

Roman Curia of a form of "spiritual Alzheimer's" during a Christmas speech to the most senior leaders in the Vatican. In the same speech he also warned against gossip, greed, self-importance, and power. Francis embarked on a long reform of the Curia, culminating in 2022 with a new constitution for the administration, *Praedicate evangelium* (Preach the gospel), which was only the fourth of its kind since 1588. It sought to enshrine Francis's vision of the Church, but the problem came in its implementation. The reforms were set out on paper but, because of Francis's distrust of the central administration, he struggled to embed deeper change. Some of the disaffection was felt when, in the heat of August 2022, when most of Rome was on vacation, the pope called a meeting of cardinals to discuss the constitution. The timing didn't help, and one cardinal was heard complaining that they hadn't been called for a discussion but were essentially being informed of what had already been decided.

In Pope Leo XIV, the cardinals have someone who will put greater trust in decision-making processes, and who is willing to work with the Vatican system. Leo relies on the Roman Curia. In his public meetings, he usually reads the speeches prepared for him by the Vatican without going off-script. While Francis would throw things up in the air for discussion, frequently setting off mini news explosions and constantly keeping people on their toes waiting for the next surprise, Leo has a more strategic approach. While Francis would merely skim through the Italian newspapers, the American pope is more conscious of what is being written in the international news media, particularly in the English-speaking world. He is the first pope to wear an Apple watch, use a smartphone, write his own emails, and use WhatsApp. When he sends emails, he's known to sign them off "Pope Leo XIV aka Bob," and he replies promptly. In meetings he is straightforward, direct, and relaxed.

Following his election, Leo signaled his new approach by restoring the tradition of paying a €500 ($580) bonus to each of the Vatican employees for their work during the papal interregnum period, something Francis had opted against due to the state of the Vatican's finances at the time and because he had succeeded a predecessor who had resigned and not died. But Leo's early speech to the Church's central administration was far more significant. One senior Vatican official told me that it was the most important intervention of the first months of his papacy because it made plain Leo's intention of working with the Roman Curia.

"Popes pass, the Curia remains," Leo told the employees of the Holy See and Vatican City State on May 24, 2025. He thanked them for their service and told them that their work ensured that "the Pope's ministry may be implemented in the best way." In other words: I can't do this job without you. I want to work with you.

But this should not be mistaken for a reluctance to reform. Leo's papacy is institutionalizing Francis's reforms, embedding them more deeply into the Church's culture and structures while ensuring that, as far as possible, the whole Church is on board. In certain respects, Leo has a chance of succeeding in reform where Francis was unable, by working with the Roman Curia and taking institutional reforms and changes seriously. Leo is seeking to execute a "both/and" approach, where he can embrace his predecessor's priorities for a Church that is missionary, which goes out to the margins of society, that stands in solidarity with migrants and the poor, while at the same time overseeing an organizational renewal. The both/and idea is deeply Catholic: it's one that rejects a binary solution and reflects the etymology of the word "catholic", meaning "universal" or "of the whole."

"Diversity is not the opposite of unity," Banks explains. "We've got to the point in the Church where [it's] a diversity which says 'we are right' as opposed to 'we need to listen to the others and what they are offering in that diversity,' and that's what he will bring." The Augustinian explains that the pendulum "probably needs to return a little to the centre of the Church," a sentiment likely to have been shared by a good number of cardinals when they elected the new pope.

Old and new worlds

The pope's early life and training took place during a period of profound reform inside the Catholic Church. Robert Prevost began his religious life as a teenager, attending a junior seminary, which to many is a feature of a Church of the past, one that existed before the reforms of the Second Vatican Council. He was born in 1955, so as a young man had some experience of the pre-Vatican II, becoming an altar server at the age of six. Both his parents were serious Catholics, and his mother was a major influence on his faith, something that is true of many priests and also of St. Augustine. His roots encapsulate the catholicity of the Church.

The future pope's mother, Mildred (known as Millie), was an educator, librarian, and an accomplished singer. She encouraged her children to attend early morning Mass, and Robert, the youngest of her three boys, was an altar server, the traditional route into a priestly vocation. According to both his brothers, Leo showed an interest in the priesthood from a very early age, with John even saying people would predict that his younger brother would one day become pope. "Around age six, I was also an altar server in my parish. Before going to school—it was a parish school—we would attend 6:30 a.m. Mass. Mom always woke us up saying, 'Let's go to Mass,'" Leo told a group of children in July 2025. It offered an insight into a devoutly Catholic family, with the pope's father, Louis, a school principal, also involved in the local parish. Such an upbringing wasn't totally unusual for that time, and it would be wrong to see the southside of Chicago, where the pope grew up, as a sort of Catholic ghetto.

As Margaret O'Brien Steinfels, a US Catholic commentator, has pointed out, the southside of Chicago was a place where "ethnicity, race, and class intersected." It was different from the sometimes embattled Irish-led Catholic communities of Boston, New York, and Philadelphia, and comprised a rich mix of migrants communities, including Polish Catholics, Bohemians, Slovaks, Italians, and Lithuanians.

Leo lived close to Bronzeville, which is home to thousands of Black people. He was there during the period of the "white flight" from Chicago, a time of demographic change and racial divides. While the young Bob Prevost grew up in a stable Catholic family, he did so within a rapidly changing culture, both in the outside world but also within the Catholic Church. The world's bishops attending Vatican II had voted overwhelmingly in favor of reforming the Catholic liturgy. Before the council the Mass was said by the priest facing away from the congregation (known as *ad orientem*) and was spoken in Latin. After the council, the Mass could be said in local languages with the focus on the "active participation" of all the people and with the priest facing toward the congregation. The reforms took place swiftly. They were aimed at recovering truths of the faith which reformers believed had been obscured over the centuries. All of this was witnessed by the young Robert Prevost, an altar server for the older form of the Mass.

"We had to learn Latin for Mass, but then it changed to English for me since I was born and raised in the US," Leo explained in a meeting with young people. "What mattered wasn't the language of the celebration but the experience of being with other kids serving Mass, the friendship, and that closeness to Jesus in the Church. It was always something beautiful."

Leo's later formation also saw him in different worlds; both in the ferment of Catholic reform in Chicago, and in the more conservative environment of Rome during the papacy of John Paul II.

After leaving school, he enrolled as an undergraduate student at Villanova University in Pennsylvania, which was run by the Augustinians. Rather than go straight into a seminary or a religious order, he was an ordinary student, living for a time on campus, and taking a course that many would not expect of a future pope. He earned a degree in mathematics while minoring in philosophy. He also took courses on Hebrew and Latin. His math studies disrupt that old stereotype that faith and science stand in opposition to one another and point to a mind that prefers order and formula. Following his graduation in 1977, Leo was clothed in the black habit of the Augustinians and became a novice of the order. He made his first vows a year later and his final vows in 1981.

The years after Vatican II were heady times for the Church as it began to implement the council's decisions. The council had been driven by two main goals. The first was to reconnect the contemporary Church with early Christianity through a return to original sources (a concept known as *ressourcement,* to better "resource" the Church for its mission). The second was to update the Church's mission for the present era (the concept of *aggiornamento,* an updating). All of this entailed a careful sifting of Catholic tradition, to determine what remained essential to the nature of the Church and what could be dispensed with. It was the equivalent of scraping away the barnacles on the barque of St. Peter so that the Church could sail more effectively.

Pope John XXIII, who presided over the council, said he wanted to open the windows of the Church to "let in more light and air" and to "let the people see in." Significantly, the council prioritized an understanding of the Catholic Church as the "People of God" with its hierarchy coming second. This moved away from the notion of the Church as a "fortress." Instead, Vatican II called for the Church to share the "joys and the hopes, the griefs and the anxieties of the men of this age, especially those who are poor or in any way afflicted." It also issued a landmark condemnation of antisemitism and opened the door to for inter-religious dialogue.

From 1977 to 1982, Robert Prevost studied at the Catholic Theological Union (CTU) in Chicago, which was founded in 1968 as a result of Vatican II. CTU was an institution imbued with the reforming spirit of the council. It provided a formation for priests alongside nuns and laypeople, an environment that was very different from the all-male seminaries, where future priests were formed together and set apart from the outside world. In the wake of the council, clergy and some religious friars and monks started to receive their higher education in universities alongside laypeople. Rev. Mark Francis, leader of the US province of the Viatorians, a religious order, studied there at the same time as the future pope and is a former president of the union.

"We were studying now with laypeople, and with women," he told me. "I remember in our own reflection group there was a woman who had given up a lucrative career and was dedicating her life to the Church, getting an MDiv degree, and she also felt called to priesthood."

According to Rev. Francis, the reflection group was led a by a nun from the Sacred Heart religious order. She was a scripture scholar, and she, too, felt called to the priesthood. "So, we were kind of surrounded by that [issue] as we started our theological studies," he explained. The teaching of the Catholic Church holds that only men can be ordained, a position reiterated by John Paul II in a

1994 ruling which he said should be "definitively held by all the Church's faithful." It was a ruling that his successors, including Pope Francis, maintained. In the years following the council, however, the ordination of women was on the agenda for discussion. And as Rev. Francis explained, it was a topic that was prevalent at CTU. In 1981, when the future pope was still a CTU student, a protest took place during the ordination of seventeen male CTU students as deacons. During the ceremony at St. Thomas the Apostle Church in Chicago each of the protestors wore a light-blue ribbon to signal their support for women's ordination. It is not known whether the young Robert Prevost attended this ceremony, but he is likely to have heard about it.

Aside from exposure to debates over the ordination question, which remains an intensely contested topic to this day, one of the benefits of the training that Leo received at CTU, Rev. Francis explained, was to see laypeople and women "as collaborators and as equals in ministry." Such a training was an antidote to the clericalism that Leo's predecessor often complained about. While Francis appointed a number of women to senior roles in the Vatican, for many senior prelates, women in the Roman Curia are not always seen as "equals in ministry." The senior positions remain male-dominated. Leo XIV, however, may be the first pope to have been trained both alongside and by women who have felt called to the priesthood. He is comfortable working alongside women in his ministry.

But the pope is not someone who has expressed firm views on contested Church issues. While he was surrounded by those pushing for women's ordination at

CTU, he is not known to have declared his position on the matter. He maintains a certain inscrutability. He listens closely but doesn't rush to conclusions. It is an approach that, like Francis's unscripted style, has made people in the Vatican nervous as they try to predict the direction of his papacy.

After Chicago, Robert Prevost went to Rome to begin studies for a doctorate in canon law at Rome's Pontifical University of St. Thomas Aquinas, known as the Angelicum. The year was 1984 and the papacy of John Paul II was at the height of its influence. It was a period when Rome had decided to press pause on some of the reforms of the council. While the Polish pope took bold steps to open a dialogue with other religious leaders, any theologians who stepped out of line faced investigations. Cardinal Joseph Ratzinger, the future Pope Benedict XVI, was in charge of the doctrine office and he was pursuing a more cautious interpretation of Vatican II. As a result, the atmospheres in Rome and in Chicago were poles apart at that time. Nevertheless, the young Augustinian enjoyed his first stint in Rome, which grounded him in an early appreciation and understanding of Church law. Respect for process and the law will be the hallmarks of Leo's papacy.

Rev. Francis remembers his young Augustinian classmate as a "rather restrained," reserved personality and also "a good guy, very approachable, easy to talk to." He pointed to Robert's natural conservatism in the sense of seeking to conserve. He sees stability as desirable and prefers to avoid grand gestures. "You also have to understand he's an Augustinian, and the Augustinians by nature tend to hew toward the conservative side, in a good way," he said. "He's going to tend to be the stable kind of person." But Prevost's training will have left him at ease with the synodal reform project begun by Pope Francis, with Rev. Francis describing it as a continuation of Vatican II. It's often said that a council in the Catholic Church takes a century to implement, and Pope Leo is now shepherding a key phase in that implementation.

Robert Prevost was ordained by two prominent progressive figures in the United States Church. He was ordained a deacon in 1981 by Bishop Thomas Gumbleton, a leading advocate for peace and social justice, and then to the priesthood by Archbishop Jean Jadot, the papal representative to the United States from 1973–80. Papal representatives play a key role in appointing bishops by drawing up shortlists of candidates, and Jadot tended to seek out candidates who were interested in social justice and a more pastoral approach to their work. Gumbleton was long considered one of the most progressive figures in the US Church hierarchy and had sometimes clashed with his fellow bishops. He was a founding member of the peace group Pax Christi USA and was arrested for civil disobedience when he protested against nuclear weapons and the 2003 Iraq War. Ordination to the diaconate by Gumbleton and to the priesthood by Jadot placed the future pope at the center of the reform-minded Catholic world. It was a time when leading figures in the US wanted a prophetic Church that spoke out about social justice. On the other hand, his time in Rome gave him another perspective: an understanding, perhaps, that reformers need to take people with them and listen to all sides of the argument. Prevost, however, was not in Rome for long before he was sent away for what was the most formative experience of his life.

The missionary pope

If Prevost's Augustinian background is one foundation stone for his papal ministry, then his experience as a missionary in Peru is the second. He is—according to the available historical evidence—the first pope in the Catholic Church's 2,000-year history to have served as a missionary in Latin America. A pope who has previously served as a missionary in the classical sense of the word is also extremely rare.

Most of Leo's immediate predecessors had all led major archdioceses before being elected pontiff. Francis led the archdiocese of Buenos Aires, Benedict XVI had led Munich and Freising, and John Paul II Kraków. The significance of a pope who has been a missionary cannot be overestimated. Throughout his pontificate, Francis had called for a Church that leaves its comfort zone, that gets out of the religious buildings and immerses itself in the suffering of humanity. He wanted, in effect, a missionary Church. In Pope Leo, the Church has a leader who has sought to put the Francis vision into action.

"Pope Francis spoke a lot about the peripheries, but Leo is the first pope from the peripheries in one hundred years, because he was a missionary bishop in a diocese like Chiclayo [Peru]," Andrea Tornielli, the editorial director of *Vatican News*, told me. Leo's missionary experience reflects a shifting vision for the Church, one that doesn't wait for the people to come through its doors but which goes out to meet the people; a Church that is less institutionally focussed and less Eurocentric. In certain respects, Leo's experience is akin to that of the early Christians who, with little institutional support, went out into foreign lands to evangelize.

It is also true that the election of the first American pope would never have been possible if a young Robert Prevost had not been sent to Peru. Nor would it have been possible without an Argentinian pontiff who identified Prevost as a leader, appointing him first as a bishop and then bringing him to Rome. Rev. Francis, Leo's former classmate, believes that Prevost's experience in Latin America is the reason he and the Argentinian pontiff got along so well and why Francis "saw in him someone to trust." But none of this was preordained. When he was a cardinal, Robert Prevost was candid in saying that he and Francis had had disagreements in the past. "I won't tell you the reason, but let's just say that when Cardinal Bergoglio and I met, we weren't always in agreement," he said in 2023, at an event organized by Peruvian bishops to mark his pastoral work in the country. The root of the disagreements has not been publicly disclosed, but one Church source told me that it concerned the deployment of Augustinian friars in the archdiocese of Buenos Aires while Bergoglio was archbishop. At the time, Prevost was prior general of the order. When Bergoglio became Pope Francis in 2013, memories of their clash prompted Prevost to tell some of his fellow Augustinians: "Well, that's very good, and thank God I'll never be a bishop." Later, as Prevost finished his time as leader of the Augustinians, he asked the pope to celebrate a Mass for the order's general chapter (the equivalent of an AGM). During that Mass, Francis spoke about the "restlessness" found in the writings of St. Augustine, and warned the friars, with a nod and a wink, about "personal interests, of the functionality of our works, of our careers," and of becoming "too comfy" or like "old bachelors." It was a provocative homily, typical of Francis, but it had prescience for the outgoing prior general, Robert Prevost, who had hoped to have time for a rest, rather than to be restless. After the Mass, the pope said to him, "Now rest," to which Prevost replied, "Thank you, Holy Father, I hope to rest."

Nevertheless, a few months later, Francis sent Prevost to Chiclayo, first as "apostolic administrator" and a bishop at the end of 2014 and then as the diocesan bishop in September 2015. Pope Francis trusted his instincts about people and, despite their past disagreements, he had identified in Prevost someone who could be handed great responsibility. Not too much should be read into their past disagreements. Francis was always happy to have a robust back and forth and encouraged people to speak their minds with him. He said he preferred that people raised problems directly with each other rather than going behind their backs and gossiping.

Although Francis had identified Prevost as a leader early on in his pontificate, he waited several years before appointing him to positions in Rome. In 2019, Prevost was chosen as a member of the Vatican department for clergy and then, in November 2020, as a member of the Vatican office for bishops. Francis would also appoint Prevost as the apostolic administrator (*de facto* bishop) of the diocese of Callao, Peru, a role he held alongside his position as Chiclayo's bishop from 2020–21.

The Dicastery for Bishops is one of the most powerful offices in the Vatican. Because it handles the appointments of bishops along with disciplinary issues and the removal of bishops from office, its work is extremely sensitive. The prefect of the dicastery meets the pope once a week, usually on a Saturday morning, to discuss appointments.

Members of the dicastery—essentially board members—take part in regular meetings, usually on Thursday mornings, where they discuss episcopal appointments. They work their way through large dossiers compiled on each candidate and make recommendations to the pope. For each diocese (local chuch) a shortlist of three candidates is drawn up and submitted to Rome by the pope's local representative. Many of the dicastery's members are cardinals, so the pope's decision to include the bishop of Chiclayo was quite unusual. It was a sign that Francis held Prevost in high esteem. During his pontificate, the pope also chose the first ever female members of the department.

Prevost's appointment to the dicastery gave him an introduction to the Vatican office he would go on to run. For three years he was exposed to the highest levels of the Church's central administration. The role also introduced to him to other cardinal members. For much of Francis's pontificate, the dicastery was led by Cardinal Marc Ouellet, a French-Canadian polyglot and theologian. In the 2013 conclave, Ouellet had been one of the leading conservative candidates for the papacy, securing twenty-two votes in the first ballot. According to Gerard

O'Connell, a respected Vatican reporter, one cardinal had been overheard urging his fellow electors to vote for Ouellet because "Bergoglio is too old!" Unfortunately for Cardinal Ouellet, just before the conclave started, he had given an interview to the Canadian broadcaster CBC, saying he would be "ready" to serve as pope if chosen. In an election where any hint of self-promotion is the deathblow for a candidacy, he did himself no favors. I was told Ouellet was left disappointed by the outcome of the 2013 conclave. Nevertheless, he remained in post for a decade.

The importance of the bishops' dicastery, and the fact it had been led by a heavyweight such as Ouellet, meant that Francis had a big decision to make when choosing Ouellet's successor. The Argentinian pope opted for Prevost. In addition, along with leading the bishop's office in the Vatican, Prevost also took responsibility for the Pontifical Commission for Latin America. Prevost confessed that he would have preferred to have stayed in Peru but had accepted the responsibility in the Vatican out of a sense of obedience. For Francis, Prevost's experience as a missionary bishop was crucial. For two years, Prevost oversaw the running of one of the Vatican's most demanding offices. It required relentless work. But it also gave him a panoramic overview of the entire Church worldwide. In many respects, this position was the ideal training for the papacy. Francis's decision to appoint Prevost to lead the bishops' dicastery and make him a cardinal effectively placed Prevost in a prime position for his election as pope. "If Francis had been able to vote in the conclave, he would have voted for Prevost," is how one Vatican official put it to me.

There was another attribute, too, that made Prevost a suitable candidate for pope. His missionary work and his global traveling have afforded him a papal superpower: the gift of languages. He can switch effortlessly between Italian, English, and Spanish and is also comfortable speaking French and German. Francis was only really happy speaking Spanish or Italian, and while he could understand English he would rely on translators. John Paul II was multilingual, as was Benedict XVI, but neither of them had great confidence in English. Leo is the first native English-speaking pope since the twelfth-century papacy of Nicolas Breakspear, an Englishman who was elected Pope Adrian IV and who led the Church from 1154 to 1159. English gives Leo a huge advantage on the world stage, ensuring that his words can easily be packaged into soundbites by the media. After a shooting at a Catholic school in Minnesota in August 2025, Leo's appeal, in English, for an end to the "pandemic of arms" was reported around the world. Nevertheless, he has at times appeared reluctant to speak too often in English, sensitive of the pope's role as Bishop of Rome and keen, like the missionaries of the past, to speak the local language.

Missionary in Peru

The role of Bishop of Chiclayo was a difficult assignment. Pope Francis's decision to send a North American Augustinian to that particular diocese in northern Peru was described to me as a "crisis appointment." For years, Chiclayo had been a stronghold of Opus Dei (Work of

God), a conservative Catholic group founded in Spain during the dictatorship of Francisco Franco. Opus Dei has a largely lay membership that includes some highly influential figures. Its central belief is that anyone—be they lawyer, politician, or businessman—can attain holiness through their daily work. Critics of Opus Dei have drawn attention to the fact that it has strong ties to right-wing political groups, questionable past recruitment practices, and a rigid spirituality. Opus Dei famously featured in Dan Brown's novel *The Da Vinci Code* as a rather sinister organization, although its portrayal was largely fictional. Pope Francis had reservations about Opus Dei. He ordered a restructuring of the order's leadership to make it more accountable to the Holy See and to put an end to the highly unusual tradition of automatically appointing its leader a bishop. These moves rattled Opus Dei's leadership, which had been accustomed to reporting directly to the pope. In Peru, Opus Dei has influence over thousands of members. It runs organizations such as schools, universities, and hospitals. Peru is also home to the first Opus Dei cardinal, Juan Luis Cipriani Thorne, a prominent conservative. In 2019, however, Cipriani was placed under Vatican sanctions following an allegation of sexual abuse dating from four decades earlier, an allegation he vigorously denies.

In appointing Prevost to Chiclayo, Francis ensured a different leadership approach, one marked by an inclusive, synodal style. Some assumed that Prevost would bring in Augustinians to run the diocese, and there was initial mistrust of the new bishop among those of the local clergy who were either linked to Opus Dei or members of the group.

American Hope

According to Elise Ann Allen in her biography *León XIV: Ciudadano del Mundo, Misionero del Siglo XXI* (*Pope Leo XIV: Global Citizen, Missionary of the 21st Century*), some of the clergy's WhatsApp group messages were full of concern for the future. One priest has revealed that Prevost was sent disrespectful messages by two members of the clergy, to which he never replied. Bishop Prevost was unconcerned by the opposition and didn't retaliate. He worked with those clergy linked to Opus Dei, even though his vision of the Church was very different from theirs. His humble, listening style slowly won many people over. He took pains to make himself well known to the people living in distant, rural communities, even visiting the most inaccessible places on horseback. Rev. José-Antonio Jacinto, a priest from the diocese of Chiclayo and a member of a priestly society linked to Opus Dei, said that he is still in contact with Pope Leo by WhatsApp. Prevost won people over with his humility, he said. What's more, Prevost appointed some of the diocese's twenty Opus Dei priests to senior positions. This style of leadership is the antithesis of the polarized positions seen in so many countries today, where people demonize each other for holding different points of view. "By the time he introduced changes to the way the diocese was run, he had the clergy of the diocese on his side," Jacinto wrote in a letter to *The Tablet*, a Catholic publication. "We worked together in the ups and downs of the new pastoral programmes and diocesan initiatives that he brought in."

Some of the disagreements with Opus Dei were over Prevost's inclusion of laypeople in positions of Church responsibility. For Opus Dei, laypeople are meant to be out in the world. It is the priests who are supposed to run the Church. They are distinct vocations. But Bishop Prevost appointed laypeople to senior leadership positions: his pastoral vicar was a layperson, and he placed women in important roles. Sister Nathalie Becquart, the first woman to be appointed to the Holy See's office for the synod, told me that as bishop in Chiclayo Prevost was "committed to involving laypeople and women in leadership roles." He was already implementing in Peru what Pope Francis was calling for in the wider Church. Sister Nathalie got to know the future pope quite well, since they both lived in the same Roman palazzo. In Rome, she says, "we have witnessed his deeply synodal style—listening attentively, working collaboratively, and consulting broadly."

As pope, Leo XIV insists that a bishop must be first and foremost a servant. "For you I am a bishop; but with you I am a Christian," were the words of St. Augustine. Leo quoted these words in his first public remarks, to make clear that his style of ministry is to walk alongside people. One of the first meetings Leo held was with members of Opus Dei's leadership, who were no doubt seeking to talk to the new pope about Francis's reforms. While Leo received them, he made no immediate decisions.

As a bishop in Chiclayo, he was known for his ability to organize and was closely involved in the charitable work of his diocese. In 2014–15, he helped respond to a huge migrant emergency as 1.5 million people fled neighboring Venezuelan to Peru due to political and social disorder. He secured oxygen equipment for people hit hard by the

Covid-19 pandemic and was pictured standing in rubber boots in floodwater as he helped people affected by heavy rains in northern Peru.

The Augustinian connection to Peru goes back to the sixteenth century, when members of the order arrived in the country from Spain. They have maintained a presence there ever since. Robert Prevost followed in a long line of Augustinian missionaries when, in 1985, he was sent to Chulucanas, in northern Peru, and later to Trujillo, on the northern coast. He was in Chulucanas at a time when the region was being terrorized by the Shining Path, a Maoist guerilla movement that wreaked havoc in rural communities, who were often caught in the crossfire of the government's counterterrorist response. It was a dangerous time for missionaries. They faced death threats and the risk of kidnapping. Prevost's period there got off to a rocky start when he caught typhoid fever and had to be rushed to hospital. He told Elise Ann Allen that at one point he was thinking: "God, either make me better or take me, because this is awful." But he recovered and gave his all to his missionary work.

Prevost never looked back. From 1985 onward, aside from a relatively brief return to the United States, Padre Roberto served in Peru until 1999. He taught at a seminary and worked in the parishes, forming Young Augustinians groups and serving the poorest communities. In the early years, a forward-thinking Augustinian bishop named John McNabb was leading the local Church in Chulucanas. McNabb was pioneering an inclusive model of the Church in accordance with the goals of Vatican II, which included the empowering of lay leaders. This was the synodal model of the Church that Francis would later take up.

By the time Prevost had served as bishop of Chiclayo from 2014 to 2023 he had spent more than two decades of his adult life in Peru. Leo retains Peruvian citizenship and loves the country. In Rome, he is close to the Peruvians who live in the city, choosing Rev. Edgard Rimaycuna, a thirty-seven-year-old priest from Chiclayo, as his principal personal secretary and closest aide. He's found a Peruvian barber, Mario Reyes, who continues to cut his hair as pope. The pope also has shoes made for him by another Peruvian, Antonio Arellano, who, with his son Daniel, runs a small shoe repair shop off the Borgo Pio, a stone's throw from St. Peter's Basilica. Leo has even admitted that if Peru played the United States in the World Cup, he would support Peru.

His former classmate Rev. Francis says that Leo's time in Peru has influenced him profoundly, particularly in "working with the poor, working with the people who are trying to get a voice in terms of society at large." Peru also exposed him to the ideas of liberation theology, a Christian approach, originating in Peru, that prioritizes concern for people who are poor and marginalized because of their race, class, or gender. Prevost became known as a dedicated pastoral leader, attentive to the needs of the people, and able to respond practically and swiftly to their concerns. As pope, he's continued that practical, hands-on style he developed in Peru. Ahead of a meeting with sexual abuse survivors in the Vatican, Leo was seen personally arranging the chairs into a semi-circle to ensure an open discussion.

Bishop Prevost didn't just win over a skeptical diocese in Chiclayo; he also earned a reputation as a troubleshooter. On one occasion he had to deal with the fallout from a bishop who had tried to impose the Neocatechumenal Way on his diocese. The Neocatechumenal Way is a Catholic group formed in the 1960s that has firm views on how to instruct people about Christianity. At one point the bishop had sent people armed with guns to threaten reluctant priests. Francis removed the bishop and asked Prevost to sort out the mess. Prevost won the respect of his fellow Peruvian bishops and was elected vice president of the national bishops' conference, an unusual appointment for a cleric from the United States.

The respect he earned was, in no small part, due to his expertise in the Church's law. While at university he studied math; as a young priest he dedicated his academic work to canon law. Once again, this points to the future pope's ordered, process-minded way of thinking—quite a contrast to Francis's spontaneity and disruptive style. A deep understanding of the Church's law informs Leo's decision-making and his governance of the universal Church, including on how to implement reforms that affect all the Church's members.

Leo's doctoral thesis, titled *The Role of the Local Prior in the Order of St. Augustine*, which he defended successfully in 1987 at the age of thirty-two, offers some insights into how he sees the exercise of authority in the Church.

Although written when he was much younger, the thesis is deeply imbued with the teachings of Vatican II. The future pope reflects on the importance of consultation in decision-making, and of leaders who listen. "Authority is service, and that service is rendered within a context of listening to what the Spirit is saying in His people so that His projects can be carried out freely and willingly," Prevost wrote. "This theology of listening as the Spirit welds the group into community provides a framework within which the Chapter's authority can be understood." In other words, authority is not a disembodied idea but is innate to the community. The thesis also emphasized unity, a priority for Leo. "One of the most important aspects of living the religious life is the communion, the unity, that is shared by the members, as a means of seeking God," he explained.

Both his academic work and his experience in Peru will build on what was started by the first Latin American pope. "We are truly seeing continuity," Sister Nathalie says, referring to the way in which Leo has been "shaped by the ecclesiology of the Second Vatican Council."

Two consecutive popes have either come from Latin America or have served for a long period of time in that region of the world. In the years after Vatican II, it was Latin America that sought to put into practice a vision of the Church as "the People of God," one that was a prophetic voice focussing on a "preferential option for the poor." Latin America became a testing ground for Vatican II's vision of the global Church, something that has became manifest through the elections of Francis and Leo. The synodal reforms Francis sought to implement are a continuation of Vatican II, and these are also deeply embedded in Leo's academic thesis. As I mentioned earlier, it is said that it takes a century to implement a Church council, the gathering which represents the highest level of teaching and legislative authority in the Catholic Church. Leo's pontificate comes sixty years after Vatican II and at a critical moment in the implementation of the council's reforms to the life, habit, and culture of the Church. The synod process is key to implementing the council.

Traditional not traditionalist

Leo is a pope who is sensitive to tradition. He has brought back a certain formality to the papacy. For example, his plan to move into the papal apartments of the Apostolic Palace once they had been renovated. Francis had spent the years of his papacy living in the Casa Santa Marta guesthouse, which had been built in 1996 by John Paul II to accommodate the cardinals during a conclave. (Previously, they had been cooped up in a dormitory inside the Apostolic Palace.) Santa Marta could be likened to a slightly spartan three-star hotel. The accommodation offers rooms with a bedroom, bathroom, and a study. Meals are taken communally in a dining room. Santa Marta is home to some Vatican officials and those visiting Rome on Church business. Francis was assigned a room there during the 2013 conclave and never left, although, when he got older and needed more assistance, he occupied a whole floor of the residence. The Argentine pope joked that he lived in the Santa Marta for "psychological reasons," so that he could remain connected with people. Living there gave him greater freedom to organize his diary, and he was not reliant on gatekeepers who would control who got to see him. Soon after his election, Francis had been shown the papal apartments but had immediately decided that he could not live there. It was a decision that communicated his vision of a papacy, which emphasized humility and a closeness to the people. Francis dismantled the monarchical trappings of the pontificate and replaced them with a servant-leader model. He intended this as a message to bishops across the world: they were not required to live in palatial residences. They should adopt a simpler lifestyle.

When Leo XIV was elected, he was living in an apartment in the Palazzo Sant'Uffizio, where the Vatican's doctrine department is based. After his election on May 8, he returned to that apartment and greeted some of his neighbors, including Sister Nathalie, who congratulated him. In fact, Leo continued to live there for several months while the papal apartments in the Apostolic Palace were given a makeover. Work was needed because no one had lived in them for twelve years.

Some have regarded his move to the old papal apartments as a repudiation or rejection of Francis. Much of Leo's decision, however, was for reasons that were both prudent and practical. First, the cost of housing a pope in the Santa Marta guesthouse was considerable due to the round-the-clock security needed to protect the residence. If the pope lives in the palace, however, the costs are reduced because security does not need to double up. Second, living in the palace makes Leo more accessible to senior figures in the secretariat of state—the engine room of the Holy See—who work in the same building.

The Apostolic Palace dates back to the Renaissance. The papal apartments include a chapel, living room, reception rooms, study, and bedroom. They have a quiet, almost monastic atmosphere. As you walk the palace's marble corridors you hear the chiming of clocks inside the offices every fifteen minutes. You pass Swiss guards in their colored stripey uniforms at the entrances and exits. For Leo, the palace offers something of a retreat, a protected space where he can gather himself and restore himself physically and spiritually.

Each morning, Leo spends time in prayer. The two closest aides who assist him are his private secretaries, Rev. Rimaycuna and Rev. Marco Billeri. The latter is a priest in his early forties from the diocese of San Miniato, Tuscany, and is a trained Church lawyer. Leo typically holds a series of official meetings each morning. These are listed publicly and are sent out by the Vatican press office each day. The meetings may be with heads of state, cardinals, bishops, or officials from international agencies. He also addresses bigger groups or delegations in the mornings. Leo has two appointments with the public each week: the Wednesday morning audience in St. Peter's Square and the Sunday Angelus prayer from the window of the Apostolic Palace. At the end of the Wednesday audience, he will greet bishops or visiting dignitaries. After lunch, his day slows down and it's an opportunity to go through documents that require his signature or to prepare longer texts he plans to publish. He'll continue to meet with people unofficially in the afternoon and in the early evening will sit down with some of the Vatican's most senior officials, including those from the Secretariat of State. The secretariat is responsible for co-ordinating the Vatican's work and handling diplomatic and political matters.

Listening Pope

Leo keeps up a relentless pace, but on Tuesdays he often takes the day off at Castel Gandolfo, the pope's country retreat. Situated above Lake Albano, it's about a forty-minute drive from the Vatican. In the summer, Castel Gandolfo is a perfect escape from the stifling Roman heat. There, the pope can use the swimming pool and tennis courts. It is a spot that has been described as an *antecamera del paradiso*, an antechamber to heaven. The use of the summer palace is another shift in style by Leo. Francis never took a holiday or a day off outside of the Vatican and didn't stay in Castel Gandolfo. In fact, he turned the palace into a museum and launched an environmental initiative in the gardens that includes a farm. Leo has restored the tradition of using Castel Gandolfo. He appreciates walking in nature and getting away from the intense life of the Vatican, taking an extended summer break there, as well as his regular weekly visits. The pope is sending a signal to priests everywhere about the dangers of overwork and burnout. He's also used his trips to Castel Gandolfo to open a channel of communication with the media by answering questions from reporters when he walks to his car on a Tuesday evening, occasions on which he is often quizzed about the latest news, including in the US.

Following tradition does not mean that Leo can't innovate. Although he makes use of Castel Gandolfo, he has not reversed any of his predecessor's changes. The papal palace remains a museum—its last occupant was Benedict XVI. Leo instead stays in the Villa Barberini, a house located in the gardens. He has also implemented Francis's wish to use the Castel Gandolfo's grounds for environmental and sustainable work, opening a new center, Borgo Laudato Si', which is named after the Argentine pope's landmark document on ecology. Leo's decisions reflect a living tradition. He does some things differently from Francis but only by building on the past. Augustinians are, by nature, conservatives with a small "c", in the sense of seeking to conserve, and to build. This is very different from notions held by those radical conservatives and traditionalists who believe that certain parts of history were superior to others, an attitude that frequently makes them prophets of doom when it comes to the present day. "Traditionalism is the dead faith of the living, but tradition is the living faith of the dead," is how the Church historian Jaroslav Pelikan put it. It holds true both for Francis and Leo.

Becoming pope demands serious personal sacrifice. Leo's movements are heavily controlled, and he cannot do many of the things he loved to do in the past. According to his brother John, one of Leo's favorite ways to relax was to drive his car. As pope, however, whenever he gets in a car someone else will be driving. One Church source told me that when he was Augustinian prior general he once drove all the way from Rome to Holland to attend a meeting.

Before his election, Robert Prevost had lived a life out of the limelight. As a cardinal, he was a member of a gym near the Vatican and stayed in shape with the help of a personal trainer. The trainer had no idea who is client was until he saw him on the balcony of St. Peter's on the day he was elected pope. Prevost was always someone who preferred to listen before speaking. At his synod round-table he was known as the person who spoke the least. Now, as pope, all his words are carefully scrutinized, and he will sometimes make several speeches a day. Being thrust onto the world stage has been a major learning curve for a naturally introverted person.

Leo's life has been formed by many different experiences, all of which have helped prepare him for the role he has today. He was rooted in the stability of a loving family. His mother and father were happily married for forty years. His experience at the junior seminary gave him an early grounding as an Augustinian, a way of life based on a fifth-century monastic rule. His time at the Chicago Catholic Theological Union opened him up to hopes of reform in the Church after Vatican II, while his time in Rome helped him to understand what was possible. His years in Peru, however, are the reason he is pope today. The decades in Latin America had a transformative effect on his ministry. An Augustinian spirituality coupled with missionary experience makes him a truly prophetic, countercultural voice on the world stage.

Leo's leadership is characterized by balance and moderation. He does not seek attention with flashy initiatives. Rather, he is a slow and steady builder of unity, someone who will strongly seek to avoid polarization. It is a leadership style that is less about "me" and more about "us." His career has given him a 360-degree perspective on today's Catholic Church and its challenges. While he is an expert listener and community builder, Pope Leo wants the voice of the Church to be heard in contemporary debates.

He wants a united Church, but one ready to speak out, and, as we shall see in the next chapter, to act as a counterbalancing force to some of the political trends in his home country.

2

Spiritual Counterweight

The first American pope in the Catholic Church's 2,000-year history did not provoke a flurry of diplomatic activity from the White House. President Donald Trump told reporters afterward that "we were a little bit surprised and very happy" about the election of the first American pope. He described the news as a "great honor for our country," saying that he looked forward to meeting Leo in what would be "a very meaningful moment."

Yet the President of the United States had no direct contact with the first American pontiff in the aftermath of Leo's election, nor in the early months of his papacy. Speaking at the end of July, Leo confessed that he had "not had direct conversations or met with the president," although he was not overly concerned about this. Trump's own position toward the pope seemed to be one of respectful ambivalence.

While Trump talked about a possible meeting with Leo a couple of months later, he said he had nothing planned and seemed in no rush to make it happen. By contrast, his predecessor, Joe Biden, who was only the second Catholic president after President John F. Kennedy, spoke with Pope Francis on several occasions during his term, including after Biden took office in 2020. In October 2021, they had a 75-minute meeting in the Vatican. Biden, in one of his final acts as president, awarded Francis the Presidential Medal of Freedom with distinction. The Biden–Francis relationship, while not without disagreements on abortion and the war in Gaza, was marked by warmth and mutual respect.

While President Trump talks respectfully about Pope Leo, signs of the underlying tensions are not hard to spot. Steve Bannon, a Catholic and an outspoken ally of Trump, described Leo's election as the "worst pick ever." (At one point, Bannon was involved in a project to turn a former monastery into a "gladiator" training school for nationalist populists.) Bannon had been deeply hostile to Francis's pontificate, describing the late pope as "beneath contempt" and reportedly advising Italy's former interior minister Matteo Salvini that the pope was the "enemy." Much of his enmity toward Francis was due to the pope's fearless advocacy on behalf of migrants. "He is very much in the line of Bergoglio," Bannon said after Leo's election. "The Curia, the globalist Curia of the Bergoglio [papacy] totally rigged this." Bannon, sensing the threat of an American pope who is not aligned with Trump, added: "All they're saying on American TV right now is that the United States has two world leaders, Donald Trump and the Pope … On Monday we are gonna turn this thing up, we will let everybody know: this was rigged."

Leo is not someone who will go looking for a public confrontation. He is measured and careful with his language, and far less provocative than his predecessor. In his first term, Trump clashed with Francis over migrants.

Spiritual Counterweight

"A person who thinks only about building walls, wherever they may be, and not building bridges, is not Christian," Francis told reporters in 2016 when asked about Trump's plan to build a wall between the US and Mexico. Francis would sometimes face the criticism, from inside and outside the Church, that he simply did not know enough about the United States.

The same cannot be said of an American pope. While Leo may not be as directly critical of the US president, his pontificate will act as a spiritual and cultural counterweight to the actions of President Trump and the MAGA movement, because what Leo does and says—often in English—has resonance and influence.

Leo is not an anti-MAGA activist nor is he trying to subtly troll the president. He will seek a dialogue with President Trump and supports his efforts to end conflicts. His papacy offers an alternative vision to the one emanating from the White House, a vision that is built on unity and spirituality and which is allergic to divisive rhetoric and polarization. I describe Leo's pontificate as a counterweight because Leo is the only American in the world today who matches Donald Trump's status in terms of global recognition.

"Pope Leo is in many respects the anti-Trump, but not in the sense that he is an active opponent or even a direct critic," David Gibson, the Director of the Center on Religion and Culture at Fordham University, New York, told me. "While Leo's exposition of Catholic teachings will contradict many of Trump's policies and statements, it is Leo's character that stands in contrast to Trump, both as a Christian and as an American." Gibson explains: "Trump is all about 'me' and Leo is all about 'we.' This is about two diametrically opposed ways of being in the world."

The contrasts between the two leaders couldn't be sharper. While Leo calls for the welcoming and integration of immigrants, the Trump administration is arresting and deporting them. While Leo says that the Christian faith is incompatible with mistreating the environment, Trump dismisses climate change as a "hoax." While Trump is routinely angered by the "fake news media," Leo has repeatedly defended journalists and the freedom of speech. As the president seeks retribution against his political opponents, Leo pursues consensus-building. While Trump pushes to exceed the limits of his presidential authority, the pope is a Church lawyer who follows due process.

If the MAGA world is often synonymous with chaos, grievance, and the shouting down of opponents, Leo's papacy seeks stability, peace, and a profound desire to listen. Everyone who knows Pope Leo says that he is not someone who relishes a fight but he has a focussed mind and a determined, natural authority. He will not be cowed by a politician. With regard to the United States, he wants the Catholic Church to act as a prophetic voice when it comes to the Trump administration's treatment of immigrants.

"The Church cannot remain silent," Leo told bishops from El Paso, Texas, after he was shown a video of the hardships experienced by undocumented migrants near the US border. He will not indulge the untruths spread about migrants, or the othering of minorities and the vulnerable—which are features of authoritarian regimes in many countries. The mistreatment of migrants, Leo says, is not the "legitimate exercise of national sovereignty" but constitutes "grave crimes." He is deeply concerned about the erosion of established facts in public discourse. "I don't have a lot of tolerance when I hear people say, 'Well, this is an alternate set of facts,'" he told his biographer Elise Ann Allen. It sounded like a reference to the notorious "alternative facts" comment made in 2017 by Kellyanne Conway, a former Trump advisor, with its suggestion that facts are partisan. In defending the work of journalism, Leo has warned about the blurring of fact and fiction and has cited Hannah Arendt's seminal work *The Origins of Totalitarianism*: "The ideal subject of totalitarian rule is not the convinced Nazi or the convinced Communist, but people for whom the distinction between fact and fiction and the distinction between true and false no longer exist."

Leo's leadership and quiet charisma have made him popular in the US. In an August 2025 Gallup poll of fourteen prominent US and global figures, including Trump, the pope was by far the most popular, with Americans giving him a 57 per cent favorable approval rating. Among US Catholics—of which there are more than 50 million—Leo's favorability rating stood at 84 per cent according to a Pew survey, even though many added they would still want to get to know him first. On social media, clips of Leo are frequently shared, with many remarking on what they perceive as his authenticity—someone who is at ease in one-on-ones, whether it's holding a baby who clings onto his cassock or chatting with newly married couples. Online, he's often called "peepaw," an affectionate term in the US for a grandfather. His gentleness, humility, and his compassion for those at the margins of the society are a consoling antidote to turbulent times, particularly in the United States, where political divisions are leading to a sharp rise in political violence.

"I think it's the case that the cardinals were looking at America's dominance on the world stage, threats to democracy and threats to the Church, and they wanted someone who would not be cowed by Trump, and who would understand how Americans think," Dawn Eden Goldstein, a Church analyst based in the US, told me.

Will.i.am, the front man for Black Eyed Peas, told me for CNN that to have a pope from Chicago is a "beautiful thing," given "all the things that are happening in America." He was speaking at a Vatican summit on human fraternity, and after a tragic incident in Chicago in which an undocumented migrant was fatally shot by an Immigration and Customs Enforcement officer while resisting arrest. "I wish we treated Chicago and inner cities better going through tough times with a human, delicate approach," he said. "The fact that we have a pope from Chicago gives me hope that other cities around the world that [are like and] reflect Chicago, that somebody's praying [for them], and those prayers can soon be answered." He added: "Pope Leo, he's awesome, I wish him the best."

Although Leo disagrees with President Trump on many issues, he has shown a willingness to engage in dialogue and compromise. When it comes to efforts to end wars—and Trump has shown a strong willingness to work for peace—the pope says he will support the president. Leo's focus is on trying to find the areas of common

Spiritual Counterweight

ground, not condemnation. The doors of the Apostolic Palace are open to President Trump should he wish to visit the Vatican. Leo refuses to be embroiled in the culture wars or do anything to fuel polarization, something that happens across the political divide and which has become more acute during the Trump presidency.

The pope, like many in the United States, has first-hand knowledge of how political divides can affect families. Disagreements over which way people voted cause heated conversations at the dinner table, and in some cases lead to feuds and family break-ups. The pope has two older brothers. His eldest sibling, Louis Prevost, is a MAGA supporter who has posted some inflammatory pro-Trump social media content in which, for example, he attacked former House speaker Nancy Pelosi. One Church source told me that Louis' wife, Deborah, is also a MAGA supporter. After his brother's election as pope, Louis conceded that he would probably "tone it down," and he has removed some posts and made his accounts private. But the Trump White House was quick to spot an opportunity. Louis and Deborah were invited to visit and were welcomed by President Trump and Vice President JD Vance.

"I really like his brother," Trump said of the pope. "His brother is a major, serious Trumper. You know that? He's MAGA all the way." Leo responded to these comments by saying simply, "That's fine," adding that Louis had been "very outspoken about his political viewpoints." Trump has had more direct contact with Leo's brother—a MAGA supporter—than with the pope himself, who is not. Actions speak louder than words.

American Hope

The American pope has made it clear that his own politics are not those of his siblings. "We're still very close, even though one [Louis] is far on one end politically; we're in different places," Leo explained. But the pope, even in his own family, proves that it is possible to disagree and stay united. He shows that political differences don't need to affect family harmony. After Leo's inauguration on May 18, Louis Prevost stepped forward to greet his brother in St. Peter's Basilica. The pair hugged each other tightly. Louis has spoken of his younger brother as a gifted communicator and mediator, someone who managed, even as a young boy, to de-escalate a scary situation in which gang members had accosted them while they were riding bicycles in Chicago. He still sees the pope as his younger brother, especially when he heard Leo make his first speech as pope. "Then he switched to Spanish, and I thought, 'OK, quit showing off, you little jerk,'" Louis joked in an interview with Newsmax. The family bonds between the Prevost brothers remain healthy.

An unprecedented letter

After his election, the *Politico* news site ran a news story headlined: "Pope Leo looks to MAGA megadonors to shore up Church finances." I showed this story to a senior Church figure, who replied: "[Leo] would throw up if he saw that."

The pope has no intention of getting involved in partisan politics in the US, or in any country. "He's not a fan of the America number 1 chant," is how one cardinal put

Spiritual Counterweight

it to me. This was also the case when he was a cardinal serving as one of Francis's closest advisers. Three days before he was admitted to hospital with severe respiratory difficulties, Pope Francis released a letter addressed to the bishops of the United States. This document would be the last major political intervention of his papacy. And it was explosive. The letter was extraordinarily critical of the Trump administration's crackdown on immigrants. It was also crystal clear in rejecting any use of Christian theology to justify anti-immigrant policies.

Francis pointed out that Christ himself went through "the experience of having to take refuge in a society and a culture foreign to his own." He quoted Pius XII, a pope acclaimed by some conservatives, who described Jesus, Mary, and Joseph as "emigrants in Egypt and refugees" and "the model, the example, and the consolation of emigrants and pilgrims of every age." He emphasized that every nation had a right to defend itself from those who have committed violent or serious crimes both in a new country or the one prior to arrival, and that every country had a right to formulate a policy of orderly and legal migration. But he insisted that "an authentic rule of law" protects the poorest and most vulnerable. "What is built on the basis of force, and not on the truth about the equal dignity of every human being, begins badly and will end badly."

Two Church sources have confirmed to me that Cardinal Prevost played a crucial role in the drafting of that letter. His involvement would make sense given that he was leading the Vatican's office for bishops at the time (the letter was addressed to the US bishops) and because he was one of only two very senior prelates from the US working in the Church's central administration. It would have been appropriate for Prevost, the former leader of the Augustinians, to advise Francis on this point. As pope, Leo referred to this letter from Francis as "very significant" and said he was "very happy" that several bishops had agreed with it, especially since it also contained a strong rebuttal of a certain theological argument that had recently been made by Vice President JD Vance.

JD Vance was received into the Catholic Church in 2019. His decision to convert had been made "slowly and unevenly," he said, and was strongly influenced by the writings of St. Augustine, whom he took as his patron (confirmation name).

In defending Trump's immigration crackdown, Vance had invoked a theological concept known as the *ordo amoris* (order of love, or order of charity), which was first formulated by St. Augustine of Hippo and later by St. Thomas Aquinas. He intended it to demonstrate that love has a hierarchy of obligations. You love your family the most, then your neighbor, then your community, your fellow citizens, and "then after that, prioritize the rest of the world." The Left he argued, had inverted this principle. "Just google '*ordo amoris*,'" Vance wrote in a post on X when challenged about the Christian justification for the immigration policy. For Pope Francis, and the Augustinian cardinal Robert Prevost, this appeal to Augustine and Aquinas could not be allowed to stand.

"Christian love is not a concentric expansion of interests that little by little extend to other persons and groups. In other words: the human person is not a mere individual, relatively expansive, with some philanthropic feelings!" Francis wrote. "The true *ordo amoris* that must be promoted is that which we discover by meditating constantly on the parable of the 'Good Samaritan,' that is, by meditating on the love that builds a fraternity open to all, without exception."

The pope couldn't have been clearer. Christian charity does not operate according to a rigid hierarchy, dispensed according to those who are most deserving. Yes, the natural bonds of family mean those closest to us are a priority, but it cannot be an either/or: either you are charitable to your family, or you are charitable to migrants. It is extremely rare for the papacy to comment on a political discourse taking place in another country, but in this instance an exception was made. Leo, at his inauguration Mass, also sent a message about Christian love. JD Vance was among those present in St. Peter's to hear it. "We are called to offer God's love to everyone," Leo stressed. "Brothers and sisters, this is the hour for love! The heart of the Gospel is the love of God that makes us brothers and sisters."

Vance is closely associated with conservative Catholics in the US, many of whom led the charge of opposition against Pope Francis. While he avoided public criticism of Francis, in summer 2021, during his run for the senate, he did speak at conference held by the Napa Institute, an influential Catholic non-profit organization. Napa blends conservative theology with free-market economics. It was founded by Tim Busch, a lawyer and real estate businessman, and attracts wealthy and politically well-connected Catholics. It has regularly hosted outspoken critics of Francis, including US Cardinal Raymond Burke. Busch is a critic of the minimum wage, saying that "when we abandon free markets, the Church suffers." In March 2025, he described the Trump administration as the "most Christian he's ever seen."

The sharp differences between Leo's vision and that of Napa came to light when the pope issued the first major document of his papacy, *Dilexi te* (I have loved you), which focussed on poverty and inequality. Leo insisted that service to the poor is non-negotiable for Christians. He lamented the rise of "a wealthy elite, living in a bubble of comfort and luxury, almost in another world compared to ordinary people." He denounced the "dictatorship of an economy that kills" and called on Catholics to eradicate "unjust structures" that cause poverty. But on the same day that Leo released *Dilexi te*, Napa sent out an email to everyone on its mailing list sharing details of a speech by Frank Hanna III, a wealthy Catholic philanthropist and financier, who said: "Blessings are not distributed equally, and wealth is a form of economic blessing." Speaking at a Napa gathering in August 2025, Hanna asked: "What if—WHAT IF, the inequality is a feature of the common good, and not a bug?" and declared, "God wants us to take risks!" While Hanna insisted that he saw faults with the "market economy, and the pursuit of profit," his speech was a world away from Leo's message. In mid October, Hanna was honored at a two-day $1,500-a-head event at the Metropolitan Club in New York, described as a "Virtuous Leadership dinner and gala." Earlier in his career, Hanna, the CEO of Hanna Capital, set up a highly profitable credit card company, Compucredit, with his brother David. In 2008,

Spiritual Counterweight

the company agreed to pay $114 million in restitution to consumers in settlement of charges that it had deceptively marketed subprime credit cards. The company also paid a civil penalty of $2.4 million.

No to ideology

JD Vance and his family came to Rome for Holy Week in 2025. On the morning of Easter Sunday the vice president was granted a brief audience with Pope Francis. Vance was the last world leader to meet him. Francis died the next day. JD Vance takes his faith seriously, and the story of his conversion, which he laid out in *The Lamp* magazine, reveals someone who has made a sincere engagement with the Catholic faith, and who wrestles with how to apply the teachings of Christianity in his life. Yet in the vice president of the United States, Leo also faces someone whose Catholic faith is tied to a political worldview. Leo's papacy has begun at a time when Christian nationalism is on the rise in the United States and in Europe. The symbols of Christianity—the cross, and the Bible—are increasingly being appropriated by politicians and activists in pursuit of a nationalist populist agenda. It is a trend that the American pope, whose faith has taken him to many countries and brought him close to many diverse cultures and peoples, strongly opposes.

In the story Vance tells of becoming a Catholic, he cites St. Augustine's famous work *The City of God*, which includes Augustine's description of the debauchery of ancient Rome. Vance likens this to today's overconsumption. He was also attracted to Augustine's teachings to Christians about being open to correction, including from reason, science, or experience. His journey to faith, he explains, made him prioritize virtue over worldly success. In this, he was influenced by the ideas of René Girard, a French thinker who converted to Catholicism in 1959. Girard's ideas, Vance says, were introduced to him by Peter Thiel, a Silicon Valley venture capitalist and later Trump backer. Thiel, a financial backer of JD Vance, reportedly expressed in private lectures his concern that Vance might become "too close to the Pope". The remark reflected his anxiety—shared by parts of the Trump coalition—about the papacy's global reach and independent moral authority, which transcends national borders. Thiel has critiqued liberal democracy and favors a more nationalist, technologically-oriented vision. Vance was taken by Girard's concept of "mimetic desire," whereby people compete for things others want and end up imitating each other. Another idea that impressed him was Girard's "scapegoat mechanism:" the way in which societies project violence onto a scapegoat who has wronged the community and is then expelled or sacrificed to restore cohesion. Girard argued that Christianity upends this narrative through the crucifixion, which makes Christ the scapegoat. Christ is then revealed as innocent, which in turn exposes the flaws of the individuals in the community. Girard argued that this breaks the cycle of violent scapegoating. And Vance says that he saw this scapegoating taking place across social media.

Some could argue that the Trump administration's policy on migrants is a textbook case of what Girard would describe as community scapegoating: undocumented migrants labeled as criminals who are perceived to be harming the community and who must therefore be deported. Paul Elie in *The New Yorker* observes, too, that Vance himself seems to have thrived through "mimetic rivalry." While he may have become disillusioned with the cut-throat competition of the legal world, his closeness to Thiel, who has financially backed his political career, shows that he "simply moved out of one elite and into another."

Vance frames his journey into the Catholic faith as a countercultural act. The article in which he describes his conversion is titled "How I joined the resistance." It is a faith deeply entwined with a political worldview. He holds beliefs similar to those of many conservative Catholics: a strong opposition to abortion and a defense of the traditional family, combined with a skepticism about liberal immigration policies and the science of climate change. He was baptized and received into the Church by Fr. Henry Stephan, a member of the Dominican order whose areas of interest include St. Thomas Aquinas. Before training for the priesthood, Fr. Henry had been an intern for Judge Diarmuid O'Scannlain—an attendee of the first "Young Americans for Freedom" event, which took place in the home of William F. Buckley in 1960 with the aim of creating a national conservative youth organization.

Vance describes himself as "post liberal." He believes that society is better served by stronger communitarian and social bonds rather than by the autonomy of the individual. To some extent, post-liberal ideas chime with a central tenet of Catholic social teaching, the Catholic

Church's doctrine on human dignity and the common good in society. Central to this teaching is the idea that government should serve the common good with policies that benefit the whole of the community. Vance is close to some prominent Catholic post liberals. In 2022, he spoke at a conference with the theme "Restoring a Nation: The Common Good in the American Tradition," held at the Franciscan University of Steubenville. The *National Catholic Reporter* described it as an event where several speakers "articulated a vision of the United States where domestic manufacturing is not only revived and globalization reined in, but where traditional Christian morality is restored to a central place in society and mainstream culture, and where leaders in government are comfortable using political power to enforce those religious values and punish 'woke' progressives."

Underlying this thinking is the idea that democratic institutions should serve an authoritative understanding of the human good determined by the Catholic Church. At the more radical end of this thinking is a concept known as Catholic Integralism, which essentially argues for the integration of government with religious authority and for policy and laws that are based on the Catholic faith. It is the equivalent of a religiously backed state authority. There is no suggestion that Vance supports such a concept.

As an Augustinian, Leo will be aware that St. Augustine's ideas are increasingly appearing in post-liberal thought. Augustine wrote *The City of God* in 410, after the fall of Rome to the Visigoths, a key event in the eventual collapse of the western Roman empire, which

Spiritual Counterweight

some blamed on Christians. The conditions of that period could, some argue, be compared to those of the present day. More and more, people doubt the future stability of long-established parties and institutions; they perceive a general decline that is leading toward societal crisis, a lack of faith in public life, and a search for meaning. Augustine juxtaposes what he called the City of Man—which is characterized by worldly power, love of self, and which is ultimately doomed to collapse—with the City of God, a community united through the love of God. The two cities intermingle but ultimately the City of God will prevail and become manifest in the eternal kingdom of heaven. Several scholars argue that Augustine's work laid the foundation for the secular world, by distinguishing between temporal and spiritual power, and by describing the notion of a pluralistic public sphere. Chad Pecknold, a supporter of JD Vance who is a professor at the Catholic University of America, rejects what he calls a "liberal" reading of Augustine. Pecknold spoke at the same 2022 conference in Steubenville. He argues that all cities are religious at their core and that Christians must work to reorder the city toward God. He accurately points out that Augustine argues that human beings and societies are inherently religious and that cities and politics cannot be religiously neutral. Pecknold says that America now needs a "new religious vision." He calls for the return of blasphemy laws to fight the "gods of social justice" and for government to "legislate in ways which privilege the recovery of opening and closing every school day with a prayer that recognizes the one true God as the benevolent cause and end of all things."

These post-liberal and integralist ideas are unlikely to find support from Pope Leo. Dawn Eden Goldstein stressed that Leo is "not out to rebuild Christendom" and "would not be in favor of an integralist understanding of City of God." Importantly, the Second Vatican Council's teaching enshrined freedom of religious thought and demarcated the lines between Church and state. One of its key documents, *Gaudium et spes*, stated that democracy is a valid form of government rooted in Catholic social teaching. The pope's namesake—Leo XIII—also affirmed the legitimacy of democracy, while Francis pushed for Catholics to be active citizens. Less than a year before he died, he said it was evident "that democracy is not in good health in today's world," while repeatedly warning against polarization. "Ideologies are seductive. Some people compare them to the Pied Piper of Hamelin," he said, referring to the German legend. "They seduce you, but they lead you to deny yourself." For Francis, the great seduction he identified was the morphing of ideology into faith. He was allergic to any form of ideology, and he insisted that Christianity is not, primarily, a set of rules to follow but an encounter with a single person: Jesus Christ.

The co-opting of Christian iconography, ideas, and symbols for political ends concerned Francis. One of the most prominent examples of this occurred in June 2020 when President Trump held up a Bible in front of the parish house of St. John's Episcopal Church in Washington, DC, shortly after law enforcement had forcefully cleared the area of George Floyd protestors. Pope Francis would liken the protesters—who were voicing their anger about the death of a forty-six-year-old unarmed

Spiritual Counterweight

African American man as he was arrested by police—to the Good Samaritan, who went out of his way to help a man left beaten up at the side of the road. In Italy, Matteo Salvini, the country's vice president, once brandished a rosary at a political rally, telling the crowd that he was dealing with the arrival of migrants in a Christian way. As interior minister, Salvini had turned away ships carrying migrants seeking to enter Italy. Francis never met Salvini during his pontificate. The late pope insisted that the cross must not be used as a "political symbol" or "a sign of religious status" and he warned against Catholic popular piety—processions, prayers and the veneration of icons—being used by political leaders to fuel "polemics, narrow-mindedness, divisions and exclusivist attitudes." President Vladimir Putin is another politician who regularly makes a public display of his faith. Under his presidency, the Russian state and the Russian Orthodox Church have become active players in today's global culture wars. The Orthodox Church, which has supported Putin's war in Ukraine, is a strong element of Putin's anti-liberal, "traditional values" agenda—one that is attractive to conservative political forces from across denomination divides. On August 1, 2025, Putin and Alexander Lukashenko, the president of Belarus, were seen lighting candles and praying together at the Valaam monastery, located on an island in northwest Russia. "When I was flying in, I thought that we have created a good tradition, with two Orthodox nations—and we as their representatives—meeting here every year, in this Church which feels like home," Lukashenko said. Iacopo Scaramuzzi, Vatican reporter for *La Repubblica*, argued in his book *Dio? In Fondo a Destra (God? Down to the Right)* that Putin looked to Orthodoxy to "give depth and spirit to his power." Francis's papacy, he argued, was an antidote to the co-opting of religion by the Right and by nationalist populists. Francis refused to be drawn into the culture wars and upheld multinational co-operation.

Leo, like Francis, is wary of ideology and anything that fuels polarization. His faith is informed by his time living outside of the US. "He struck me as not an ideologue in any shape or form or [someone who is] influenced by right-wing thinking," Mark O'Connor, a Catholic writer from Australia, told me. O'Connor is a member of the Marist religious order. He had spent time with Cardinal Prevost in the month before his election and, as I have mentioned, had talked of him as a potential future pope.

Right-leaning nationalist populism, which seeks to co-opt religion, is often pushed by the intellectual elites. While for some, Catholicism is part of a cultural battle of ideas, Leo's faith is rooted in a lived experience among the poorest communities in Peru. While Vance pursues policies which deport Latin American immigrants, Leo has immersed himself among those people who now face removal from the US. "My own story is that of a citizen, the descendant of immigrants, who in turn chose to emigrate," Leo told diplomats. "All of us, in the course of our lives, can find ourselves healthy or sick, employed or unemployed, living in our native land or in a foreign country, yet our dignity always remains unchanged: it is the dignity of a creature willed and loved by God."

When JD Vance met Pope Leo in the Vatican's Apostolic Palace on the day after Leo's inauguration, he was accompanied by US Secretary of State Marco Rubio, a Catholic with a Cuban immigrant background. Leo said he discussed the importance of respecting people, regardless of where they were born. The vice president handed Leo a letter from the President of the United States and the First Lady, which Leo simply placed to one side. As he presented the letter, Vance said that it was "inviting you," although the video from the Vatican feed then cuts off before he says what the invitation concerns. Karoline Leavitt, the White House press secretary, later explained that the letter was an invitation to the pope from President Trump and the First Lady to visit the White House as soon as he possibly could. The meeting between Leo and Vance was something of a reset in relations, an opportunity for Leo to build a rapport with the vice president, and a channel for dialogue. To his credit, Vance has admitted that, as a relatively recent convert to the Catholic faith, "there's a lot I don't know" and that he tries "to be humble as best I can when talking about the faith."

"Leo handles JD Vance as a political leader who happens to be a Catholic," Dawn Eden Goldstein says. "As pope, Leo's role is to be concerned about the salvation of Vance's soul, so he's going to be careful about admonishing him publicly because he doesn't want Vance to close his ears to the voice of the Church. It is a delicate situation for Leo, but if anyone can handle it, Leo can."

While the pope is not out to push his personal political views, his X account, (@drprevost) leaves no doubt about where Leo stands. The account, now defunct, shared several articles that were critical of Trump's immigration policies. One of those was an article from the *National*

Catholic Reporter on the *ordo amoris* debate. It was headlined "JD Vance is wrong: Jesus doesn't ask us to rank our love for others." On another occasion he reposted a tweet in 2018 from Cardinal Blase Cupich of Chicago condemning the separation of immigrant children from their parents and an article by Bishop Evelio Menjivar-Ayala, a Salvadoran-born priest who is an auxiliary (assistant) bishop in Washington, DC. The article compared the suffering of migrants with that of Jesus Christ, describing the "disturbing actions" that immigration enforcement had taken against "peaceful and productive migrants and refugees across the board."

Pope Leo has received a warm invitation to the White House, and he is already likely to have met many people from the US who have urged him to make the trip home. However, the pope will have to weigh very carefully the political implications of such a trip.

"I don't think he's going to be coming to the United States anytime soon, because of the political implications of a pope visiting and the fact that the president would have something to say about his schedule, and what he would have to do, and presenting him in a certain sense back to the American people," his friend Rev. Mark Francis says. "I don't think he's going to risk that."

The first American pope's visit to the United States will be a momentous historical event. Of course, visits abroad by the pope are common. They are a means of spreading the papacy's soft power, a chance for the pontiff to address the country's leaders, its Catholic community, and society more broadly. But an American pope has never before set foot in the US. Such a visit is likely to generate spectacular levels of public interest. One can only imagine the size of the crowds when Leo returns to his home city, Chicago. But Leo will be careful: papal visits can be vulnerable to exploitation for political gain. I recall traveling with Francis to Uganda in 2015 and seeing posters of President Yoweri Museveni, dressed in white, placed side by side with posters of the pope in his white cassock. Because of the risk of being co-opted by politicians, popes avoid traveling to a country during an election cycle. Leo will be acutely sensitive to the ways in which his visit to the US will be perceived, so the locations he will visit and the people he will meet are matters that must all be worked out sensitively in advance. But, without doubt, a trip by Leo to the US, where most of the country's eyes will be fixed on him, and not on President Trump, will provide a unique opportunity for him to offer a message of unity, peace, and hope.

Influence by appointments

Choosing bishops is one of the surest ways the pope can exercise influence on the leadership of the Church in any given country, which in turn can impact on the way the Church engages in a country's politics. Leo's appointments to the Church hierarchy in the US will be crucial in ensuring that bishops are in line with his vision. It's important, too, given that the bishops lead the church of around 53 million in the US, with around 20 per cent of the population identifying as Catholic. As pope, he has insisted that it is up to the US bishops to take the lead in engaging with the Trump administration. Yet it is Leo who decides who those bishops will be.

In the first months of his papacy, Leo appointed four bishops to the Church in the US, three of whom were not born in the country. The message this sent was clear: that new arrivals in a country, when they are integrated and welcomed, can enrich their new home. The three migrant bishops are living examples of what is possible. The timing of the appointments—while federal agents were arresting and deporting migrants—was also significant. But Leo's appointments also have a deeper, longer-term aim. He is gradually reshaping the leadership of the US Church, a Church that included those who have often been fiercely opposed to Francis.

The pope's first appointment was Bishop Michael Pham, whom Leo chose to lead the diocese of San Diego, in southern California. Pham was a child when he fled Vietnam in the early 1980s, along with his older sister and younger brother. They were at sea in a rice barge for four days and three nights, with communist forces pursuing them, before ending up in a refugee camp in Malaysia. Eventually, an American family sponsored them to relocate to Minnesota. Pham's parents and the rest of his siblings later joined them, and they moved to San Diego.

Pham's story makes vivid and personal the threats migrants face. As a bishop, he now offers pastoral support to people brought before immigration courts. On June 20, 2025, Pham and other religious leaders turned up at a federal building in San Diego where masked US Immigration and Customs Enforcement (ICE) officers had

Spiritual Counterweight

gathered to make arrests. When the officers saw Pham, they dispersed. "Today, I stand as a leader of the Catholic Church thanks to these opportunities that allowed me to contribute to society," he said during a Mass beforehand. "When I was ten years old, living in Vietnam, I witnessed this situation. It involved seeing people being taken away without an obvious reason."

Leo's next appointment was Bishop Pedro Bismarck Chau, who became the United States' the first Nicaraguan-born bishop. Chau entered the US illegally in 1984 at the age of sixteen after the Nicaraguan regime drafted him into military service during a period of revolution in the country. His mother feared that he would be sent, with minimal training, into mountain combat with guerillas, so she arranged for him to be smuggled, with his brothers, across the border. Chau worked in a women's clothing factory while he studied English, then he became a US citizen, earned degrees, and was ordained at the age of forty. On September 8, 2025, just over forty years after he left Nicaragua, his mother witnessed her son being ordained an auxiliary bishop for the Newark Archdiocese.

A month after appointing Chau, Leo chose Simon Peter Engurait, the first Ugandan-born bishop for the US, to lead the diocese of Houma-Thibodaux, which covers southeastern Louisiana. Engurait is the first black bishop of the diocese, a place where endemic racism has long affected the justice system, education, policing, and community relations. Engurait had an eleven-year career working for the Ugandan government, while at the same time studying for a master's in business administration

(MBA) in the Netherlands. After "a long period of prayer and discernment" he was accepted as a trainee priest for the Houma-Thibodaux diocese.

The pope and the Church's leaders in the US support each country's right to manage its own borders and execute policies that ensure orderly migration. The Trump administration is insisting that it is tackling illegal immigration. It has sought to bring the flow of migrants arriving at the southern border under control. The removal of undocumented migrants, including those with criminal records, has had widespread public support, although the policy quickly became much more contentious when it transpired that many of those being arrested by ICE possessed a legal right to live in the US. They had been swept up in a deportation dragnet that often had scant regard for due process.

Cardinal Robert McElroy, the Archbishop of Washington, DC, spoke to me about Trump's immigration policies in an interview for CNN. He said that the government had a right to deport those who had committed "serious crimes, especially violent crimes," but said that the problems with immigration were rooted in an American political system that had failed to address immigration law and reform over the last fifteen years.

"However, what's going on now is something far beyond that," he explained. "It is a mass, indiscriminate deportation of men and women and children and families which literally rips families apart and is intended to do so." What's going on, he added, is "morally repugnant."

Cardinal McElroy leads the archdiocese which covers the US capital. He said that people were now afraid to attend Mass for fear of being arrested and deported. For the same reason, in the diocese of San Bernardino, California, Bishop Alberto Rojas made the extraordinary decision to dispense with the requirement that Catholics attend Mass on Sundays. It's a move without obvious precedent. Meanwhile, in Chicago, Cardinal Cupich has stated simply: "the Church stands with migrants." Cupich, an ally of Leo's, spoke out after ICE (Immigration and Customs Enforcement) started making arrests in the city, and soon after Leo said that the Church cannot be silent in the face of mistreatment of immigrants. "I will insist that you be treated with dignity. Americans should not forget that we all come from immigrant families."

On November 1, 2025, a gathering of priests was prevented from entering a makeshift ICE facility in Chicago. They had been hoping to give holy communion to the migrants detained inside, but were turned away by Homeland Security agents. Later, outside Castel Gandolfo, Leo had significant words for those carrying out Trump's deportation agenda. Citing the Gospel of Matthew, he said: "Jesus says at the end of the world we are going to be asked, 'How did you receive the foreigner, did you receive and welcome him, or not?'" He added that a "deep reflection" was needed on what was happening. "Many people who have lived for years and years and years, never causing problems, have been deeply affected by what's going on right now. The spiritual rights of people who have been detained should also be considered and I would certainly invite the authorities to allow pastoral workers to attend to the needs of those people. Many times they have been separated from their families for a good amount of time, no one knows what's happening, but their own spiritual needs should be attended to."

McElroy says that while Leo speaks about migration "in a universal context," his words have relevance to the US. The cardinal in Washington, who has criticized Trump, holds a doctorate in political science from Stanford University. He said that he fears that one of the "main things" behind the immigration crackdown is that "people who are coming to our country now are [perceived to be] of a different kind." He added, "That's been a great theme in American culture and history all through our country's immigration, when the Irish came, when the Italians came, when the Poles came, the refrain has been the same, 'These are inferior people,' and that's what's going on now ... it's an outrage." A White House spokeswoman rejected the cardinal's criticisms, saying that "the American people elected President Trump, not a DC Archbishop, to serve as their president."

Leo's early appointments to the US hierarchy are not simply a case of rubber-stamping decisions made by Francis. It's crucial to remember that Leo led the Vatican's department for bishops and was closely involved in episcopal appointments. From early 2023 until Francis's death on April 21, 2025, Prevost, as a trusted aide to Francis, had a hand in in all major appointments to the US Church. Among them was the appointment of McElroy to lead the Washington Archdiocese, a decision made in January 2025, just days before Trump's inauguration. Another significant appointment was that of the archbishop of Detroit, Edward Weisenburger, an outspoken advocate on behalf migrants, who has even suggested that "canonical penalties" be imposed on any Catholics involved in separating children from their families at the US–Mexico border. Weisenburger also supported Francis's efforts to protect the environment; he shared the late pope's vision. But not everyone in the archdiocese felt the same. In the archdiocese's seminary, for example, three prominent, long-serving professors had been hostile to Francis, even accusing him of sowing disunity in the Church and demeaning Church doctrine. What made their opposition to the pope so unusual was that they were teaching at a faculty for training future priests. Weisenburger removed all three soon after taking up his post.

The Detroit incident is just one example of the extraordinary opposition to Francis in the United States. Leo is acutely aware of this. "What fuels so much of the resistance to Pope Francis in the United States?" Cardinal Prevost once asked Vatican reporter Christopher White. For his part, the future pope saw that at the heart of the resistance was a deep aversion to Francis's critiques of unfettered free-market capitalism. The opposition wasn't so much theological as economic.

Prevost had made an insightful observation. Concerns about Francis surfaced early on. Church donors were unhappy about his pronouncements on unrestrained capitalism. They also complained that they could no longer get access to the pope. During the papacy of John Paul II, donors would meet the pope after his early morning Mass in the Vatican. But no one could buy their way into the early morning Masses celebrated by Francis, which he reserved for members of the parishes around Rome, Vatican workers, couples celebrating anniversaries, and visiting clergy. You were more likely to be in a private Mass with Francis if you were a Vatican gardener than if you'd donated millions to a Church project. Powerful and wealthy Catholics used to have a key to the Apostolic Palace, as it were, but Francis changed the locks.

Skepticism of Francis often went hand in hand with support for Trump. Soon after his election, the Argentine pope released *Evangelii gaudium,* a document that criticized trickle-down economics, and called on the Church to reject an economy that gave rise to exclusion and indifference. Soon afterward, Ken Langone, a billionaire who was leading efforts to refurbish St. Patrick's Cathedral in New York, told the city's archbishop, Cardinal Timothy Dolan, that one potential seven-figure donor was alarmed by the pope's statement on market economies. He told Dolan: "This is one more hurdle I hope we don't have to deal with. You want to be careful about generalities." Langone is also a donor to the Republican Party and a supporter of President Trump.

In my book *The Outsider*, I described the resistance to Francis in some circles as a phenomenon that had not been seen in centuries, if ever. Francis's opponents were engaged in a kind of guerilla warfare against him. What made this opposition even more extraordinary was that it was coming from conservative Catholics who, in the past, had demanded absolute obedience to the papacy. Previously, it has been liberal Catholics who have criticized popes, especially those whom they felt had not gone far enough with reforms. Now, with a Latin American pope whose style of ministry and priorities made them uncomfortable, a new group of conservative dissenters had

Spiritual Counterweight

emerged. Some of their objections were theological. They didn't like Francis loosening the rules to allow divorced and remarried Catholics to receive communion. They didn't like the welcome he extended to LGBTQ Catholics, or his defense of migrants, or his amending of Catholic teaching to make the death penalty inadmissible. It has to be said that most ordinary Catholics strongly supported Francis. The fiercest resistance was coming from sections of the Church hierarchy and the US Catholic media. Among the US bishops, the opposition to Francis could take the form of outspoken criticism, quiet resistance, or simply expressions of confusion about the pope's pastoral agenda. Early in his papacy, Francis signaled an end to what might be described as the "culture-war approach:" by which he meant a relentless focus on political opposition to abortion, same-sex marriage, and other so-called "pelvic" issues. "We cannot insist only on issues related to abortion, gay marriage, and the use of contraceptive methods. This is not possible," the pope said soon after his election. "The teaching of the Church, for that matter, is clear and I am a son of the Church, but it is not necessary to talk about these issues all the time."

It was a statement that pulled the rug from under some in the US Church. Charles Chaput, the influential retired archbishop of Philadelphia, was one of the fiercest critics, repeatedly accusing Francis of sowing confusion and being unclear in his teaching. I am told that in private Chaput found it hard to hide his frustration with the late pope and these frustrations would sometimes bubble out into the open. Even on the day Francis died, Chaput wasted no time in voicing harsh criticisms of him, saying that Francis had a "temperamental and autocratic" personality whose "loose words" had sowed "confusion and conflict." A few days later, Chaput spoke to *The Pillar*, a conservative Catholic news site. While he praised the late pope's personal generosity and kindness, he said that Francis "was often a cause of disunity because of his style and temperament" and that he "created ambiguity around important matters of doctrine, Christian practice, and Church law. And that never ends well." These were strong words from Chaput. It is extremely rare for an archbishop to speak of a pope in such terms on the day the pope dies. According to Catholic teaching, bishops are supposed to be in communion with the pope and the pope is the "visible source and foundation of the unity" between the bishops and the whole Church. That teaching was gravely tested in 2018 when some American bishops gave their support to the sensational dossier released by Archbishop Carlo Maria Viganò (mentioned in chapter one), which called upon Francis to resign. The fallout from the dossier was so serious that it was regarded by some as a "quiet schism." In later years, Francis's synodal reform process—focussed on listening and more participatory forms of Church governance—received only a lukewarm response from the US bishops.

Viganò's successor as the papal ambassador to the US was Cardinal Christophe Pierre, who had worked closely with Cardinal Robert Prevost to help rebalance the US hierarchy with moderates. As ambassador—or nuncio—it is his task to draw up a shortlist of three candidates whenever a diocese needs a new bishop. In an interview with the Jesuit publication *America*, Pierre admitted that some priests and bishops "are terribly against Francis" but that he was "shocked" to learn that many US bishops were unaware of the fact that Francis's synodal reforms were rooted in Church decisions taken in South America decades ago. The need for bottom-up governance, lay inclusion, and the insistence that the Church becomes a prophetic voice against injustice were all matters that were established during major Church gatherings in Medellín, Colombia, in 1968 and in Puebla, Mexico, in 1979. More recently, as archbishop of Buenos Aires Francis took a leading role at the 2007 Aparecida Conference in Brazil, which laid out a blueprint for the Latin American Church that prioritized the poor, the marginalized, and the environment. The experience of Catholicism in Latin America can feel very different from the experience of the European or US churches, but it's one that Pope Leo knows intimately. The outcome of Aparecida, Cardinal Pierre said, was the "development of a pastoral plan" that resulted from a synodal, listening approach. It formulated a means of transmitting the Catholic faith from one generation to the next in whatever cultural context. This was now an especially current challenge for the United States, with Hispanic immigrants reshaping the American Catholic Church and calling for a shift in approach. The dilemma for the Church, Pierre says, is that it is "at a change of epoch," which can lead some to start looking backward rather that forward, seeking security in the past.

Francis was aware of the dynamics of the opposition he faced and spoke of it numerous times. He was the first pope chosen from the Society of Jesus—the Jesuits— a religious order renowned for their missionary work, engagement with the culture, and in education. While the Jesuits do live in community, they can be focussed on their individual missions and work. The emphasis is different in Pope Leo's Augustinian order, which strongly emphasizes community and living in collective harmony. The pioneering, sometimes outspoken Jesuit spirit was often evident in Francis's pontificate, and it provoked strong reactions.

"In the United States the situation is not easy," he said in a discussion with his fellow Jesuits in August 2023. "There is a very strong reactionary attitude. It is organized and shapes the way people belong, even emotionally." The pope coined a new word to describe the attitude of his critics: *indietrismo* (being backward-looking). For several of Francis's critics, the Church was better in the "good old days," although he himself confessed to the temptation of nostalgia. "I would like to remind those people that *indietrismo* is useless and we need to understand that there is an appropriate evolution in the understanding of matters of faith and morals," he said.

During his papacy Francis chose cardinals who shared his vision. In the US, these included Blase Cupich in Chicago, Joseph Tobin in Newark, and Robert McElroy first in San Diego and then Washington, DC. Later appointments, with the help of the future Pope Leo and the nuncio Pierre, have helped make the United States Conference of Catholic Bishops (the overarching body of US bishops) more aligned to the pastoral priorities of Francis and Leo. This was underlined when the US bishops issued a rare statement expressing their concern about the "vilification" of migrants. It was also Cardinal Prevost who oversaw the Vatican bishop's office at the time of the removal of Bishop Joseph Strickland of Texas, who had set himself against Francis and had aligned himself with the MAGA movement.

Spiritual Counterweight

But there is work still to do. In November 2025, the US bishops' conference elected Archbishop Paul Coakley as their president. Coakley is an adviser to the Napa institute and among those who issued support for Archbishop Viganò's "integrity" in 2018, although he has said he does not support Viganò's later views. Coakley has also spoken up for immigrants. Leo's early appointments show that he understands how immigration is reshaping the US Church. And the choice of an American pope is hugely significant, given the past opposition to Francis. "The fact that I am American means, among other things, people can't say, like they did about Francis, 'He doesn't understand the United States, he just doesn't see what's going on,'" Leo says.

Pope Leo underlined this message with his most significant appointment to the US Church: his choice of Bishop Ronald Hicks to lead the Archdiocese of New York. This position, like the archbishop of Washington, DC, has a *de facto* national role in the Church's engagement with US culture and politics, and is influential among fellow bishops. In Archbishop Hicks, Leo chose a fellow Chicagoan who, like him, has spent time in Latin America and has firsthand experience in countries from which many have emigrated to the US. Hicks spent five years in El-Salvador working with orphaned and abandoned children, along with an earlier stint in Mexico, and has a devotion to Oscar Romero, the martyred former archbishop of San Salvador I mentioned at the beginning of the book. The new archbishop is someone out of the Leo mold: a good listener and bridge builder who has worked with bishops of different theological persuasions and can navigate ideological divides. He has been shaped by the church's social teaching, expressing his solidarity with migrants while his experience in El Salvador and Mexico reflects the growing influence of the Hispanic Catholic community in the US. And his appointment came at a time when the Trump administration was ramping up its anti-immigration policies to which the leadership of the church in the US—with the support of Leo—has responded with more vocal criticism.

Hicks's appointment also opened a new era for church leadership in the US. The archbishop took over in New York from Cardinal Timothy Dolan, a talented communicator and something of an ecclesiastical media star, who is often interviewed by news networks for his insights. He has a gift for making Church teaching accessible to a wide audience and is quick-witted and jovial. The cardinal is now past the episcopal retirement age of seventy-five, when, according to the Church's law, bishops must offer their resignation to the pope. However, it is also normal for those leading archdioceses such as New York to be asked to stay on beyond seventy-five.

Dolan was appointed to New York and made a cardinal by Benedict XVI. He was considered a rising star. In 2012, he was asked to address the German pope and the College of Cardinals on the topic of the "New Evangelization." During the Francis era, things were different and Dolan's role in the global Church was reduced. In the meantime, Dolan had become friendly with President Trump, once joking that he called Trump more often than he called his mother. In 2025, he offered one of the invocations at Trump's inauguration. While Dolan didn't publicly criticize Francis, in 2020 he forwarded to his fellow cardinals copies of a book entitled *The Next Pope: The Office of Peter and a Church in Mission*. Some of them were left "speechless" by the decision to distribute

Spiritual Counterweight

this book, given the strict rules against campaigning for a papal candidate. The author, George Weigel, was a critic of Francis. He pointed out that the book discussed no candidates nor any conclave strategy: it was simply a reflection on the office of the papacy. Nevertheless, it left the impression that Dolan was already thinking about the post-Francis Church.

Dolan also raised eyebrows after the shocking death of Charlie Kirk, the conservative activist who was assassinated at Utah Valley University on September 10, 2025, during a public dialogue with students. On *Fox News*, the cardinal likened Kirk to a modern-day St. Paul. While Kirk had often made compelling defenses of Christianity in his speeches, Dolan's comparing of him to one of the most transformative figures in the Christian Church felt to many like an inappropriate exaggeration. Kirk had also been critical of Pope Francis, saying on one occasion: "I can't get over the idea of this Marxist who calls himself the head of your Church being a representation of Christ our Lord." It made Dolan's comparison even more baffling. His remarks were met by a significant backlash, including from the Sisters of Charity in New York, a congregation founded by Elizabeth Ann Seton, the first American-born saint. The sisters, while condemning Kirk's murder, said that Cardinal Dolan's comparison was ill-advised given Kirk's anti-immigrant rhetoric and support for Christian nationalism.

The bottom line is that Leo is looking for bishops who don't become embroiled in the political culture war. For the diocese of Albany, Eastern New York, he selected Bishop Mark O'Connell. O'Connell is a pastoral moderate who in 2021 opposed a document from his fellow bishops which would have sought to ban Catholic politicians from communion if they supported pro-abortion legislation. This was aimed at President Biden and his support for abortion laws. O'Connell opposed any blanket ruling on this topic, saying it should be left to private conversations between an individual politician and his pastor and local bishop. O'Connell said the formulation of such a document by the bishops could "further polarize our people," something that is likely to be echoed by the pope. The choice of O'Connell, and the bishops with immigrant backgrounds, shows that Leo wants Church leaders who speak out against injustices, but stay out of the boxing ring of partisan politics.

Roman politics

Leo regularly meets heads of states and government leaders visiting Rome, and the Vatican is highly experienced in diplomacy.

The ninety foreign embassies based in Rome regularly host events where senior Vatican officials and diplomats meet informally—part of the papacy's soft power. And, as I have mentioned, the Vatican has long been considered a good "listening post" by foreign offices, a place to pick up information from seasoned diplomats both inside and outside the Church. The Vatican carries out much of its diplomacy through the ambassadors based in Rome, particularly when it comes to pushing for solutions to global conflicts. When Russia invaded Ukraine in 2022, Pope Francis made the unheard-of decision to drive to Russia's embassy to the Holy See to make his feelings

Spiritual Counterweight

known. Leo, who has met President Volodymyr Zelensky on several occasions, has offered the Vatican as a neutral ground for talks between Russia and Ukraine, although he expressed doubts about whether he could broker a peace. In any event, Russia dashed diplomats' hopes by saying that the Vatican was not an appropriate venue for negotiations.

The Holy See embassies will often host and accompany visiting heads of state, leaders of governments, and other government ministers to the Vatican, where they will meet the pope or senior Vatican officials. In October 2025, it was the United Kingdom's embassy to the Holy See that arranged the historic state visit to the Vatican for King Charles and Queen Camilla, rearranging a visit that had been postponed due to the ill health of Francis (the king and queen did manage a brief meeting with the pontiff shortly before he died). British Prime Minister Gordon Brown visited the Vatican in 2009 to formally invite Pope Benedict XVI to visit the UK in 2010. And in 2018, Penny Mordaunt, then the UK's International Development Secretary, urged senior Vatican officials to relax the Catholic Church's ban on artificial contraception and to do more to support LGBTQ rights, saying that the Church's voice can have an influence in ending hatred. I understand that Mordaunt's intervention was not received favorably as it was seen as an outside attempt to influence Church policy, but the incident is illustrative of the fact that governments recognize the Church's worldwide influence, and the need to engage the Vatican. Since 2014, the Holy See's foreign minister has been Archbishop Paul Gallagher, a Liverpool-born priest who has served in Burundi, Guatemala, Uruguay, and Australia before taking up his current post.

Alongside his native English, Archbishop Gallagher speaks Italian, Spanish, and French fluently, an ability unlikely to be matched by many of his counterparts in the UK. The Vatican has a special diplomatic training school in Rome, the Pontifical Ecclesiastical Academy, known as the Accademia, where it sends some of the brightest and best priests to be trained in languages and law. The Vatican has its own embassies across the world which are led by ambassadors, known as apostolic nuncios.

The US and the Holy See have had formal diplomatic relations since 1984. Forty years on, the newly re-elected President Trump named Brian Burch as his ambassador to the Holy See, a decision that put some pressure on the relationship with the Vatican. Burch is the co-founder of Catholic Vote, a political organization that supported Trump in the 2024 presidential election. He had previously been critical of Pope Francis, saying that Francis had created "confusion" after he authorized blessings for same-sex couples. Burch had also criticized Francis's governance for what he described as a "pattern of vindictiveness."

The election of Leo offered a chance to reset the relationship with the US, with Burch taking up his position several months after the 2025 conclave. The new ambassador presented his credentials to Leo the day before the pope's seventieth birthday and brought with him a chocolate cake from Portillo's, a restaurant chain headquartered in Chicago. Burch's strong family values are likely to endear him to officials in the Vatican: he is a married father of nine who says that his Catholic faith has made him who he is.

Leo maintains warm relations with Ambassador Burch,

and vice versa. After their first meeting, the ambassador told people at a reception that the pope had pointed out to him that he was not an "American pope" but "a pope from America for the world." During their conversation, the ambassador also raised the assassination of Charlie Kirk. Later the US embassy to the Holy See posted on X that the pope "underscored that our political differences can never be resolved with violence and told Ambassador Burch that he was praying for the widow of Mr. Kirk and his children." It was through the embassy, rather than through the Vatican's official channels, that any insight into what Leo thought about the shooting was revealed.

Discussing the tragic death of Mr. Kirk was understandable given the huge impact it was having on the US. But it also shows how Leo could come under pressure to comment on major incidents in the US. The new ambassador to the Holy See is very much a Trump appointment, something emphasized at a reception held in Rome to celebrate the presentation of his credentials to the pope. The most senior Church figures at the event were two Wisconsin-born US cardinals. The first, Raymond Burke, the former head of the Church's supreme court, was a public critic of Francis and a supporter of Trump. The second, James Harvey, a former Vatican diplomat who oversees the papal basilica of St. Paul-Outside-the-Walls, is very discreet but is friendly with key conservative critics of Francis.

Another area in which Leo is likely to come under diplomatic pressure is in the Holy See's attempt at a diplomatic rapprochement with China. In 2018, the papacy and Beijing signed an historic agreement on the matter of appointing of bishops. The deal was controversial. Its details have never been made public, although it appears to give a role to the Chinese state in the appointment of bishops. Several popes have sought to normalize the situation for Catholics in China. The Chinese Catholic Church is, in effect, a state-sanctioned Church. However, many Christians in China balk at worshipping in churches run by state-compliant priests, and instead seek to join underground churches, with services often held in people's homes. Francis's aim was to ensure there is one Catholic Church in China, even if it means making compromises with Beijing. Leo has said that he will continue the arrangement in the short term, although he has listened to "Chinese Catholics who for many years have lived some kind of oppression or difficulty in living their faith freely," which suggests that he may be open to a change of direction. As leader of the Augustinians from 2001 to 2013, Prevost has spent some time in China, a country that no pope has yet visited. Some Catholics are strongly opposed to any deal with Beijing. The Vatican's approach was also deeply unpopular with the first Trump administration. In September 2020, Secretary of State Mike Pompeo accused the Vatican of risking its "moral authority" should it renew its deal with China, which the Holy See nevertheless went on to do. Pompeo traveled to Rome to urge Vatican officials to reconsider, and at an event held at the US embassy to the Holy See he denounced China's record on religious freedom. However, he was denied an audience with Pope Francis, because, the Vatican told him, the pope avoids meeting political figures in the run up to elections.

When it comes to the culture wars, Leo's position, like Francis's, encompasses the "both/and" approach of

Spiritual Counterweight

Catholic teaching. Like Francis, Leo, too, is facing criticism from conservative Catholics who want to make opposition to abortion the most pressing issue for the Church's engagement in politics. In 2023, the bishops of the United States reiterated their position on abortion as their "pre-eminent priority." On the other hand, there are those who argue that a Catholic's defense for life in the womb must also extend to a defense of all life, and that means opposing the death penalty and supporting migrants. Pope Francis, who strongly opposed abortion, ruled that the death penalty was "inadmissible" and changed Catholic teaching on this topic. Some conservative Catholics resisted this, and maintained that the Church can support the death penalty. But once again, Leo's position on the matter is clear. In 2011, Rev. Robert Prevost personally emailed the then governor of Illinois, Pat Quinn, to thank him for abolishing capital punishment in Illinois, Prevost's home state.

"THANK YOU for your courageous decision in signing into law the elimination of the death penalty," Prevost, then prior general of the Augustinians, wrote. "I know it was a difficult decision, but I applaud your vision and your understanding of the very complex matter. You have my full support!"

Leo spelt out his position on life topics when he was asked about a certain controversy in Chicago. In September 2025, Cardinal Cupich had decided to give a lifetime achievement award to Senator Dick Durbin in recognition of his work on immigration reform. At least ten bishops objected to the award because of Durbin's support for legal abortion (although he personally opposes abortion). Leo replied by questioning whether a Catholic can truly say that they are pro-life while supporting the "inhuman" treatment of immigrants in the US, and added that it is "not really pro-life" to oppose abortion and support the death penalty. He also said that the entirety of Senator Durbin's forty-year service should be taken into account before judging him. Leo remains close to Cupich and while the Chicago cardinal faced criticism for the Durbin award, the pope appointed him as a board member of the Vatican City State administration not long after.

On life issues, including abortion, this pope's approach is close to what is known as the "seamless garment" understanding of Catholic teaching—meaning that every issue is connected—and the "consistent life ethic," which fosters a culture of defending life rather than any overt focus on a single issue. In other words, it is inconsistent for Catholics to campaign against abortion while saying nothing about child refugees dying at the US–Mexico border or on the shores of southern Europe. Conservative commentators have criticized Leo for his support for the consistent life ethic, with one saying that his views are "disappointing" and "largely irrelevant." His comments on immigration and his support for protecting the climate led one influencer who is supportive of Trump to write simply: "Some popes are a blessing. Some popes are a penance."

Leo remains a US citizen and is still registered as a voter in the Chicago suburb of New Lennox. Voting records show that he's cast ballots regularly in both Republican and Democrat primaries but is not registered with any political party, despite a claim by the late Charlie Kirk on X that "he's a registered Republican" and "a strong Republican." His affiliation is, in fact, "undeclared."

Spiritual Counterweight

Most recently, he voted in the 2024 presidential election, although it is not known which candidate he favored. Kirk was, however, correct in saying that the pope is "pro-life," which is rather stating the obvious. In 2016, Prevost's Twitter account retweeted an article criticizing Hillary Clinton's "extreme abortion position," which it said had alienated voters, including Democrats. As pope, Leo has warned against the "pandemic of arms large and small" following a shooting at a Catholic school in Minnesota in August 2025 which killed two children. He made his remarks about gun control in English so that they would be heard in the right places.

While Leo's style is quiet and measured, it doesn't mean he won't take a stand. As bishop of Chiclayo, he publicly questioned the decision by President Pedro Pablo Kuczynski to offer a pardon to the disgraced former president Alberto Fujimori, who had led the country during the internal conflict and had used lethal force to crack down on the Shining Path guerilla group.

As pope, he made a robust diplomatic intervention both before and after his September 2025 meeting with the President of Israel, Isaac Herzog. Ahead of a papal audience, Herzog's office said the president was traveling to the Vatican at the pope's invitation. But the Vatican then issued a highly unusual statement. "It is the practice of the Holy See to grant requests for audiences addressed to the pope by heads of state and government," a spokesman explained. "It is not the practice to extend invitations to them." It made it clear that Leo had not been the one to initiate the audience.

Leo's approach is to try to engage leaders directly, rather than simply make bold statements. He has kept a channel of dialogue open with Israel, condemned the rise of antisemitism, and spoke to Prime Minister Benjamin Netanyahu after an Israeli missile struck the Catholic Church in Gaza. He has a diplomatic strategy that seeks to persuade or mediate through dialogue, but he won't allow himself to be used for political ends. When Rafael López Aliaga, the founder of a right-wing populist party who hoped to be a candidate in Peru's 2026 presidential elections, sought a private meeting with Leo, he was denied. "I think Leo is aware that this is the fight of his life and that if he wants to be like his namesake Leo XIII—who was one of the longest-serving popes—then he has to save his strength for the battles to come," Dawn Eden Goldstein explained. "He knows where the winds are blowing, he's been speaking about suffering Ukraine, and suffering Gaza. He has spoken against polarization."

Leo says he doesn't believe that his primary role is to solve the problems of the world. He is aware of his limitations, and those of the Church. The pope says that his most important task is to "confirm others in their faith." While he prioritizes the spiritual nature of his ministry, he insists that the Church has a voice and a message that needs to be "spoken and spoken loudly." This message, he believes, offers a response to humanity's crises that is rooted in faith. Leo's pontificate—gentle, firm, and non-confrontational—makes him very different from any other world leader. At a dark and turbulent time in world history, when a president is leading the United States along a path that many believe is fraught with chaos and uncertainty, here is one of the world's most visible Americans saying there is a different and better way.

3

Unifying the Church?

Leo's first appearance on the balcony of St. Peter's contained a message. It wasn't only in his words, but in what he wore. "He dresses like Benedict, speaks like Francis," is how one senior figure put it.

Over his white cassock Leo had donned a short red cape, known as a mozzetta, over another white vestment. Pope Francis, who'd wanted a simpler, more modest papacy, had dispensed with that traditional papal attire in 2013, reportedly remarking, before making his appearance on the balcony, that "the carnival is over." Red was a color Benedict XVI had been known for. His red papal loafers became iconic in the fashion world, even though the color was meant to symbolize Christ's sacrifice and the blood of the martyrs. Benedict had also worn a wide-rimmed red hat at public audiences in summer, and in winter had sported a red velvet cap with a white ermine trim, not unlike that worn by Santa Claus. Pope Leo also wears the red mozzetta and white vestment when he receives heads of state in private audiences, and he also puts on an additional vestment, a stole, which is used when giving a blessing.

Leo's choice of dress doesn't simply demonstrate a respect for protocol. It is a message that he wants to bring the whole Church with him, that there is room for everyone. During the Francis pontificate, some younger priests and trainee seminarians had felt alienated by the pope's rebukes about their dress. The late pope told a gathering in the Vatican that it was a "scandal" to see young priests in Rome's ecclesiastical tailor shops trying on hats and elaborate robes, while on another occasion he told priests to stop wearing "grandma's lace." To the senior, experienced figures in the Church, Francis had correctly identified a serious problem—that some clerics had the wrong priorities. An old-fashioned Jesuit, the late pope was as tough on himself as he was on others.

On the other hand, as Robert Mickens, a long-time Catholic commentator has pointed out, a good number of clergy were "unable to hear" what Francis said because they were "not mature enough to accept his rebukes."

By adopting certain formalities of office, Leo has smoothed some of these tensions. He wears a more classical type of pectoral cross, and his ability to sing well in Latin has helped win over those who found Francis's criticisms of clerical culture hard to take. The pope's choice of vestments, his comfort with Latin, and his gentler, more moderate style has been seen by some as a deliberate break with Francis. For them, the twelve years of the last pontificate were an anomaly and now, with Leo, the Church can go back to "normal."

But this is not what Leo is doing. When I asked one senior prelate whether Leo's choice of vestments and his singing in Latin were signs that he was a secret traditionalist, he replied with a smile: "They call it a head fake," meaning an action that tricks an opponent by mimicking an intended movement in one direction before going in another. Ironically, while many perceived Francis as a "liberal" his instincts were quite conservative, but he moderated by being bold and radical. Leo, on the other hand, has more progressive instincts but moderates by seeing the conservative point of view.

The pope's willingness to take on board different points of view—and to listen to everyone—makes it harder for those who might wish to oppose a decision they disagree with later down the line. "He is like a religious superior," the senior figure explained. "He will say, 'This is the approach we are going to take; I listened to you and now I am asking you to get behind this decision.' He will expect this to be done as a matter of accountability." As a young man, the future pope had talked about this in his doctoral thesis when he explored the nature of power and authority in the Augustinian order. It still applies now he is pope. "While great emphasis is placed upon the necessity of seeking consensus among the members of a community in the last analysis there must be an authority figure whose decision will be recognized and accepted by the group," he wrote.

Prevost, in his thesis, explained that good decision-making involves the "creative combination" of the will of the superior and the contribution of the community member. On this point, he cites Ladislas Orsy, an internationally respected Church lawyer who served as an adviser to the archbishop of Salisbury (now Harare, Zimbabwe) at the Second Vatican Council. Prevost quoted Orsy when he wrote that "a discerning superior will find a balance between imposing his own will on another person and letting him formulate a responsible decision."

Inside the Catholic Church different groups are making great demands upon Leo. On the one hand, traditionalists want him to move the Church in a more conservative direction, and essentially to reverse some of Francis's most consequential decisions. On the other, progressive Catholics want Leo to go further and faster on reforms, especially those concerning the ordination of women and the reframing of Church teaching on sexuality and LGBTQ questions.

Leo has become leader of the Church at a time when debate on a range of highly controversial topics has only really been taking place for a relatively short period. When Francis was elected, certain topics—the ordination of women, married priests, and homosexuality—were not openly discussed. For thirty-three years, John Paul II and then Benedict XVI maintained theological red lines. Any theologians or bishops who crossed them could find themselves in hot water. There was Bishop Bill Morris, removed—without due process—from his leadership of the Diocese of Toowoomba, Australia, after he wondered whether ordaining married men and women might solve the problem of an acute shortage of priests in a diocese that covered a landmass larger than California. Other cases included Fr. Jacques Dupuis, placed under a two-and-half-year investigation by the doctrine office for his pioneering work in inter-faith dialogue, and Sister Jeanine Gramick, a nun who was censured by the Vatican for her

Unifying the Church?

ministry (with a priest) to LGBTQ Catholics. (Francis later rehabilitated her, and praised her work as following the "style of God.") Criticisms of popes John Paul II and Benedict were not tolerated.

All this contributed to a climate of fear and silence inside the Church. But when Francis was elected, it evaporated, and suddenly everything was on the table. The Argentine pope's election was like a father walking into a huge family gathering and asking why no one was talking. Francis complained about this attitude in Rome, recalling his experience as a cardinal at a major Church synod in 2001. He had been given the key role of gathering the material for the synod and arranging it, only to find a senior official would "remove this or that thing, which had been approved by a vote of the various groups." It was, he said, a "pre-selection of materials." But Francis said: "Today, we have moved forward and there is no going back."

Suddenly, the spinning plates of disagreement started to fly and smash. Francis himself faced serious criticism at times—but he allowed his critics the freedom to speak. He even appointed cardinals who held views very different from his own into senior Vatican positions. The windows and the doors of the Church had been flung open, and a healthy atmosphere of debate ensued.

On the other hand, Leo takes over a Church at a time when discussions have, occasionally, become polarized. Different groups are pushing their agendas and in response to their demands, Leo holds private audiences with leaders from across the Church. Where needed, he shows generosity and welcomes those who come from different ends of the Church spectrum. No one is being shut out of the conversation. He is purposefully not taking strong positions on issues, instead doing all he can to be a "pontifex," a bridge builder. Should his approach be successful, then he will ensure that the Church—as a largely unified body—is able to renew and reform. The risk, of course, is that his pontificate ends up in the middle of the road, getting knocked around by major events.

Traditionalist hopes

One group that has been lobbying Leo persistently and directly is that seeking a reversal of Pope Francis's restrictions on the so-called Traditional Latin Mass, the rite of the Mass codified in the sixteenth century, following the Council of Trent, and celebrated until the reforms mandated by Vatican II. As I mentioned earlier, in the pre-Vatican II Mass, the liturgy was spoken in Latin by the priest facing away from the people (technically known as *ad orientem*, or facing east), with parts of the liturgy said in silence by the priest, inaudible to the people. Women could not offer readings or be near the altar. Following Leo's election there were wild—and unsubstantiated—rumors that Cardinal Prevost had celebrated the older form of the Mass while a cardinal in Rome. This raised traditionalists' hopes that the older form of the liturgy could be more widely celebrated. Leo, however, is a friar, priest, and bishop formed in the teaching of Vatican II, and will have had little, if any, exposure to the Traditional Latin Mass while he served in Peru. According to a Mass

Unifying the Church?

listings site, the country does not have a single officially sanctioned and regularly celebrated traditional Mass.

Vatican II's liturgical reforms allowed for the Mass to be said in local languages. Priests started to face the congregation; the liturgy focussed on a "noble simplicity" in worship and a stronger sense of participation from the people. These changes reflected an understanding of the Church as the "People of God" and followed the Latin axiom *lex orandi lex credendi*—the concept that says "the way we worship" is "what we believe." Cardinal Cupich, the archbishop of Chicago and, as I have mentioned, a friend of Leo, argued in 2025 that, over the years, the Catholic liturgy had "incorporated elements from imperial and royal courts." This, he said, had transformed its "aesthetics and meaning" and had made it "more of a spectacle rather than the active participation of all the baptized [members] in the saving action of Christ crucified." The attempted reforms of the liturgy were a way of going deeper into the tradition, sifting out what was essential, and then renewing Catholic worship.

Not everyone saw it this way. A small yet vocal group resisted the changes and over the years they pushed to allow greater freedom to celebrate the older liturgy. They disputed the reforms and would frequently criticize so-called "abuses" in celebrations of Mass since the 1960s, such as the inclusion of dancing, "clown Masses" (in which priests try to bring some playfulness into the liturgy), the ignoring of liturgical rules, and the inclusion of inappropriate music, while insisting that the older form was a more reverent and respectful way to worship. The Traditional Latin Mass has developed a strong following among groups of young people in France, the UK, and the US. Young people are frequently talking about the silence and mystery of the older form, which is attractive to them because it is so completely different from contemporary life. More traditional forms of worship, which follow a precise ritual, seem appealing and consoling at a time of deep uncertainty.

In the years after the reforms were authorized, Pope Paul VI allowed elderly or aged priests to carry on celebrating the older liturgy in private, although he widened the permission after a special appeal was made from cultural figures in Britain, including Agatha Christie and Graham Greene. This became known as "the Agatha Christie indult [permission]." In 2024, a similar request to protect its celebration was made to Pope Francis by cultural figures in the UK. The signatories included Lord (Andrew) Lloyd-Webber, the composer; Tristram Hunt, director of the Victoria and Albert Museum in London; and the author Lady Antonia Fraser.

The signatories also included non-Catholics and non-believers, who seemed primarily concerned with ensuring access to the "magnificent spiritual and cultural heritage" of the older rite, an appeal based on protection of patrimony rather than theology. It is almost as if the pope was being asked not to close to the public an historic house containing wonderful works of art so that people could still be allowed to visit. In the Catholic understanding, tradition is not simply something to "preserve," it is something living, rooted in the Latin word *tradere*, meaning to hand over. Official teaching sees the current form of

Unifying the Church?

the Mass as the liturgy that has been celebrated from the beginning, albeit in different forms updated over time.

To accommodate those who preferred the older form, John Paul II widened permissions for the Traditional Latin Mass celebrations. Benedict XVI went even further, lifting restrictions on the old rite in 2007. Fourteen years later, Francis reimposed restrictions, saying that Benedict's generosity had been exploited by those seeking to foster division in the Church. Francis's decision—which did not ban the older Mass outright but restricted it and left decisions in the hands of local bishops—received a deeply hostile response from traditionalists. Francis believed that the older rite was being used to reject the teachings of Vatican II, a serious situation given that a council's decisions have the highest legal authority in the Church. Francis said he'd made his decision after circulating a questionnaire to bishops. The French hierarchy, which was leading a Church in which the Traditional Latin Mass was popular, said that Benedict's opening had "failed to deliver on its vision for unity in the Church," and had created "rigid mutual mistrust" between the different forms of the Mass. The issue, the French bishops said, was primarily "ecclesiological," meaning that it concerned how the Church was understood by supporters of the traditional Mass, rather than the forms of worship. Since Pope Leo's election, however, a journalist sympathetic to the traditionalist case published a document written inside the Vatican revealing that a majority of the bishops surveyed in the questionnaire had not seen a case for restrictions on the older rite of the liturgy. The disclosure of the document—which gave only a partial picture of the situation—looked like a strategic leak designed to exert pressure on Leo.

"You can say Mass in Latin right now. If it's the Vatican II rite, there's no problem," Pope Leo says. He is wary of polarization and ideology when it concerns the liturgy but says he's willing to talk to traditionalist groups. As Leo suggested, the issue is not about the use of Latin—which is used in Masses said by the pope—but about an understanding of the Church. With Francis, traditionalists opposed virtually everything he did. In 2017, a group of critics issued him with a "filial correction" (a respectful request that he correct his doctrinal errors) for allowing the spread of heresies in his teachings on marriage and family life. Two years later some priests and scholars accused him of the "canonical delict of heresy," and urged the world's bishops to act. This latter charge was much more serious. It effectively accused Francis of obstinately denying the truths of the Catholic faith.

Pope Leo must judge for himself how far traditionalists and conservative Catholics are willing to compromise. Support for the Traditional Latin Mass continues to come from high-profile figures in culture and the media, among them Harrison Butker, the NFL American football kicker, who has been photographed with Cardinal Burke, and movie star Shia LaBeouf. Michael Knowles, the US conservative political commentator, has spoken in favor of the older liturgy and has observed that support for the Traditional Latin Mass often goes hand in hand with certain political positions.

Given how vociferously the traditionalist groups opposed Francis, will they shift under Leo? Mike Lewis,

Unifying the Church?

the editor of the website "Where Peter Is," follows the traditionalist Catholic movement closely. He believes it will be difficult for Leo to get everyone on board, although he sees a distinction between those who attend the older liturgies and its leaders.

"I think that most of the faithful—the rank and file, not the super-online traditionalists—go to the older liturgy because they like the atmosphere, the Latin, and the reverence, and they are not so aware of the ecclesiastical and theological battles in the Church," he explained. "The problem is that many of the traditionalist clergy and the spokespeople for the groups have a strong ideological and theological aversion to the reformed Mass. They would react very badly to any situation that requires them to participate in the reformed liturgy. It is likely to result in a loud and aggressive reaction."

Lewis says that traditionalists are working to convince Leo that he should make the older liturgy more widely available. But he said that for many the real end goal is the full restoration of the pre-Vatican II Mass, with some priestly groups refusing to celebrate major liturgies with priests who use the reformed Mass.

Any concession or gesture by Leo will be embraced—even pushed—to the maximum limit by those who want wider use of the older liturgy. Leo will have to keep this in mind given that the most significant, formal fracture to Church unity in recent Catholic history concerns the traditionalists who were led by a French archbishop, Marcel Lefebvre. He rejected several key teachings of Vatican II and was excommunicated in 1988 after he consecrated four bishops without Rome's approval. Lefebvre's followers still congregate today as the Society of St. Pius X. Several popes have tried, unsuccessfully, to return them to the fold. Francis made overtures to the SSPX, although its leader, Bishop Bernard Fellay, later signed the 2017 filial correction that asked Francis to stop spreading heresies. Healing the rift with the SSPX is fraught with difficulty. Benedict XVI lifted the excommunications on the four bishops illicitly ordained by Lefebvre, but it later turned out that one of them, the late Bishop Richard Williamson, had recently denied the Holocaust. The decision to lift Williamson's excommunication provoked global outrage and caused a crisis in Benedict's papacy. Williamson, who was British and had been educated at Winchester College and Cambridge before converting to Catholicism, was known for his outlandish views. He once condemned *The Sound of Music* as "soul-rotting slush" and said that trouser-wearing women were a "revolt against the order willed by God."

Leo has to tread carefully in this area. In Rome, the two figures leading the traditionalist push are US Cardinal Raymond Burke and Cardinal Robert Sarah, the former prefect of the Vatican's liturgy office. Leo has met privately with both Burke and Sarah to hear their points of view. Both of them have formidable and well-resourced followings of conservative supporters. They get their message out through statements, books, and interviews given to carefully selected media outlets.

Cardinal Burke wants a return to how things were under Benedict and is pushing Leo to make the "more ancient usage" of the liturgy more widely available. He is a canon lawyer and a former prefect of the Catholic

Unifying the Church?

Church's Apostolic Signatura, the equivalent of a supreme court. Burke had consistently opposed Francis, who, toward the end of his pontificate, removed some of Burke's privileges, including a subsidy on his 4,488-square-foot Vatican apartment and a monthly stipend of around £4,300 ($5,900).

Burke has wiped the slate clean with Leo. Following their private audience, permission was granted for a group of traditionalists to celebrate an older-rite Mass at one of the main altars in St. Peter's Basilica. For defenders of the older liturgy, the sight of thousands of people attending the Mass in St. Peter's was a sign that they were "back," and even that restrictions might lift in the future. The event was reported on with a certain triumphant tone on traditionalists sites. A Vatican source, however, described granting permission for the Mass as an act of generosity on Leo's part, but that the pope was also testing the water to see how the group acts. Can they enter into a meaningful dialogue, and compromise, over the liturgy?

Over the same October weekend that the traditional Mass in St. Peter's was celebrated, a meeting focussed on the Church's synod renewal process took place. Two different visions of the Church that Leo is leading were on display. The first, celebrating an older form of liturgy, saw dozens of priests seated around the altar and the cardinal celebrating the Mass dressed in magnificent white and gold vestments. They represented a strongly hierarchical Church with a message that the Church's future lay in rehabilitating the styles of worship used in its past. Several of the clergy taking part in the Mass were young, as were the families who attended. The second was a gathering of representatives from across the world: bishops, laypeople, and cardinals who were taking part in discussions about how to implement reforms focussed on the Church's living tradition, including Vatican II's description of the Church as "the People of God." While still respecting hierarchy, the synodal vision, according to Leo, offers "a more humble Church" that is open and listening. While traditionalist groups have frequently criticized the synod, Leo has suggested that the disagreements are handled by synodal-style discussions.

Cardinal Arthur Roche, the British prefect of the Vatican office in charge of liturgy, is a moderate and is likely to be someone Leo listens to closely. The two worked together in the Vatican before Leo became pope. Cardinal Roche is the equivalent of an opening batsman when it comes to liturgical questions. Because he's been central to implementing the restrictions on the older form of the Mass, he has faced down a torrent of aggressive bowling, including bouncers and other fast deliveries. The Yorkshire-born prelate has managed to defend his wicket and pick up runs where needed. He's also been unafraid to speak out against those "stubbornly" opposing the reforms of Vatican II and says they risk adopting a position that is no longer Catholic.

Cardinal Sarah ran the same department as Roche, but his positions on the liturgy were at odds with those of Francis, who even publicly corrected Sarah on several occasions. "I wonder if a ritual that is over a thousand years old can be 'banned,'" Sarah said in an interview several months into Leo's papacy and just a few days ahead of a private audience with the pope. "If liturgy is also a source for theology, how can access to 'ancient sources' be prohibited? It would be like prohibiting the study of St. Augustine to those who want to reflect correctly on grace or the Trinity." The reference to St. Augustine during the papacy of an Augustinian pontiff was quite pointed.

Sarah is one of the most prominent African prelates in Rome. He has led an extraordinary life. Born in Guinea in 1945, he grew up in mud huts in a mountainous bushland region of the country. He was ordained at the age of twenty-five and became archbishop of Conakry at thirty-four. He was in post during the hostile dictatorships of Sékou Touré and Lansana Conté, against whom he spoke out for their mismanagement of the country. It later emerged Touré had planned to arrest and execute Sarah. He was called to work in the Vatican in 2001 but now, at the age of eighty, he is a retired cardinal living in Rome. Retirement allows him time to give speeches, travel, and make his case. Other cardinals in Africa will look to him for guidance. At a synod assembly in the Vatican, he denounced "Western homosexual and abortion ideologies and Islamic fanaticism." In one of his books, written with the conservative French author Nicolas Diat, he warned that the West is opening itself to "new, barbaric civilizations" by allowing immigration. Sarah presented himself as a sort of parallel authority during the Francis pontificate, an alternative vision of leadership, even while he continued to work for the pope. Despite being publicly corrected, he insisted that he "never opposed" Francis, but when the pope was considering a request from bishops in the Amazon region to ordain married men, Sarah made an extraordinary intervention. He published a book—presented as jointly authored with Benedict XVI—defending the status quo on mandatory celibacy for priests. It later turned out that Benedict had simply provided an essay for the book and asked for his name to be removed as co-author in future editions. The politics of the Eternal City are subtle, but they can be brutal. Leo will need to be on his guard. Intriguingly, following their meetings with the pope both cardinals Burke and Sarah have said little about what was discussed. Of course, it is protocol not to reveal private conversations with the pope, but they could have agreed with Leo in the meeting about releasing certain details. The lack of information suggests that the pope was careful to do most of the listening, while giving little away. Listening to someone is not the same as agreeing.

Traditionalists make up a tiny percentage of the world's 1.4 billion Catholics. However, they have an outsized influence in Rome, and they are trying to shift the conversation. They have the support and ears of influential bishops, and there is a noticeable drift toward traditionalism among younger clergy and those training for the priesthood. Leo must consider not just the traditionalists' views but the conservative shift in the clergy's thinking in the US and Europe.

LGBTQ *flashpoint*

Traditionalist liturgy is not the only area in which Leo is facing intense lobbying. Cardinal Sarah and other African prelates are pushing for a repudiation of Francis's

Unifying the Church?

approach to gay Catholics, in particular his landmark decision to allow individual priests to bless same-sex couples. In the aftermath of this decision, Cardinal Fridolin Ambongo Besungu of Kinshasa, in the Democratic Republic of Congo, sent Pope Francis a seven-page letter and flew to see him in Rome. The decision to allow blessings, the cardinal later explained, had caused a "shockwave" in Africa. "We didn't understand what was happening at the Church level," he said. In consultation with the pope and the Vatican's doctrine office, a statement was released: "No blessing for homosexual couples in all Churches in Africa." At the same time, it said gay people must be treated with "respect and dignity" and offered pastoral care. Francis's ruling essentially allowed for brief, informal blessings to be offered outside of a Church context. Priests are permitted to bless cars, animals, and houses without controversy, but when it comes to same-sex or "irregular" relationships, the reactions can be extremely emotive. Although Cardinal Ambongo won an exception from Rome on blessings, he had overstated his case by claiming to speak for the whole of Africa. A grouping of bishops from North Africa contradicted the Congolese prelate with their own statement, saying that blessings would be offered in their dioceses. The North African bishops said that Francis's ruling, titled *Fiducia supplicans* (Supplicating trust) would help "deepen the concrete paths of a pastoral ministry of reconciliation and communion."

Since Leo's election, both cardinals Ambongo and Sarah have been strongly criticizing the blessing of same-sex couples. The Congolese cardinal described it as "a bad chapter" in Francis's pontificate, which had "caused a lot of harm to the Catholic faithful, and even beyond." Sarah, meanwhile, said it is time to "clarify and perhaps reformulate" the blessings document, which, he says, "endangers the unity of the Church" and "is a document to be forgotten." Cardinal Ambongo is an influential figure. He leads one of the largest local Catholic churches in the world (the archdiocese of Kinshasa has more than 7.5 million Catholics). I witnessed for myself the Church's influence in the DRC during Francis's visit to the country in 2023. The streets of Kinshasa were lined with crowds of people, several rows deep, who had come to greet the pope. Later, he addressed a gathering of 65,000 young people, who filled the country's largest stadium. The cardinal and the Church leaders play a hugely important role in the DRC. They are the providers of healthcare and education; they are voices for civil society and they defend democracy and human rights.

Given the rapid growth of the Church in Africa and its increasing influence on global Catholicism, Leo must pay close attention to leaders such as Cardinal Ambongo. Inside the major synod gatherings attended by Cardinal Prevost in 2023 and 2024, the welcome of LGBTQ Catholics became one of the most difficult topics of conversation. Synod delegates heard testimony about a young LGBTQ person who had not felt welcomed by Catholic Church officials and subsequently took her own life. Many of the delegates wept. But there was also strong resistance, mainly from African and eastern European prelates, to any significant shifts, including some fiery interventions in 2023. Rev. James Martin, a priest and author who ministers to LGBTQ Catholics, was one of the synod delegates.

Unifying the Church?

He said that one delegate didn't want to sit next to him, one didn't want to use the word LGBTQ, and others used the words "disgusting" and "appalling" in conversations with him about the topic. The collective synod documents did not specifically mention LGBTQ Catholics, although pastoral support for those in polygamous marriages—a particular concern of the African Church—made it onto the agenda. But Rev. Martin did notice that during the synod process attitudes started to change, and that today the LGBTQ issue is up for discussion. Watching all this was the future pope. He was in the synod listening to the debates, hearing from delegates who talked about LGBTQ family and friends.

During the Francis pontificate the tone and approach of the Vatican towards homosexuality changed. The fact that the issue was discussed at all during the synod was significant, as was the fact that attitudes started to shift during the gathering. It is also true that within virtually every Christian denomination the recognition of same-sex couples—whether in the form of blessings or marriage—is a contested topic that has strained unity. Francis sought to welcome gay people into the Church without changing doctrine. Leo looks set to do the same. In past pontificates, gay Catholics had felt alienated and hurt by some of the harsh language coming from the Vatican on homosexuality. Francis signaled a new approach when he famously said, "Who am I to judge?" when asked about gay priests. He insisted that LGBTQ people were "children of God" and invited transgender women to the Vatican for lunch. He went further than mere words and gestures. His decision on same-sex blessings came alongside his support for the civil recognition of same-sex couples—something the Vatican had opposed in the past—and his call for the decriminalization of homosexuality in the DRC and South Sudan, a call he made before and after his visit to those countries. Francis's intervention on decriminalization—the first by any pope—was highly significant given that around thirty-one African countries criminalize same-sex relations. Despite the pope's statement on decriminalization, cardinals Ambongo and Sarah have remained silent on this topic.

Leo continues to face public pressure in the form of letters and petitions. One of them, entitled, "A Filial and Apprehensive Supplication to His Holiness Pope Leo XIV," warned, in dramatic language, of "an open offensive to impose the acceptance of homosexual unions" while claiming that "some forces are striving to reinvent the Catholic Faith according to worldly passions, making it unrecognizable." They called upon Leo to "annul" Pope Francis's move to allow communion for remarried divorcees in certain circumstances, and his move to allow same-sex blessings. The group behind the appeal was the American branch of the Society for the Defense of Tradition, Family and Property, an international coalition founded by Plinio Corrêa de Oliveira, an ultraconservative Brazilian layman and activist who had opposed Vatican II. The group, which was condemned by Brazilian bishops in 1985 for its "esoteric character, its religious fanaticism, the cult of personality," had strongly resisted Francis's reforms. Some hoping for a change of direction from Leo had cited a speech that he himself—then Rev. Robert Prevost—had given at a Church

Unifying the Church?

gathering in 2012 in which he had lamented the media's promotion of the "homosexual lifestyle" and "alternative families." Eleven years later, when he was made a cardinal, he was asked if his views had changed. "I would say there has been a development in the need for the church to open, and to be welcoming," the new cardinal said.

The American pope is unlikely to be swayed by petitions. By meeting officially with Fr. James Martin, a Jesuit priest and leading advocate for LGBTQ Catholics, he has sent a message indicating that he will continue Francis's legacy of openness and a welcoming attitude toward same-sex couples.

Rome in early September 2025 saw the fruits of that legacy. At the Church of the Gesù in central Rome, a senior Italian Bishop, Francesco Savino, presided at a Mass for hundreds of LGBTQ Catholics. "Go, celebrate the Mass with them!" is what Leo said, according to the bishop. Later in the day more than a thousand LGBTQ pilgrims walked in procession up the Via della Conciliazione and through the Holy Door of St. Peter's Basilica. It was the first time this had happened. Francis DeBernardo, Executive Director of New Ways Ministry, a US organization that advocates for LGBTQ pilgrimages, recalled Pope John Paul II condemning the first World Pride events taking place in Rome in 2000 and the "anti-gay rhetoric" coming from parts of the Vatican. A quarter of a century later, to see LGBTQ Catholics being welcomed into St. Peter's was a "big change" and something "he never would have imagined." While not an official jubilee event (2025 was a jubilee year, a special year of remission of sins), the LGBTQ pilgrimage was listed on the calendar of events and wouldn't have happened without Leo's permission.

I walked with the pilgrims and interviewed some of them as they processed into the basilica. A number emphasized the importance of the welcome that was being offered, and how it wouldn't have been possible without Francis. It felt nothing like a political rally, but simply a group of pilgrims seeking to deepen and confirm their faith. As we walked, however, a reporter for some of the traditionalist Catholic platforms was standing at the side and taking photos, looking to identify any source of "scandal" from the event. A photo later appeared of a male couple holding hands, with one wearing a bag which said "F*** the rules." This was seized upon, but the vast majority of those taking part showed no sign of wanting to provoke or score political points.

Pope Leo is aware of the polarization on the issue and is not planning to change Catholic teaching on sexuality, at least in the short term. According to the Catechism of the Catholic Church, sex is only permitted between a man and woman who are married. The Church's official principles describe homosexuality as "intrinsically disordered"—wording that some Catholics want to see altered to "differently ordered"—but they also state that gay people must be treated with "respect, compassion and sensitivity" and all "unjust discrimination" must be avoided.

"We have to change attitudes before we can ever change doctrine," Leo said in an interview, when asked about LGBTQ issues. It's an intriguing remark that suggests doctrine *might* change in the future—the sort of

Unifying the Church?

remark that Francis might have shied away from. When Leo met Rev. James Martin in the Apostolic Palace, the audience was listed on Leo's official calendar—which was papal code for his support for Martin's ministry.

Rev. Martin told me that it is notable that Leo has used the acronym LGBTQ in an interview, something Francis never did. The Jesuit priest says Leo's challenge is to both reach out to the LGBTQ community while at the same time responding to the strong action against Francis's ruling on same-sex blessings.

"It's that balance between prophecy and unity," he says. "Prophetic would be in moving the Church ahead and unity would be in remembering that this is not an issue that he wants to break the Church over." Rev. Martin, who says he would continue to support Leo even if he did something he disagreed with, explained: "This is a smart, experienced, compassionate pastor who understands this community is part of his flock. I'm very hopeful." Martin pointed out that the pope can do things which don't require any changes to teaching: speaking out on the decriminalization of homosexuality, violence against gay people, and conversion therapy. On decriminalization, Martin says: "I asked Pope Francis once, 'What would you tell a bishop who disagreed with your stance [on this topic]?' The pope replied, 'I would tell him he's wrong.'"

Church sources say that Leo will not overturn Francis's ruling on same-sex blessings. While Leo is going to continue in the Francis mold, he's likely to do so in a more cautious and consolidating manner. He has warned against churches in "northern Europe" offering blessings in a way that contradicts the pope's ruling. As a Church lawyer, he will expect bishops to stay within the bounds of what is permitted. His cautious approach isn't welcomed by all. Liberal Catholic groups in Germany, such as We Are Church, described Leo's remarks on homosexuality as "extremely disappointing". A Church lawyer, Thomas Schüller, told the KNA news agency: "There will be no significant changes to Catholic doctrine during his pontificate." Germany has been at the forefront of progressive reforms in the Church, pushing for same-sex blessings, the ordination of women, and a different model of power and authority in the Church. These reforms were resisted strongly by Rome, although a dialogue between Germany and the Vatican was established, thanks in part to the then Cardinal Prevost. Mary McAleese, the former president of Ireland, meanwhile lamented in *The Tablet*, a Catholic publication, that Leo "is more Benedict than Francis," although she quipped that "the latter's reputation as a reformer was well over-egged." McAleese also suggested that Leo was courting "MAGA money," although, as I pointed out earlier, this was disputed by a senior Church official. In short: progressive Catholics, looking for major changes, are likely to be disappointed, but they have a pope who understands their concerns.

Leo's priority for the Church is unity. Rev. Martin believes that he has the potential to achieve this. For example, he points to the pope's personal manner. "He's very still, quiet, and reserved. It makes the other person feel listened to and instils a sense of calm." Leo's decision to wear the traditional vestments and sing in Latin, Rev. Martin believes, was canny. He's "very smart in making gestures, showing that he's not on one side or the other,"

Unifying the Church?

and this could be a healing message for the US Church, where divisions between conservatives and progressives run deep, and for the polarized nation as a whole. In his own family situation, too, there is a parable for a divided country. Even though his political views are very different from those of his eldest brother, he remains close to him and to all his siblings. While Trump has said, "I hate my opponent and I don't want the best for them," in Leo's family, political differences have no effect on its love and unity. The American pontiff's words and actions offer a stark contrast to those of Trump. American Catholics may take note of this.

"He's the one, he can bring unity to the US Church. They look to him and say 'you can do it,'" Rev. Martin says. The risk, however, as Rev. Martin points out, is that he does something that leads one part of the Church to disengage from him.

Ordination of women

In 1994, Pope John Paul II ruled against the ordination of women as priests. He stated that "the Church has no authority whatsoever to confer priestly ordination on women" and that "this judgment is to be definitively held by all the Church's faithful." It's a ruling that effectively closed the door on the ordination of women to the priesthood, at least in the short term. Theologians may debate whether John Paul II's ruling can be considered an infallible statement. However, it is certainly meant to be one "definitively held" by everyone in the Church.

Nevertheless, in recent years the possibility of ordaining women as deacons—who are members of the clergy but do not celebrate Mass or hear confessions—is back on the agenda. The diaconate is distinct from the priesthood: deacons provide service, while priests represent Christ *In persona Christi capitis* (In the person of Christ the head), a role that confers a distinct authority on priests and requires them to be male.

Pope Francis ordered two commissions on the subject of women deacons, while various synod gatherings, in 2019, 2023, and 2024, discussed the matter as a possibility. Proponents argued that ordaining female deacons would give women a greater visibility in leadership roles, and, significantly, that there was precedent in Catholic tradition. From early Christianity until the thirteenth century, there were deaconesses serving the Church, most prominently Phoebe, a first-century leader mentioned by the Apostle Paul. Among ordinary Catholics, there is support for women's ordination. A 2024 Pew survey showed that a majority of Catholics in Brazil, Argentina, Chile, Peru, and Colombia were in favor, while 64 per cent of Catholics in the US were also in favor. In Italy, France, and Spain, too, a majority was in favor.

However, the topic remains a highly sensitive one in the Vatican. There is deep resistance to female deacons—and any form of female ordination—inside parts of the Church hierarchy. That sensitivity was on display during the 2024 synod assembly gathering when Bishop Anthony Randazzo, an Australian cleric who worked for five years in the Vatican's doctrine office, told reporters that female ordination was a "niche issue" that Catholics in the global north had become "obsessed" with. He even made the bold assertion that focussing on topics such as women deacons meant that "women who in many parts of the Church and world are treated as second-class citizens are totally ignored." Some of those at the synod, and earlier ones, countered the bishop's argument by pointing out that were the Church to confer official ministerial responsibility on women in those parts of the world where they are "second-class citizens", it could be a bold, helpful and prophetic move in favor of women.

The question of female deacons remains under review. A document produced by the synod gathering—with a stamp of authority from Pope Francis—describes it as an "open question." But the question has been caught up in Vatican politics.

Leo has tried to take the heat out of the issue. He has said that he will not change teaching on female deacons in the short term, but will continue to listen to people, to "examine the theological background, history, and will wait to see what the Vatican study commissions come back with". A Vatican commission reported to Leo that it had voted against ordaining women as deacons, although it said further study is necessary and that their judgment is not "definitive." As a young friar in Chicago, he was formed with and by women who wanted to see women ordained. He is aware of the strength of feeling on the topic. He's familiar with all sides of the argument.

Leo's approach to the women's ordination question reveals a determination to follows a process, something that Helena Jeppesen-Spuhler, a Swiss synod delegate, said is crucial. Leo "speaks to the process," she said, and this was "important" because it points to a pope who is ready to co-ordinate and guide. She said that during the synod Cardinal Prevost was always well-prepared before making interventions and, unlike some prelates, didn't feel the need to be at the center of everything.

Leo says that two questions need to be examined before making a decision on female deacons. First is whether the role of a deacon has been developed and understood properly (Vatican II restored the office of permanent deacon and opened it to married men, but the take-up globally has been patchy). Second, Leo also wonders whether female deacons would end up "clericalizing" women by making them part of the clerical system.

Phyllis Zagano, a member of the first female deacons commission, told me that Leo is up against some "entrenched negative attitudes toward women, all cultural and non-theological," and that a combination of "historical, anthropological (cultural), and theological negativity" about the topic will be difficult to overcome. But, she pointed out, the pope will need to navigate relations with the Eastern Orthodox churches, some of whom "have maintained or restored the tradition of ordaining women as deacons," adding that "in Catholicism, there is no doctrine forbidding ordaining women as deacons"; the tradition is restricted by a "merely ecclesiastical law." It is significant that Leo has entrusted the question of female deacons to a process of listening and study, and that he is open to taking on board their contributions.

Unifying the Church?

Can Leo keep the peace?

Leo's methodical and ordered approach to difficult topics is helping him maintain unity. He is unafraid to wait before making up his mind, or simply to remain undecided about the best way to approach a thorny issue. Francis could sometimes move in two different directions on a disputed question, leaving people unclear about where things were heading. While he opened a discussion on ordaining women as deacons, he said that he personally was opposed to the move. He wanted to welcome LGBTQ Catholics, but didn't seek to change teaching. In 2019, at a gathering of Amazonian bishops in the Vatican, he allowed a debate on the ordination of married men, but then refused to authorize any action. His opening to allow divorced and remarried Catholics to receive communion was relegated to a small footnote in a major document on marriage and family life. In some respects, this strategy was deliberate. He wanted to get the discussions going without starting a revolution. Sensitive Catholic topics had been buried in the freezer for years until Francis started urging bishops and others to speak with *parrhesia*—a frankness.

Also, the Argentine pope did not want the Church to become fixated on certain issues: sexuality, female ordination, married priests. He warned the well-organized German Church, which was pushing for major changes in these areas, that they couldn't simply "reorganize things, change them and 'put them back together,'" as this would not solve underlying problems. Francis, like Leo, was wary of polarization and division within the Church. Both popes have also shown awareness of a much deeper question that must, sooner or later, be answered: how will the Church carry out its mission in a multitude of different cultures and contexts and still maintain its unity? While blessings of same-sex couples are welcome for churches in northern Europe, they are rejected in Africa. For some countries, poverty and climate change are matters of urgency, while in others it's secularization. In societies where women are on an equal footing with men, giving women authority makes sense, but in countries with a male-dominated power structure, this is harder to do.

Leo is seeking to harmonize these approaches, to allow for unity within diversity, where one Church doesn't run ahead of the other. He is a pope who won't let a single-issue topic threaten the Church's communion, but he is willing to listen to all sides of a discussion. He's opened St. Peter's Basilica, the home of the popes, both to LGBTQ pilgrims and to those attached to the pre-Vatican II form of the liturgy. The renewal process begun by Francis—the synod—is crucial and one that Leo is going to lean on heavily. It allows for listening and dialogue between different groups and for the development of a consensus. The pope has even described the process as an "antidote" to polarization, a way of getting people around the same table.

For those who felt left out during Francis's papacy, particularly conservative communities and younger clergy, Leo has offered an olive branch. He's not going to rebuke them in the way Francis did, and the deference he's shown to the traditions and styles of the papal office has given encouragement to conservatives who had been concerned about institutional fraying during the previous pontificate.

The demands and requests for Leo to act or decide in a certain way are coming in thick and fast. But he is not easily lobbied, and his red lines remain the reforms of Vatican II. While he listens to people, he is also pointing the way for an inclusive and outward-facing Church, the type he experienced as a missionary in Peru, and which was called for by Francis, the first Latin American pope. Leo will not reverse the course of travel charted by his predecessor, but his first aim is to bring the Church together, to heal the wounds of polarization and division through the medicine of listening and dialogue.

As a personality, Leo has a gift for appealing to different groups in the Church, for reassuring Catholics hopeful for reforms and those wary of too much change. His monastic, contemplative style echoes the teaching of St. Benedict, the father of Western monasticism, who said that a good abbot of a community "must so arrange everything that the strong have something to yearn for and the weak nothing to run from." It is what Leo is aiming to do.

4

Quiet Reformer

Don't make any big changes in your first year. This is the advice given to trainee priests or young clergy when they take up the leadership of a new parish or institute. Pope Leo has also followed this advice. He's used his first twelve months, for the most part, to adjust to his new role, to observe, and to try better to understand the complexities of leading the 1.4-billion-member Catholic Church.

But taking your time doesn't mean you don't have a strategy. Leo's aim is to build on the reforms begun by Francis, to take meaningful steps to tackle the most pressing issues facing the Catholic Church. He is doing so by working closely with the Church's central administration, the Roman Curia, and through a process-based method grounded in his knowledge of the Church's legal system. All of this gives him an immense opportunity to effect reforms, such as expanding the role of laypeople—particularly women—and tackling the clerical sexual abuse crisis. He has a chance to embed a renewed model of the papacy and a new style of governance at the center of the Church. Leo is the arguably the first pope since Paul VI (1963–78) to work seriously with the Roman Curia. John Paul II essentially left the Curia alone as he traveled the world extensively, devoted his time to the Cold War and the fall of communism, and built relations with other faiths. His successor, Benedict XVI, was unable to get a firm grip on the Church's central administration. Although the "professor pope" had led the Vatican's doctrine office for decades, he preferred to communicate with the wider body of believers through his theological works. Francis instinctively distrusted the Curia and often tried to work around the system. Paul VI, however, had worked in the Vatican for thirty-two years and had served as archbishop of Milan before his election. He ushered in the contemporary papacy and oversaw reforms that were some of the deepest and most impactful the Church had seen in centuries. Papa Montini, as he was known, was the first pope to travel on an airplane and to visit six continents. He removed the monarchical trappings of the papacy by relinquishing the papal tiara; he reorganized the Curia; he set a retirement age for bishops and cardinals, and he promoted dialogue with other faiths and Christian denominations. In 1966, he became the first pope to meet an Archbishop of Canterbury since the Reformation.

Paul VI's most significant achievement was the conclusion and implementation of the reforms of the Second Vatican Council. The council was called by Pope John XXIII, who opened it in 1962, but he died less than a year later. It fell to Paul VI, therefore, to shepherd the council through its final two years, including the publication of its constitutions and decrees, and then to implement them. Among its most significant rulings was the council's declaration on the Catholic Church's relationship with other religions, including an historic condemnation of antisemitism. It opened the Church to a new co-operation with religions, and saw the papacy convene major gatherings with leaders of different faiths, and state that religion cannot be used to justify violence. Leo has taken up this call for inter-religious harmony, making his first foreign trip to Turkey and Lebanon, including a visit to the Blue Mosque in Istanbul.

Paul VI was renowned for navigating a careful path between the different groups within the Church and received criticism from both traditionalists and progressives.

It was Pope Paul who promulgated the reformed liturgy, something that affected Catholics across the world, and Pope Paul who opened a more collegial style of papal governance involving the world's bishops. He pushed for peace during the war in Vietnam and oversaw the emergence of a Church that had a bolder voice in matters of social justice and human rights. Paul VI established the synod structure that became the main vehicle for Francis's pastoral agenda, and which has been taken up by Leo. Many felt that John Paul II and Benedict XVI had pressed pause on the reforms that Paul VI had begun with the council. Francis pressed the play button again and began the synod process, a renewal that sought to involve the entire global Church. But Francis had only managed to get the synodal car into third gear by the end of his papacy. In March 2025, from his hospital bed, he signed off the next phase of the synod process which, he ruled, would culminate in an "ecclesial assembly" in Rome in 2028. Leo now takes up the baton.

"He's the Pope Paul VI to [Pope] John XXIII," is how one cardinal described Pope Leo to me, underlining just how significant Paul VI's papacy had been.

Like Paul VI, Leo has an opportunity to bring to fruition a major Church reform initiative, and like Paul VI, he has shown the ability to navigate between progressives and traditionalists. Like Paul VI, he takes over from a prophetic, John XXIII-style pope in Francis and is tasked with making an ecclesial vision a reality. The American pontiff has the advantage of knowing how Rome works. Sometimes when faced with the Roman Curia, a pope can feel as if they are in the British political satire *Yes Minister*. "Holy Father, that's a wonderful idea, but I am not sure it's going to work effectively that way," is the sort of thing the Curia might say to a reforming pope. In Rome, there's the concept of *Romanitas*, a Roman style and way of doing things that is rooted in the Church's central bureaucracy. Francis, an outsider who had never lived or studied in Rome before his election, ignored *Romanitas* and did things his own way. Leo, on the other hand, understands Rome. He has worked in the Curia as a cardinal and was based in the Eternal City for twelve years as prior general of the Augustinians. As pope, Leo is playing by the rules but once he makes a decision, the discussion is over. "Once this lion roars, nobody is going to be able to convince him 'no, Holy Father, we don't do things like that,'" Dawn Eden Goldstein said. Leo's style makes him a quiet, but formidable, reformer. Although he doesn't generate headlines in the way Francis did, Leo has said things about reform that his predecessors did not.

Quiet Reformer

While Leo says he'll continue to listen and to study the question of female deacons, Francis gave a simple "no" in a CBS interview with Norah O'Donell when she asked him about the possibility of women in holy orders. In his decision-making, the pope has said he wants to continue in a "synodal" way: listening, discerning, building consensus and deciding. None of this is foreign territory for him; it builds on his time in Peru. When he was the bishop of Chiclayo, he said he held "diocesan assemblies" in a "synodal style" for seven of his nine years there. These were essentially local Church gatherings with representatives from the different parts of Chiclayo's Catholic community. Priests and laypeople worked together to search for "the kind of Church that we are looking for today, reaching out to the poor, to the neediest, to those on the margins, to those who do not frequently come to church."

He has shown that he trusts the synod process, perhaps even more than Francis did. Inside the Paul VI synod hall in October 2025, he sat at a table with a mixed group including a cardinal, bishops, a religious sister, and laymen and -women as he took part in an open discussion on the reform topics opened up by the synod. He switched between English, Spanish, and Italian, and, speaking without a script, looked at home in this environment. Leo stressed that the synodal principles of listening and dialogue are not simply applicable to the Church. Responding to a Canadian bishop, he stressed the need for a synodal approach in light of the deteriorating relationship between the US and Canada: countries, he said, once considered the closest of allies but which now "grow distant from one another." He was speaking after President Trump had broken off trade talks with Canada. Leo didn't get into the specifics of trade, but his words sent a message: the Church must lead by example in holding up ways of navigating disagreement in an increasingly fractured world.

Seven weeks after his election Leo went to the synod office in person (popes don't often visit Vatican offices) to encourage the office in its work and to point out that the synod is aimed at building up "participation and communion" in the Church. Sister Nathalie said that during that meeting "we had an excellent dialogue with him."

Deepening the participation of Catholics in the mission of the Church was at the heart of the Francis renewal, which Leo is now overseeing. At the top of the agenda is the role of women.

Female leadership

In the Catholic Church it is the all-male hierarchy—the priests, bishops, and cardinals—who have the authority to run local churches (dioceses) and parishes. In the Vatican, most departments are led by cardinals and bishops. Although female ordination has been ruled out, the issue of promoting women to leadership roles—giving them greater visibility and recognition in ministry and decision-making—has become one of the most pressing issues for Church reform.

Finding creative ways for women to serve as non-ordained leaders will be high on the agenda during Leo's papacy. During the previous pontificate, Francis broke several Vatican glass ceilings with his appointment of the first female leaders of major departments. Sister Simona Brambilla, who holds a doctorate in psychology and has worked in Mozambique as a missionary, was appointed to head the Vatican's office with responsibility for members of religious orders: monks, friars, nuns. And Sister Raffaella Petrini, who studied at the University of Hartford, Connecticut's business school, was appointed to run the Vatican City State. Francis tapped into the often-ignored talent pool of religious sisters to help with the running of the Vatican office. Many religious sisters are highly competent leaders who have run schools and hospitals—often in very poor, conflict-ridden countries—and who have led their own complex, global religious communities. In recent centuries the Catholic sisters and nuns have played an enormous role in education and healthcare in Europe, the United States, and Australia. Going back even further, the female abbesses of the medieval period (such as those of Santa María la Real de Las Huelgas in Spain) held vast authority—they were the equivalent of a bishop and had priests under their jurisdiction. For those seeking a more prominent role for women in the Catholic Church, this is not a question of innovation but the recovery of tradition. Despite the manifest skills of religious sisters, it was not until the Francis pontificate that women began taking on serious executive authority in the Vatican. Sisters were already working for senior figures in the Church, but often as poorly paid domestic helpers in the residences of archbishops or the cardinals working in the Curia. Francis chose sisters for senior Vatican roles, while he appointed laywomen and sisters to board-level positions in Vatican offices.

Leo is following in Francis's footsteps by appointing women to senior Vatican positions. Two weeks after his election he chose Sister Tiziana Merletti, an expert Church lawyer, as the secretary, or number two, of the Vatican department for religious orders. This meant that, for the first time, a Vatican office had an all-female leadership team. But the opposition to women in the Roman Curia can be cultural as much as structural. An all-male atmosphere can be difficult even for women appointed to senior positions. It was noticeable, therefore, that Francis chose a supportive cardinal, Ángel Fernández Artime, to work alongside Sister Brambilla and help smooth out any problems. One Church source I spoke to described Brambilla as a highly capable leader who works closely with the clergy in her office. Leo comes from a religious order which includes religious sisters. As a bishop, he worked closely with women. And when he was prefect of the Dicastery for Bishops, he collaborated with the department's first three female members appointed by Francis. One source said that the women who worked with Leo in the department all spoke positively of him because he treated them as trusted collaborators. He does not look down on women, which, unfortunately, isn't always true of those in the highest positions in the Church.

"It was easy to approach him," Helena Jeppeson-Spuhler, a voting member of the 2023 and 2024 synod assemblies, told me. "He's one of those cardinals you could talk to during the breaks." She also said that Leo was aware of the instances when laypeople played an active role in the selection of bishops, including in two dioceses in Switzerland.

Pope Francis's appointments might look like small steps from the outside, but inside the Church they were giant leaps and Leo was on board with them. Francis's constitution for the Church's central administration officially opened the way for any layperson, man or woman, to run a Vatican department, a move that some in the hierarchy resisted.

Francis also appointed, for the first time, women as voting members in synod gatherings, including those in 2023 and 2024. Since Paul VI introduced the synod, the assemblies in the Vatican have been known as "Synod of Bishops" meetings. Francis's inclusion of fifty-four female voters, and some laymen, received the inevitable pushback from conservative clergy. Cardinal Gerhard Müller, a member and former leader of the Vatican office, said the inclusion of laypeople meant that the status of the gathering was "unclear." Müller, a frequent critic of Francis, had previously described the pope's synod reforms as a "hostile takeover" of the Catholic Church and a step toward "Protestantization." Francis responded to this "storm of chattering" by saying that the inclusion of laypeople was consistent with tradition and showed that bishops cannot take decisions "without others." The sheer angst about the inclusion of women voters pointed to a deeper issue, however. The moves toward a more participatory Church that gives every member a voice has left some people feeling nervous and threatened. Leo put his finger on the problem: "Sometimes bishops or priests might feel, 'synodality is going to take away my authority.'" But, he added, firmly: "That's not what synodality is about, and maybe your idea of what your authority is, is somewhat out of focus, mistaken."

The involvement of laypeople in decision-making does not threaten the roles of priest and bishop. If anything, it can strengthen a bishop's authority because it shows that decisions have been taken following genuine consultation. Priests and bishops are going to retain a distinct, sacramental role and a role in leadership.

Leo's remarks about those who misunderstand their authority indicate that he is wary of clericalism, where authority becomes disconnected from the community, and where those in power lord it over others without listening to those whom they've been called upon to serve. He takes over the Church at a moment when his predecessor had opened a serious theological discussion about the role laypeople might have in the governance of the Church—but it was a discussion that was left unresolved. Francis made appointments, and he started processes. Leo must take those processes forward. One critical question is this: how can laymen and women exercise actual governance in the Church? The Church's 1983 *Code of Canon Law* says that laypeople are permitted to "co-operate" in the power of governance, rather than "share" in it, which was the word that had originally been proposed. The decision to use the weaker, and more ambiguous word "co-operate" was taken after a commission had been set by John Paul II—which included the then Cardinal Joseph Ratzinger (later Pope Benedict XVI)—to make final revisions.

The debate is not simply an academic one. Many parts of the world, including Europe, the US, and Latin America, face an acute shortage of priests. In parts of Switzerland, Jeppesen-Spuhler explains, female theologians are leaders of parishes and are performing baptisms. "A lot is possible without ordination," she said. Leo has been codifying Francis' openings to women such as changing the law to allow a woman to serve as president of the Vatican City State administration. Francis had appointed Sister Petrini to that role, but the law had said only cardinals could hold the position.

With the ordination of women and married men off the table, the question of lay ministry and leadership becomes more important. If women can exercise true leadership roles (not simply advising a bishop or working in finance, legal, or administrative positions), then it could be a major step toward solving the urgent issue of female inclusion. Francis's moves allowed laywomen to lead Vatican offices because they were given the authority by the pope. Others argue that laypeople can exercise authority by virtue of being baptized members of the Church and if they have been identified as having a specific gift (charism). The authority in the Church doesn't simply flow from the top down—it also flows from the bottom up: everyone has the capacity to exercise leadership because the true source of authority is the Holy Spirit, which is given to each person at baptism.

The final document of the synod 2023–24 assembly, in which Leo participated, called for laymen and laywomen to be "given greater opportunities for participation," including in "all phases of decision-making processes (drafting, making and confirming decisions)" and to take "positions of responsibility." It also stated that it was "urgent" to make sure that women can "assume roles of responsibility in pastoral care and ministry."

This document was approved and authorized by Francis, which gave it authority. But Rev. Tom Reese, a respected Church commentator, has observed that if these reforms are to move beyond a "pious wish," which will be ignored or obstructed by those keen to keep the status quo, it will be crucial to make amendments to the Church's law. Bishops are bound by canon law. This is where Pope Leo, a trained canon lawyer, will be on firm ground. The synod says that the 1983 *Code of Canon Law* needs to be revised. In addition, a study group has proposed a series of ways by which a more participatory Church can become a reality. These include making it mandatory for bishops and priests to consult and include laypeople in decision-making, while not excluding those who are in "complex personal and/or marital situations." It is significant that Leo's first major appointment to the Roman Curia was an experienced Church lawyer. He chose Archbishop Filippo Iannone to serve as his successor as leader of the Dicastery for Bishops in the Vatican. Iannone is widely seen as someone who supported Francis's reform of the Roman Curia and his synodal vision of the Church. Like Leo, he is a low-key, low-visibility prelate and a member of a religious order, the Carmelites, who are known for their life of contemplative prayer. Leo is drawing on experienced Church lawyers who are willing to act as impartial civil servants in implementing reforms and tackling problems.

In his doctoral thesis, written decades before the current debates were taking place in the Church, Robert

Prevost examined the nature of authority. His dissertation focussed on the role of the prior in the Augustinian order. At one point, however, he touched on the question of lay leadership. Most Augustinian friars are ordained priests, but some remain as "brothers"—members of the order but without the authority that comes with ordination. Leadership positions are, however, reserved for priests. In 1977, the Augustinians decided that all the friars would be eligible to all offices in the order, regardless of ordination. Prevost, in his thesis, writes that the Vatican was petitioned to allow this change "to eliminate the distinction between priests and lay brothers." But the request was denied by the Vatican. Prevost wrote in his thesis that "the requirement of priesthood remains a requisite for the office of Prior, not by choice of the Order, but by virtue of the common law of the Church."

Decades later, in 2022, Francis issued a legal ruling that allowed lay brothers to lead orders as religious superiors. Two years later, a Benedictine community, St. Anselm's in New Hampshire, elected their first brother as the community's abbot.

Prevost's thesis demonstrates that he has grappled with, and lived, the principles of a synodal Church for decades. He reflects on the importance of superiors consulting with their community before making major decisions. "There is no room in Augustine's concept of authority for one who is self-seeking and in search of power over others," he wrote.

If Leo can make concrete changes to the role of women and lay people in the governance of the Church, it could become one of the signature reforms of his papacy.

Jeppesen-Spuhler stresses the importance of the fact that he listens to churches at the grassroots level, which is where creative models of Church leadership are being explored, all of them within the bounds of Church law. In the Amazon region, for example, women are already taking on leadership roles in communities where there are no priests. They lead services and baptize children. The Amazonian Church could become something of a laboratory for reform. A new structure has been established, the Ecclesial Conference of the Amazon, which includes bishops, laypeople, indigenous leaders, and priests, while proposals for a special Amazonian liturgy include a call for the ordination of married men and for women to "occupy spaces as preachers and officiants of sacraments." Could other churches follow suit with similar lay-bishop bodies?

In local churches the push for reform is bubbling away. In Germany, a new council is in the works for laypeople and bishops to sit together on an advisory and decision-making body that will make decisions about the Church's future, including its finances. The German synod's more controversial push for the ordination of women and for public blessings for same-sex couples was stalled by Rome, but its proposals also include a greater separation of powers within the Church, including a greater accountability of bishops and clergy, and more involvement for laity in the selection of bishops. The German synod, while controversial, has been influential.

Other local reform processes have also been noticed by Rome. One in Australia involved a long consultation that culminated in a national Church gathering—a plenary council—which saw laypeople and bishops gathered around small tables to vote on a range of topics. These included a call for women to be represented in the "decision-making structures of Church governance" and, significantly, a resolution that Australian bishops would install female deacons if this were permitted. But it didn't all run smoothly, as I saw for myself. Halfway through the gathering in Sydney, some delegates threatened to walk out when the motion on female deacons failed to attract enough support from the bishops. In the end, they found a compromise. Meanwhile, in Ireland, a woman, Julieann Moran, has been appointed general secretary of a national synod process which the country's bishops hope will bring about renewal.

Abuse crisis

The push for reform inside the Catholic Church is taking place during the gravest crisis to face the Church in 500 years. The clerical sexual abuse scandal has rocked the Church to its foundations in ways not seen since the Reformation, and this has only strengthened the call for profound and far-reaching reforms. The scandal doesn't simply involve the appalling abuse of children and vulnerable adults by priests, but the mishandling and cover-up of their crimes by bishops and Church leaders. It is no coincidence that the countries that have seen wave after wave of abuse cases are those that have been the most vocal in the calling for reform.

The first major exposures began in the 1980s. Prior to that time, few cases ever came to public attention—they were handled discreetly by the Church and the victims were often silenced. By the mid 1990s, investigative reporters and survivors' groups had started to document the abuse and the cover-ups. In the early 2000s, the crisis went global, with waves of revelations from around the world. Ireland is the ground zero of the crisis. In Australia, Germany, France, Ireland, and the UK, state and Church-funded independent inquiries have conducted multiple investigations into abuse inside the Church. All of them have revealed similar patterns of failure to tackle the crisis by those in authority, including a defensive and secretive attitude by bishops whose main priority was to protect the Church institution.

In the United States, the Catholic Church has paid out more than $4 billion in abuse case settlements, with the archdiocese of Los Angeles alone reaching an $880-million settlement in October 2024. (Its total payouts stand at $1.5 billion.) Grand jury reports, such as those in Philadelphia in 2011 and Pennsylvania in 2018, laid bare the extent and horror of the abuse in those states. In 2002, the *Boston Globe* reported on a series of individual cases, which blew the scandal wide open and suddenly brought it into mainstream public awareness. The story of how the Boston reporters uncovered the abuse was later dramatized in the Oscar-winning 2015 film *Spotlight*. The payouts and settlements in US dioceses continue.

Several major inquiries revealed serious structural failures when it came to tackling abuse: predatory priests were often protected by a system that had little accountability or scrutiny. The crisis exposed profound moral and spiritual failings in those individually culpable in the crimes and in the hierarchies and culture that allowed it to happen. "Sexual abuse is above all also an abuse of power," was the conclusion of a major research project undertaken by German bishops. "An authoritarian-clerical understanding of the ministry can lead to Church leaders regarding a priest who has committed sexualized violence more as a threat to their own clerical system than as a menace to other children or juveniles, or to other potential persons affected."

A gross misuse of power requires an examination of how power should function inside the Church. For reformers, such as those in Germany, it means ensuring transparency and accountability to counter the underlying structural problem. For ordinary priests and bishops there are few accountability mechanisms: bishops are simply asked to submit their resignation to the pope at the age of seventy-five. A religious order, of the type in which Pope Leo was formed, is different. Augustinian friars live in community and have a degree of accountability to each other. The leaders are elected for limited terms and can be voted out of office.

Building accountability into Church structures and leadership is something Leo must address. The 2023–24 synod meetings called for bishops to give "an account of pastoral activity in various areas"—this was a new idea—while pointing out that clericalism, which Francis regarded as the root cause of abuse, is "based on the implicit assumption that those who have authority in the Church are not to be held to account for their actions and decisions." It has often been remarked that the scandal of abuse wouldn't have festered for so long in the Church if women—wives and mothers—had had a seat at the decision-making table. This was borne out in the detailed, 449-page Vatican report into the abuse and misconduct perpetrated by the former archbishop of Washington, DC, Theodore McCarrick. The report described how, in the mid 1980s, a woman named as "Mother 1" wrote anonymous letters to members of the Church hierarchy complaining about McCarrick after witnessing him "massaging [her sons'] inner thighs" in her home. McCarrick was removed from the priesthood following a Vatican trial in 2019 and was charged in Massachusetts and Wisconsin with sexual assault. However, he was deemed mentally incompetent to stand trial. He had always denied the allegations against him, and died in April 2025.

Calls for reforms to decision-making, the role of women, and the inclusion of lay people in governance have intensified in the wake of the abuse scandals. Such reforms may help offer a solution to the crisis if implemented. In addition, the Church must continue to support and listen to the victims—people who will carry the trauma of abuse for the rest of their lives.

Leo is tasked with carrying on what Francis started. Francis made serious reforms to the way in which the Church handled abuse. Among the changes he made were the following: a new framework for holding bishops and religious superiors accountable for their actions (*Vos estis lux mundi*), new systems for reporting abuse, changes to the Church's canon law to recognize that vulnerable adults can be victims of abuse and that laypeople in official positions, as well as priests, can be held responsible. For the victims, however, the lack of transparency in the

Quiet Reformer

Vatican and beyond remains a problem. Survivors still complain about Church leaders dismissing their stories and showing a lack of sensitivity and care. Leo is faced with the difficulties of some countries, particularly in Africa, where robust reporting structures have not been established. Meanwhile, on his doorstep in Italy, a Vatican commission has found that a "cultural resistance" to tackling abuse remains. Some survivors believe that the Catholic Church in Italy has not adequately faced up to abuse scandals.

Francis was also the first pope to acknowledge the abuse of nuns by priests, revealing that his predecessor, Benedict XVI, had sought to shut down a French congregation of sisters due to the scale of the abuses.

But Leo's predecessor also faced criticism for the way he dealt with some cases. The case of Marko Rupnik, a Slovenian Jesuit and prominent Church artist, revealed serious inadequacies in the Vatican's handling of cases involving priests accused of abusing adult religious sisters. Rupnik was accused by dozens of nuns of "sexual, psychological, or spiritual" abuse and was briefly excommunicated for one of the gravest sins in Church law: using the confessional to absolve a woman with whom he had engaged in sexual activity. He later recanted and the excommunication was lifted, although he was expelled from the Jesuits in 2023. In October 2025, the Vatican announced that judges had been chosen for a Church trial of Rupnik. The Slovenian artist has not responded publicly to the allegations made against him, although one of his supporters has said Rupnik had been subjected to a media "lynching." Inexplicably, despite the allegations, the Holy See's communications department continued to post Rupnik's art on its website and social media channels.

Some criticized Francis for sometimes allowing personal relationships, rather than established reporting systems, to color his judgment. For example, he initially defended Gustavo Zanchetta, an Argentine bishop and friend, and created a job for him in the Vatican. Zanchetta was later convicted in Argentina and sentenced to four and a half years in prison for the abuse of two former seminarians.

Leo's background in canon law, and his concern for obtaining justice for those wronged, means that he will be clear-eyed in dealing with cases of abuse. One abuse survivor I spoke to said that Leo's quiet personality is reassuring. Matthias Katsch, a German management trainer and philosopher, pointed out that abusers often tend to be "charismatic personality types." He described Leo as "structured" in his approach to the crisis. Katsch, who is a founding member of the group End Clergy Abuse, was among the survivors and advocates who had a private meeting with Leo in the fall of 2025. "He was very open, and he didn't answer like a politician who was looking to cover his back," Katsch said. "He said 'I want to work with you. I'll tell you when I don't agree with you but let's discuss it.'" Katsch said that Leo reacted in an "empathetic way" to the stories of survivors and referred to those experiences later in the conversation. Leo told them that being pope was still a new experience for him. Katsch described him as someone with a "very practical, hands-on attitude." The pope, he said, emphasized the limitations of his role: it's not simply a case of the pope making a decision and everything changing. Katsch said Leo was conscious that in a polarized world people will quickly take to social media to say why they disagree or have a different view.

Tackling a problem like sexual abuse inside the Church gives us an idea of the enormity of the responsibility facing the pope, which must sometimes feel isolating. Leo's meeting with Katsch and other abuse survivors was only known in advance by a very select group inside the Vatican and not by those in the wider Church government.

In Peru, Prevost was the leader of the Peruvian bishops' safeguarding commission. He told the bishops that when people come forward with allegations, they will, for the most part, be telling the truth. He knew what he was talking about. During his time in Peru, he'd dealt with one of the worst abuse cases in the Church's recent history.

The case concerned a hugely influential Catholic society in Peru known as the Sodalitium Christianae Vitae (SCV), or simply as the Sodalitium. It was a case in which abuse and power were deeply intertwined, and it required decisive action on the part of Prevost, first as bishop and later cardinal, to put an end to it.

The Sodalitium had close ties with the Peruvian elite. Founded in 1971, its aim was to counter the influence of liberation theology in Latin America. At one point, it had 20,000 members across South America, a community in Colorado in the United States, and connections with conservative Catholic media. Details of the abuse inside the society came to light in 2015 in a book entitled *Half Monks, Half Soldiers* written by Pedro Salinas, who was one of the victims, and Paola Ugaz, a very courageous and tenacious reporter. In the wake of the book's revelations, an independent report was commissioned by the Sodalitium. It alleged that Luis Fernando Figari, its founder, and three former members of the society had committed sexual abuse against nineteen minors and ten adults. Figari, who was not a priest but a consecrated lay leader of the society, was also accused of carrying out sadistic physical, spiritual, and psychological abuse for decades. CNN later reported on the allegations, including the testimony of one victim who recalled Figari leading him to a room and raping him, saying it was "the only way to correctly see his aura." Figari's lawyer, Jorge Ernesto Villa Avila, told CNN that Figari maintains his innocence, and pointed out that he has not been convicted in a court of law.

But the Sodalitium had powerful connections within the Church and the political establishments who helped to keep the scandal under wraps. Although he has said that he was unaware of abuses in the society, one of its most important Church protectors was reportedly the archbishop of Piura, José Antonio Eguren, a member of the Sodalitium, who served in a diocese neighboring Chiclayo. Robert Prevost had been the bishop of Chiclayo for about a year when the scandal surfaced. According to several sources, including Ugaz, a contact in the Vatican, and the survivors themselves, it was Prevost who made sure that the Church took action against the society. Of the Peruvian bishops, it was Prevost who organised a meeting with the victims. The bishops and the victims signed a joint statement, which they planned to take to Rome, where they would meet Pope Francis and present a list of their needs. But senior Church officials prevented this from happening, which, according to Ugaz, caused Bishop Prevost "great frustration." She also told me for CNN, however, that "his character is not one to burn down the house. He accepted what had happened, made his frustration clear."

Things changed when Pope Francis appointed Prevost to run the bishops' office in the Vatican in January 2023. Two top investigators were dispatched to Peru. Their findings resulted in the expulsion of fourteen members from the society, including Figari and Eguren. Prior to the expulsions, Pope Francis had accepted Archbishop Eguren's resignation, seven years sooner than the retirement age for bishops. Eguren denied that Prevost had removed him, but Prevost's office would certainly have been involved in the decision. One Vatican source close to the investigation of the Sodalitium said: "As prefect of the dicastery, he was very efficient in evaluating the evidence and obtaining the resignation of Archbishop Eguren."

In early 2025, it emerged that Francis was dissolving the entire Sodalitium society for serious wrongdoing—a remarkable act that has happened only rarely in the history of the Church. The decision was formalized in the final days of Francis's papacy. In response, the Sodalitium released a statement asking for "forgiveness from the entire Church and society for the pain caused" and "forgiveness for the mistreatment and abuse committed within our community."

Ugaz believes that Prevost played a major role in ensuring that this powerful Peruvian society was dissolved completely. He also put pressure on the Sodalitium to compensate the victims. Katsch said that with the dissolving of the Sodalitium, Leo had "helped to achieve something that hasn't been done in Church history"—

the shutting down of a society due to abuse. "Normally processes like this would have gone on for an eternity without a decision, but he helped the survivors and find the right door to open to be listened to."

Prevost knew Ugaz and Salinas well. Before his transferral to the Vatican, he had sent them a message of support after they were sued for defamation by Archbishop Eguren, who had not taken kindly to them accusing him of protecting the Sodalitium despite knowing about the alleged abuses. (He later dropped the case.) But Eguren's lawsuit was just one of many. Over the years, Paola Ugaz had suffered a relentless campaign of legal harassment over her investigations into the Sodalitium. She had even received death threats. But her reporting had made her well known to the public. In 2025, a play called *Proyecto Ugaz* (*Project Ugaz*), which was inspired by her work, was being staged in Lima.

A few days after his election, Leo met with media representatives in the Vatican. Among those present was Ugaz. She presented him with a Peruvian scarf and a box of chocolates. After everything she'd been through, this must have been a marvellous moment for both of them. Leo spoke about the importance of journalism in uncovering abuse. Later, he sent a message to be read aloud during a live performance of *Proyecto Ugaz*: "Wherever a journalist is silenced, the democratic soul of a country is weakened," Leo said, adding that those who had reported on the Sodalitium had done so with "courage, patience, and fidelity to the truth" and had faced "unjust attacks." These were Pope Leo's first public remarks on the sexual abuse crisis. "It is urgent to ingrain throughout the Church a culture of prevention that does not tolerate any form of abuse—neither of power or authority, nor of conscience or spirituality, nor sexual," he said. It requires, he went on, "active vigilance, transparent processes, and sincere listening to those who have been hurt." The message was read on stage by Monsignor Jordi Bertomeu, one of the Vatican officials who had investigated the Sodalitium, with Ugaz sitting next to him.

Leo understands the importance of robust journalism. He is aware of how information can become weaponized when it comes to abuse scandals. In 2018, the dossier released by Archbishop Carlo Maria Viganò calling on Pope Francis to resign was first published—in full—by two conservative Catholic media outlets, neither of which had given any indication as to whether they had been able to verify the claims.

Among those who had been expelled from the Sodalitium was Alejandro Bermúdez, the founder of the Catholic News Agency, based in Denver. A Vatican investigation found him to have committed "abuse in the exercise of the apostolate of journalism," a canon law term meaning the abuse of journalism by a Catholic, especially when it harms faith, morals, or the Church's mission. Bermúdez, known for a combative style on social media, retorted that he was kicked out simply for "telling the truth" in his reporting. Since then, he has worked for Catholic Vote, the MAGA-supporting group set up by Brian Burch, who is now the US Ambassador to the Holy See (see chapter two). Even after the scandal broke, the Sodalitium retained powerful supporters. Following the news of the expulsions, the archbishop of Denver, Samuel Aquila, said he was "shocked and saddened," while a longtime adviser to Archbishop Charles Chaput (the former archbishop of Denver and a critic of Francis) wrote that "something is deeply wrong with Rome's latest treatment of the SCV (Sodalitium)."

Cardinal Prevost's action against the Sodalitium made him some powerful enemies. Those upset with him have briefed against him in the Catholic media. The Sodalitium's displeasure was on full display when, two days before Pope Leo's election, Bermúdez posted on X, linking to an article titled: "Prevost and Co, anyone involved in sexual abuse should not be pope." On another occasion he mused that it was strange that some media outlets were running stories suggesting Cardinal Prevost would be "a 'great' papal candidate." *InfoVaticana*, an ultra-conservative Spanish-language site, ran critical pieces on Prevost's handling of abuse cases, while the College of Cardinals Report, an initiative that sought to promote the prospects of conservative cardinals ahead of the conclave, argued that "continued questions over his handling of sexual abuse have also cast a cloud over his prospects." The report offered profiles on forty papal candidates and a copy was handed to each cardinal ahead of the conclave. The authors said that they were simply helping the cardinals get to know each other; however, the profiles heaped praise on a traditionalist candidate while describing one involved in Church reforms as "controversial."

Meanwhile, *The Pillar*, a Catholic news site often skeptical of the priorities of the Francis pontificate, ran an article three days before the conclave entitled "Why Prevost's papal prospects prompt pushback," written by one of its editors JD Flynn, a former chancellor of the archdiocese of Denver (the archdiocese which had said it was saddened by the Vatican's action against the Sodalitium). Flynn quoted abuse survivors in Peru who raised concerns about the way in which their case was handled. It also reported that Prevost—during his time as provincial (regional leader) of the Midwest Augustinians in 1999–2001—had "allowed" a priest accused of abusing minors, Rev. James Ray, to live in an Augustinian friary near a Catholic school. Lawyers for the Augustinians said that the decision to place Ray in the friary was taken by officials of the archdiocese of Chicago, that there were no allegations against Ray during that time, and that those who lived in the friary were the responsibility of the prior of the house. Ray was removed from public ministry in 2002 and then from the "clerical state" a decade later.

The most serious criticism made against Pope Leo concerns his handling of the case of three biological sisters who claimed that he had not properly investigated their allegations of abuse by priests when they had been minors. The sisters said that the then bishop of Chiclayo had failed to punish the priests and that the investigation had been superficial. One of the accused priests was seen publicly celebrating Mass while under investigation by the Church, according to a *New York Times* report. Prevost's former diocese has denied that he acted improperly, saying that the allegations were sent to the Vatican's doctrine office in July 2022, which found insufficient evidence to pursue the matter. Peruvian prosecutors also investigated the case. They, too, found insufficient evidence, and said that the statute of limitations had expired.

Some have suggested that the negative reporting of Prevost's handling of abuse is a repercussion of his actions to dismantle the Sodalitium. Pedro Salinas believes that the Sodalitium and its supporters have fanned the flames of bad publicity against Prevost. Ugaz and some in the Vatican agree. Leo himself has said there has been "a lot of manipulation."

A Vatican source close to the investigation of the Sodalitium told me that the accusations of a cover-up originated in part with Ricardo Coronado, a Peruvian canon lawyer, ex-priest, and former member of the Augustinian order who, the source said, was very close to the Sodalitium leadership in Denver. He was the one, the Vatican source said, who "accused Prevost of a cover-up in relation to a case involving three victims of abuse in Chiclayo." Coronado told me that he has "no ties with the Sodalitium," although he said in another statement that he has "known and had friendly relations with members [of the Sodalitum] over the years," including with its founder, Figari. Coronado knows the case in which Prevost has been accused. He represented the three female abuse victims, saying that he did so to "give them a voice and to hold the Church hierarchy accountable for alleged misdeeds."

The same Vatican source insisted that Prevost "had investigated the facts, offered psychological help to the victims, and urged them to file a civil complaint," saying, "he had handled the cases well." The source said that the allegations against the future pope, which were amplified by sites such as *InfoVaticana*, could be described as the "revenge of the Sodalitium" and, in the end, a "retaliation" against the Vatican investigation that ended in the group's ultimate suppression. "The worst part is that it was an exploitation of the Sodalitium of the victims of Chiclayo," the source said. "Why did Prevost have to endure this defamation for more than a year and why was the Church almost deprived of an excellent pope? Because of the Sodalitium. The Church must be very attentive to these powerful groups and movements."

Coronado has rejected the claim of retribution, saying that "Prevost was not pope at the time; the conclave had not happened when I brought the case of the victims ... was I not obliged to so present it?"

Austen Ivereigh, a Church commentator and a biographer of Pope Francis, heard a similar account. "My understanding from good sources in Peru is that Coronado has had a kind of vendetta against Prevost for many years, seeing him as typical of the 'left-wing foreigners' whom conservative Peruvians blame for taking the Church in a progressive direction," Ivereigh told me. Ivereigh added that the accusations against Prevost were also used by "Sodalitium-adjacent lobbies" as "part of their failed dirty-tricks campaign to stop Prevost at the conclave." For his part, Coronado has accused the pope of "cynicism" and "subterfuge" in his handling of the case involving the sisters, even accusing Prevost of having "misled the cardinals." He insisted to me that Leo was "afraid of the truth" in the case, and rhetorically asked: "If you would ask me if I believe that Prevost covered up [for the priest accused of abuse] while he was bishop of Chiclayo, my firm response is YES."

When asked if there was an attempt to highlight the accusations against Prevost ahead of the conclave in the media he told me: "I wasn't part of that" and said that he didn't know if those close to the Sodalitium were involved in a campaign against the future pope. He said, however, there was "no Sodalitium house or work in Chiclayo."

Even if a case is exploited by those with an axe to grind it doesn't mean that the pope, or any Church leader, shouldn't face scrutiny in how a case is handled, nor does it mean that it was handled perfectly. Given the risk of abuse being weaponized, and the different agendas at play, it affirms the need for the Church to have robust, independent, and transparent processes for investigating abuse. In the case in which Leo has been scrutinized, the Church authorities say that he investigated and referred the case. The civil authorities also investigated. Rev. Hans Zollner is a Jesuit priest and one of the leading authorities on the Church's battle against abuse. A German theologian and trained psychologist and psychotherapist, he heads the Institute of Anthropology's Interdisciplinary Studies on Human Dignity and Care at Rome's Pontifical Gregorian University.

"Nobody can claim that he is without fault in this world, and we can't know for sure that [Leo] has always done the right thing, but from what I can see his record is good on these issues," Zollner told me, referring to Leo's support for the victims of the Sodalitium and his support for reporters investigating scandals.

In 2012, Zollner was one of the main organizers of an international symposium on clerical abuse for Church leaders held at the Gregorian University. This was the first of its kind. One of those who attended was the then prior general of the Augustinian order, Rev. Robert Prevost. His attendance at the event—which the Holy See had kept at arm's length—demonstrated his seriousness in addressing the problem. "By nature, and profession, he is a person who favors things that follow due process and clear guidelines in our area of concern," Zollner added.

Pope Leo has acknowledged that the abuse crisis is far from solved. He has said that victims must be supported and that bishops should seek the advice of professionals when dealing with cases. After his experience of dealing with the Sodalitium, he understands the complexities of abuse scandals, which, at their heart, are an abuse of power. But some of his remarks have come in for criticism. At a Vatican press conference in 2023, the then Cardinal Prevost said that the abuse scandal needed to be "kept in the proper perspective" and that the "whole life of the Church" doesn't revolve around this one issue. Some wondered whether he was downplaying the scandal. Similarly, as pope, he has said in an interview that abuse cannot become the central focus of the Church, which has its own mission. His remarks were questioned by Bishop Peter Kohlgraf of the German diocese of Mainz. "I would like to put a question mark over the Pope's statement on the mission of the Church and the Gospel," he said in a speech reported by the Catholic news agency KNA. "Sexualized violence is a crime against human beings and a betrayal of the Gospel." He said it should continue to be the focus of the Church to "take responsibility" for failures.

While Leo may not want abuse to become the Church's central focus, the scandal does hit at the very heart of the Church's mission. Many Catholics have walked away because of abuse, and, in the public's perception, the

Catholic Church is now commonly associated with abuse. The crisis has severely damaged the Church's credibility at a time when Leo wants it to be a prophetic voice.

Papacy in a time of AI

Pope Leo is hoping that the Church can offer a moral contribution to the major technological advancement of our age: artificial intelligence. Leo's papacy takes place not just in an era of change but in a change of era. Rapid advances in technology are opening up some profound ethical and social questions about the ordering of societies. The Vatican has long been talking to tech companies about the need to develop AI ethically, and has been pushing for what it calls "algorethics"—ethics for algorithms. It has persuaded big tech corporations such as Microsoft, IBM, and Cisco Systems to sign a "Rome Call for AI Ethics." The Vatican expert on this is Father Paolo Benanti, a Franciscan friar and professor who is a member of a UN body on AI. Pope Francis pushed for a global treaty that would regulate the development of AI, while Vice President JD Vance has warned Europe against heavy regulation of the technology. Francis raised the subject of AI when he addressed the G7 summit of world leaders in Puglia, southern Italy, in 2024, the first time a pope had spoken at the summit. He called for stronger guardrails on the technology, and the need for human oversight of AI. He also expressed his fears about automated weapons systems. Both Francis and Leo have recommended reading *Lord of the World,* an apocalyptic novel published in

Quiet Reformer

1907. It was written by Robert Hugh Benson, who was the son of a former archbishop of Canterbury. In Benson's story, a secular, humanistic ideology takes hold through a charismatic leader, who offers a utopian peace in exchange for blind obedience. The offer is resisted by a faithful few, including the Catholic Church, and ends in a final confrontation with the leader. Francis mentioned the book frequently. He saw it as a prophetic warning of a future in which machines replace human beings. Leo has said that the sci-fi novel offers food for thought. What, after all, would happen in a world where faith is lost?

Leo can influence the debate on AI in two ways. The first is through the convening power of the papacy: the Vatican has the ability to bring together the world's best thinkers in the field of AI. Few people, no matter how high their profile, turn down an invitation to the Vatican for a special event in which they meet the pope. An added bonus is that such gatherings are often held in extraordinarily beautiful venues such as the Casina Pio VI, a Renaissance villa in the Vatican gardens. At an event in September 2025, the Vatican gathered thinkers from various scientific fields, including AI. Speakers included Geoffrey Hinton, known as "the Godfather of AI," physicist and author Max Tegmark of MIT (Massachusetts Institute of Technology), and Will.i.am, front man of the band Black Eyed Peas, who also owns an AI company. Such gatherings give the pope an opportunity to address leading thinkers directly and to hear their ideas. A few weeks after his election, Leo gave a message to the executives of corporations such as Google, OpenAI, and Anthropic, who had gathered in the Vatican's Apostolic Palace, along with

Church representatives and academics from Harvard, to discuss AI. Echoing Francis, he called for AI to be developed according to an "ethical criterion" and warned about its impact on the "intellectual and neurological development" of children.

The second way Leo could influence the AI debate is through his own teaching. When Francis issued his landmark encyclical letter on the environment, *Laudato si'*, it had an impact not only on the Catholic Church but on discussions around the world. He placed the weight of the papacy's moral voice behind efforts to tackle climate change, and this included an important shift in Church teaching that made stewardship of the natural world a moral priority. In the past, Francis wrote, "we Christians have at times incorrectly interpreted the scriptures" to argue that because we were created in God's image we have "dominion" over the earth and therefore "domination" over other creatures. Francis argued that this must change and "instead, our 'dominion' over the universe should be understood more properly in the sense of responsible stewardship."

Leo could write a similarly influential encyclical letter on AI, one that updates Catholic teaching and applies the Church's social doctrine (the body of teaching that engages with politics) to the new technological advances. Such a document could be dubbed a "*Rerum novarum* for the Digital Age*,*" taking up the name given to the major nineteenth-century encyclical written by the pope's namesake, Leo XIII, to address the changes brought by the industrial revolution. A new industrial revolution, perhaps even more far-reaching, is already underway.

Quiet Reformer

An encyclical by Leo could cover a variety of themes, including the dignity of work in the age of AI, the regulation of the technology, how to promote the common good, and solidarity with poorer nations. Crucially, he would want to emphasize that technology cannot replace what it means to be human.

"If we lose sight of the value of humanity, and we think that the digital world is the be-all and end-all, and then the extremely rich people who are investing in artificial intelligence totally ignore the value of human beings and of humanity, I think the Church has to speak up there," he told Elise Ann Allen in his first interview after becoming pope. The pope is likely to frame what he says in the context of growing inequality. He has voiced his concern about the huge gulf between CEO pay and that of ordinary workers, at a time when Elon Musk is on his way to becoming the world's first trillionaire. "What does that mean and what's that about? If that is the only thing that has value anymore, then we're in big trouble," he said. The concept of solidarity—support for the poorest—is a central theme of Catholic social teaching, as is finding policies that support the common good, not just the a select few.

The two most recent popes have come to the papacy from a scientific background. Francis's early training was as a chemist. Leo is a mathematician who wants to maintain a fruitful relationship between faith and science, which are sometimes placed in opposition to each other. He insists that the Church is not against the development of technology, and he is supportive of AI's advances in the field of medicine. While faith and science operate in different spheres, at their best both are searching for the truth about humanity's place in the universe. Science offers the *how*, whereas faith tries to answer the *why*. Leo's fear is that if scientific technology pursues its aims without reference to faith, then it becomes empty and does damage to humanity. Notorious episodes, such as the seventeenth-century Church's condemnation of Galileo for demonstrating that the earth revolves around the sun, suggest that religion opposes the search for scientific truth. But this obscures the work of the Church in the field of science. Figures such as Georges Lemaître, the Belgian priest who formulated an early Big Bang theory, or the Vatican observatory, founded in 1891, which Leo visited in July 2025, show that faith and science are two sides of the same coin. The observatory, located in Castel Gandolfo, demonstrates the Church's support for the science of astronomy. It hosts summer schools, giving young students the opportunity to learn with leading experts.

Leo's undergraduate studies in mathematics have given him a useful qualification for entering the AI discussion. A major teaching document from him will need to demonstrate a credible understanding of the technological developments and the ethical questions they raise, such as: how do we respond to deep-fakes and misinformation? Popes themselves are increasingly the subject of fake, AI-generated images and videos. A fake picture of Francis sporting a stylish white puffer coat went viral. Other images showed him riding a motorcycle and even enjoying himself at the Burning Man festival in Nevada. Leo has also been subjected to fakes: on one occasion

Quiet Reformer

someone asked him how he was feeling because they'd seen a video of him falling down the stairs. He refused to authorize a pope avatar that would grant "private audiences" to people and to which they could ask questions. The growth of conspiracy theories and misinformation is, he says, "very destructive, very destructive." It is likely to be a subject on which he will continue to speak out. One source told me that Leo would like to address the ethics and purpose of communication at some point.

At the age of just seventy, Leo potentially has a long papacy ahead of him. He has time to implement significant internal reforms while at the same time giving the Church a voice and an input into the epoch-shifting developments of the century. Popes build on what they have been left by their predecessors: for Leo, it will be Francis and Paul VI when it comes to implementing Vatican II and changes to the role of laypeople, while he'll look to Leo XIII when it comes to his reflections on Catholic social teaching and technological change. Leo's job is not to come up with big novelties. In the Catholic understanding, reforms build on the past; they reinvent and reimagine but are always linked to a living tradition. They reflect, in some ways, the histories of extraordinary cathedrals and churches, where some parts have been knocked down and rebuilt while others have been updated and refurbished. But the foundations and original purpose remain. Leo's pontificate will add his mark to the great building of the Church's tradition, while making sure the doors remain open, and the interior is habitable.

5

Balancing the Books

Court 19 on the fourth floor of the Rolls Building in London's Royal Courts of Justice feels a world away from the frescoed halls of the Vatican. This modern, efficient court building was opened in 2011 to handle complex commercial disputes, and the Vatican had become embroiled in one.

It was here, in July 2024, that the Holy See, for the first time and very much against its wishes, was standing trial in a foreign court. This extraordinary moment was testimony to the fact that the Vatican's dubious financial practices were now being scrutinized as never before.

The saga of the Vatican's finances has sometimes resembled a plot from a Dan Brown novel. On July 4 and 5, Archbishop Edgar Peña Parra, the papacy's equivalent to a chief of staff, entered the witness box in Court 19 to give evidence in a dispute concerning the Holy See's disastrous investment in a London property. In the past, the Vatican would have avoided the unpleasantness of a court appearance by claiming diplomatic immunity as a sovereign state. Under Francis, that changed. Church leaders—whatever their rank—were increasingly told to co-operate with secular justice. In the Vatican, Francis also changed the Vatican City State legislation so that cardinals could face prosecution by lay judges. No one would be above the law. Still, sending Archbishop Peña Parra to give evidence in the Royal Courts of Justice was a high-risk move for the Vatican.

The Holy See had invested about £300 million ($400 million) in a vast property in Chelsea, southwest London, which had originally been built as a car showroom for the Harrods department store. Everything about this investment had gone wrong. The Holy See claimed that it had been the victim of a crime and had lost roughly £100 million ($150 million). The property price had been overinflated, the Vatican said, and the middlemen involved had been fraudulent bad actors.

Pope Francis decided that those responsible for this debacle—including a once-powerful cardinal who had been Peña Parra's predecessor—would be prosecuted by the Vatican City State Tribunal.

One of those put on trial by the Vatican was an Italian financier named Raffaele Mincione. Toward the end of 2023, the Vatican found him guilty of embezzlement and "self-laundering." It was Mincione who had introduced the Vatican to the Chelsea property deal. Mincione was, however, acquitted by the tribunal of other charges and has sought to appeal his convictions. He has said that the Vatican case against him "rests on nothing." Strenuously insisting on his innocence, Mincione decided to try and clear his name in the London courts by bringing an historic civil action against the Vatican. This was how Peña Parra ended up in the witness box. Mincione was seeking to have the court in London rule that he had acted "in good faith" in his dealings with the Holy See, something that the Holy See had disputed.

Peña Parra faced hours of intense, and, at times, hostile cross-examination in the witness stand. It was unlike anything either he or his predecessors would have experienced before. In the Vatican hierarchy, Peña Parra is the number three. He helps to run the Church's central administration and the Vatican's foreign policy. He works in the Apostolic Palace, and may meet with the pope whenever he wishes. He also holds the high-ranking role of Sostituto (Substitute), which, among other things, allows him to help oversee the pope's agenda and correspondence—a role that gives him huge authority in what is a deferential, hierarchical Vatican culture.

But when Charles Samek, KC, the barrister representing Raffaele Mincione, began questioning the archbishop about the property deal, all deference went out of the window. Archbishop Peña Parra had arrived at the court in good form. He said that he was staying in Wimbledon, the home of the papal ambassador to the United Kingdom, but had "not been able to watch any tennis." The lightheartedness quickly evaporated.

Mr. Samek's opening exchanges were polite. He asked Peña Parra how he would like to be addressed, to which the Vatican official said that he had no preference. Then things quickly became more heated. Mr. Samek put "Monsignor Peña Parra" under intense pressure with a series of questions about the Vatican official's own conduct. Several times, Samek raised his voice incredulously in reaction to the answers he was hearing. "You are making that up as you go along, aren't you?" Samek said to Peña Parra. "That last answer, I suggest to you, is a lie." The archbishop was stunned. He tried to contain the onslaught by answering more slowly, pausing before each reply. And, presumably on advice from his lawyers, he directed his answers to the judge, Mr. Justice Robin Knowles. In answer to Samek's questioning, the archbishop insisted, "I did not lie." He did, however, make a serious admission. When asked why he had paid an invoice for €5 million ($8.3 million) that he had known to be "completely fictitious", Peña Parra replied: "You said that I was not honest. I accept that." That admission, it seemed then, would severely damage the Vatican's case. Nevertheless, as the questioning went on, Archbishop Peña Parra seemed to recover his mettle. Although he had an interpreter on hand, he spoke in English, which is his third language.

Peña Parra has one of those calm, measured personas that belie a fiery determination and resilience. In the courtroom, he put up a fight. By submitting himself to cross-examination he was risking his stellar, thirty-year career as a Vatican diplomat, but he managed to acquit himself. Despite being accused of lying, and admitting that on one occasion he was "not honest," Peña Parra was considered by the judge to be an honest and credible witness. Justice Knowles, in his judgment, said that he accepted the "honesty of [Peña Parra's] evidence at trial" and on the point where the archbishop had admitted not being honest: "In my judgment it involved acceptance of personal imperfection or a degree of failure, and not of bad faith or dishonesty in the ordinary sense of the word."

Peña Parra's risk had paid off. The judge ruled that the Vatican could "consider itself utterly let down" by

Mr. Mincione and his companies, which had taken "no care towards" the Holy See, had "put their own interests first," and had "made no attempt" to protect it from "fraudulent bad actors." Crucially, the judge refused to accept that Mr. Mincione had acted "in good faith" in his dealings with the Vatican, saying that his conduct had been "misleading" when he had stated the value of the London property. The ruling by Justice Knowles was a significant victory for the Holy See because it confirmed the prosecution case and the convictions in the earlier Vatican trial. Here was a British court establishing that those contracted by the Vatican had not acted in good faith. "How did you manage that, Edgar?" Pope Francis is said to have remarked after the ruling. Peña Parra replied: "I don't know!"

It wasn't the cleanest of victories for the Vatican. The judge rejected the Holy See's allegations that Mr. Mincione was guilty of "dishonesty and conspiracy," and later ordered it to pay half of Mr Mincione's £7 million ($9.3 million) legal costs. Both sides had employed teams of lawyers (about nine on each side) and had racked up costs of millions.

The case had shone a light on the sheer messiness of Vatican finances. How had they gotten themselves into this position in the first place? "Bad choices," is how Leo has described what happened. But these bad choices had resulted from serious structural weaknesses in the Vatican financial system. The main one was highlighted repeatedly to me by the late Lord (Tom) Camoys, a veteran UK banker who for years had served as an adviser to the Administration of the Patrimony of the Apostolic

See (Apsa). Apsa managed the Holy See's assets, properties, and investments. It also operated a sort of general accounting service, which included paying salaries and acting as a purchasing office.

The major problem, Lord Camoys told me, was that large investment portfolios were being overseen by clerics who were not trained in financial management or administration. This created a dangerous situation that left the Vatican vulnerable and exposed. Lord Camoys, who was from one of the oldest Catholic families in England and who had served as the first Catholic Lord Chamberlain since the Reformation, had managed the Vatican's London property portfolio for years without problems. The company he oversaw, British Grolux Investments, runs twenty-seven properties in London, including shops in Kensington High Street and New Bond Street. But Lord Camoys, who died in 2023, was never consulted about the Vatican's investment in Chelsea.

The origins of the London property saga go back to 2012, when a man named Antonio Mosquito suggested that the Holy See's Secretariat of State—the central, co-ordinating office of the Holy See which also handles foreign relations—invest $200 million in his Angolan oil company. Mr. Mosquito was aquainted with the then papal chief of staff, Archbishop (later Cardinal) Angelo Becciu, from Becciu's days as papal ambassador to Angola. Mr. Mincione, who had experience of managing investment funds, was brought in to facilitate the deal. In the end, the oil venture was considered too risky, so Mr. Mincione proposed investing the same amount in an attractive property at 60 Sloane Avenue in Chelsea,

Balancing the Books

London. The property was owned by Mr. Mincione's property investment company. It had great redevelopment potential and, the court was told, a supposed value of £275 million ($366 million). In fact, as the Vatican later learned, Mr. Mincione had bought the property for the much lower price of £129 million ($165 million) at the end of 2012. The £275 million figure, the Vatican said, had "no basis in reality."

In 2014, the Vatican invested its $200 million in Mr. Mincione's property investment fund, much of which was linked to 60 Sloane Avenue. In return, the Vatican obtained a 45 per cent stake in the property. Initially the plan was to turn it into apartments, in the hope that this would be a shrewd, long-term investment for the Church. But the Vatican ended up becoming one of the few entities unable to make money from the London property market. By 2018 it had become clear that Mr. Mincione's fund had performed poorly and that the Vatican was losing money on its investment. The Vatican sought to exit the arrangement with Mr. Mincione's companies by purchasing the property outright. It then paid another £40 million ($53 million) to Mr. Mincione, which, the Vatican later claimed, was an overpayment on a property with an overinflated value. The London judge said that while Mr. Mincione had been "ambitious and opportunistic" in seeking this payment it did not show "serious wrongdoing." (In December 2023, the Vatican court, too, had acquitted Mr Mincione of charges of fraud and embezzlement relating to the overvaluation of the property.)

Buying the property meant that the Vatican found itself saddled with a mortgage of £128 million. (The mortgage had been attached to the property for pre-development financing.) One Church source said that the Holy See faced paying £1 million ($1.2 million) each month in interest on the loan.

Archbishop Peña Parra had taken up his position in October 2018 and had quickly sought to solve the problem by trying to take full ownership of the property. But he had been under pressure to act quickly and the Vatican found itself doing business with a questionable figure. This was the Italian financier Gianluigi Torzi, who had a complex financial relationship with Mr. Mincione. Torzi was brought in to help negotiate the purchase. In the Vatican trial, Torzi was accused of structuring the deal in such a way that left him in control of the building, with the Vatican effectively purchasing an "empty box." Essentially, Torzi had brokered a deal where the Vatican owned the London property through a company in which he retained the controlling shares. To make matters even worse, Torzi was then accused of extorting €15 million ($17.4 million) from the Vatican in return for control of the building. These were the fictitious invoices that Peña Parra admitted paying (one for €5 million and the second for €10 million) and why he said he was not honest. The archbishop felt he had to pay the money to Torzi because otherwise the financier would "lie and lie." Peña Parra conceded that some of his staff had been "superficial and naïve" but in court he insisted: "I would give Torzi nothing, and I would put him in jail several times." A legal source told me that the Vatican had little choice but to pay Torzi, adding that Torzi could easily have sold the building without the Vatican's consent. The London judge described Torzi's actions as a "breach of duty, unscrupulous, and dishonest."

In the end, 60 Sloane Avenue was sold for £186 million ($223.6 million), at a very significant loss.

In what was a legal first, Pope Francis authorized a Vatican trial of ten defendants including, for the first time, a cardinal of the Catholic Church, the once hugely powerful Cardinal Giovanni Angelo Becciu. Mincione and Torzi were among the others. Becciu had been responsible for overseeing the London property deal. He was accused of approving and authorizing Vatican money for a dubious investment that had involved a high-risk fund. The judge-led trial in the Vatican convicted nine out of the ten defendants in December 2023, including Becciu, who became the first cardinal to be convicted in the Vatican's criminal courts. Torzi was convicted of extortion and fraud, although he is appealing his convictions. Becciu was found guilty of a range of charges, including embezzlement, and sentenced to five-and-a-half years in prison. And Becciu had not only been on trial for his role in the London property investment. He had also been accused of transferring €575,000 ($670,000) to Cecilia Marogna, a "security consultant," purportedly to help free a Colombian nun kidnapped in Mali, Africa. Vatican prosecutors argued that this money was in fact spent by Marogna on items such as clothing, footwear and fashion accessories from high-end brands, including Prada, Gucci, and Hermès, along with furniture and luxury hotels. Marogna, who is in her forties, was dubbed the "cardinal's lady" for her association with Becciu. During the trial, the court was shown images she had posted on social media showing the inside of the cardinal's Vatican apartment with the captions "feeling at home" and "my paradise." Marogna was convicted for misappropriating funds and sentenced to three years and nine months in prison. She denied wrongdoing, telling the Italian newspaper *Corriere della Sera* that she legitimately spent the funds on her work, which included a "network of relationships in Africa and the Middle East." Both Marogna and Becciu denied any improper relationship. Torzi was convicted of extortion and fraud and was sentenced to six years in prison, while Mincione's convictions landed him with a five-and-half year prison sentence.

Although the Vatican had handed down prison sentences, no one went straight to jail; everyone was free pending an appeal. The Vatican does not have a jail but it does has some pre-trial detention cells. Technically it could use jail cells in Italian prisons. When Benedict XVI's butler, Paolo Gabriele, was convicted of theft for leaking sensitive Vatican documents, he served his sentence in the Vatican cells.

Becciu, Mincione, Torzi, Marogna and some other defendants continue to assert their innocence. In the Vatican legal system, as in Italy's, both the prosecution and the defense may file appeals after the first judgment. In a victory for those convicted, the Vatican court allowed the defendants' appeal to go forward but denied the prosecution's appeal for a reconsideration of counts that had been dismissed in the trial or in which the defendants were had been found not guilty.

The prosecution and the Vatican criminal system has faced criticisms over procedure and fairness. Some also question whether the system is sufficiently independent, given that the pope hires and fires judges. Nevertheless, the trial was considered an important moment. It signaled that the Vatican was willing to ensure accountability for financial wrongdoing.

Out of their depth

Although Becciu continues to stress his innocence, it can't be denied that the London property investment was a massive risk. The Vatican court found that Becciu had breached the Church's law which states that all "administrators are bound to fulfil their function with the diligence of a good householder," and to "exercise vigilance" to ensure that what is under their care is "in no way lost." The court believed that Becciu had been "highly speculative" and irresponsible to have authorized the $200 million investment. Given that Becciu had a doctorate in canon law, he must have been aware of his responsibilities.

At the very least, Becciu was, as Lord Camoys warned, unqualified to oversee such vast sums of money. According to a 2019 report, the Holy See's Secretariat of State was managing assets worth approximately €928 million ($1 billion).

In the London trial, Justice Knowles put his finger on some of the deeper problems. He noted that Archbishop Peña Parra and Mr. Mincione (who, curiously, was once engaged to the former model Heather Mills, ex-wife of Beatles legend Sir Paul McCartney) were from "different worlds." Mincione, the judge said, was a "flamboyant deal maker, stimulated by the world of business," while the "steadier" Peña Parra found "himself and his office out of their depth or overwhelmed in terms of financial administration."

On the manner in which the Vatican went about making its investments, the judge said: "Remarkably the line of decision-making as regards investments and their management reached His Holiness the Pope [Francis] himself. This brings further into question the realism of the [Holy See Secretariat of] State itself managing successfully to sustain the type of involvement in investment it was attempting."

But the judge also remarked upon the problems of not having sufficient expertise when it comes to managing a complex portfolio of financial assets: "Peña Parra found himself tangled in a world of business in which he was inexperienced and inexpert and with insufficient time at his disposal … The pursuit of return on investment had taken the eye of the [Holy See Secretariat of] State off the nature and consequences of its investments. It found itself involved in the type of investment that required a close and experienced assessment of how to engage, step by step, and with whom, individual by individual. The reality today is that the management of wealth on the scale involved needed greater strategy, experience and expertise than it had. The descriptions available to me did not show that these attributes could be found within the [Holy See Secretariat of] State."

Justice Knowles emphasized the three things the Holy See needed when managing finances: "strategy, experience and expertise." Francis's pontificate saw more competent lay professionals brought into manage the Vatican's investments. He also ordered that the Secretariat of State's investments should in future be managed by Apsa, whose secretary, Fabio Gasperini, has spent thirty years in the financial services, advising banks and asset management companies. One of his previous employers had been Ernst and Young. It will be crucial for Leo to draw on professional expertise if he is to avoid a repeat of the London property disaster.

Vatican shortfall

Although the Vatican owns many priceless works of art, it is a common misconception that it has limitless wealth. The Vatican City State and the Holy See cannot simply call in cash from the worldwide Catholic Church—they are responsible for their own income and expenditure. According to figures from 2022, the Holy See's annual income stood at €769.6 million ($894 million) while expenditure was €803 million ($933 million)—a budget similar to that of a large university.

By contrast, in 2015 the Catholic archdiocese of Cologne, Germany, revealed that it was worth €3.35 billion ($3.89 billion), making it much wealthier than the Vatican. The German Catholic Church has far more resources than the Vatican. Its wealth is largely derived from a Church tax, which collects 8 to 9 per cent of the income tax of its members.

The Vatican's income comes from a variety of sources.

There are contributions from believers and donors, incomes from properties and investments, and, crucially, the Vatican museums. But the Covid-19 lockdown affected this dramatically. For months, no visitors came through the doors. On the other side of the ledger, the Holy See has around 5,000 employees (including those working in the Church's central administration and the Vatican City State infrastructure). It also has the major costs of supporting a worldwide network of diplomatic missions and a department for communications, which includes a multi-language news outlet responsible for the broadcasting of papal events.

Pope Leo faces two major financial difficulties. The first is a structural budget deficit of tens of millions of euros. The Vatican accounts for 2024 showed a structural deficit of €44 million, although this had reduced significantly from €83 million. The second is a ballooning pension black hole. In November 2024, Francis wrote to the College of Cardinals saying that there was a "serious prospective imbalance" in the fund, and he appointed US Cardinal Kevin Farrell as the fund's sole administrator. Farrell, a Dublin-born former bishop of Dallas who became a naturalized US citizen, is one of the few cardinals with an MBA. He is highly trusted in financial matters. The Vatican's pension shortfall was put at €631 million ($734 million) in 2022 but the hole is thought to have grown larger since then. Cardinals and Vatican officials are living longer, and retirement ages may need to be recalculated.

Another worry has been a decline in donations to the Holy See's main cash fund, Peter's Pence, which supports

Balancing the Books

the pope's mission and his charitable endeavours. Catholics from across the world are encouraged to make an annual donation to the Peter's Pence fund—the equivalent of sending the collection basket around the world's 1.4 billion Catholics. In recent years, however, most of fund's annual expenditure has gone on funding the Vatican's shortfalls. In 2024, €58 million ($67 million) was raised in annual donations, while €61.2 million ($70.6 million) of the €75.4 million ($86.9 million) paid out by Peter's Pence that year went on funding Vatican costs. It was a similar scenario the year before. While over the last two years the income has increased, the donations to the collection declined during the Covid pandemic. A former Vatican finance tsar, Rev. Antonio Guerrero, has pointed out that there was also a decrease of 23 per cent between 2015 and 2019. The capital from the fund was being used to pay the Vatican's expenses. Guerrero said that things could no longer go on like this.

The state of the Vatican's finances was a topic of discussion for the cardinals gathered in Rome for the conclave that elected Leo. They were asking themselves how on earth the Church was going to save money. Leo's experience of running a religious order globally, which involved the oversight of money in different jurisdictions, would have been a factor in the cardinals' perception of him as a strong candidate. A priest who knew Bishop Prevost in Peru described his "mathematical" mentality, recounting to the Associated Press that the future pope would often be on the lookout for used cars. He would then fix them up himself, often going to YouTube for advice. It's worth remembering that Leo once taught mathematics and physics at St. Rita of Cascia High School in Chicago. Recently, he demonstrated his head for figures during a meeting with young people in the Vatican. "Allow me to do some calculations with you," he told them. "Do you know how many stars there are in the observable universe? An impressive and wonderful number: sextillion stars — that is, a 1 followed by 21 zeros! If we divided them among the 8 billion people on Earth, each person would have hundreds of billions of stars. With the naked eye, on clear nights, we can see about five thousand."

He's not someone who can be bamboozled by figures or have the wool pulled over his eyes when it comes to the Vatican's financial reports.

It is likely that Leo will adopt a methodical and prudent approach to the Church's finances. He has already received some good financial news. The property asset management arm of the Vatican (Apsa) has reported a €62.2 million ($72.3 million) profit for 2024, up by €16 million ($18.6 million) from the previous year, while a further boost has come from the millions of pilgrims visiting Rome for the special 2025 jubilee year, a twelve-month-long celebration focussed on forgiveness and spiritual renewal that takes place every twenty-five years. A jubilee always attracts large numbers to the Eternal City, more so in a year when one pope has died and another has been elected. The Vatican also reported that in 2024 it made a surplus of €1.6 million, the first for years.

The Holy See has more than 5,000 properties managed by Apsa—in Rome, Switzerland, Paris, and London. The portfolio in Italy includes 4,051 properties, many of them apartments, mostly in Rome and Castel Gandolfo, along with hundreds of buildings used as shops and offices. Around 60 per cent of the apartments are occupied by Vatican employees who pay a reduced rent (described by a former Apsa president as "a form of social housing.") Francis made efforts to change this and tried to get more of the properties rented out at the market rate.

American advantage

With the Vatican facing a budget and pension shortfall, some senior Church figures will hope that an American pope will bring a major boost in income. One way to do this would be an appeal to donors. The Vatican regularly receives donations from organizations and individuals who support specific projects, and toward the end of his papacy Francis set up a special commission dedicated to raising money from believers, bishops' groups, and other benefactors.

A US pope is likely to have an advantage when it comes to raising money from American Catholics, the biggest contributors to the Peter's Pence annual collection. Almost $16 million was given in 2024 from the US church. Some of the most generous individual supporters of the Holy See's work are in the United States. These include groups such as the Papal Foundation, which supports various charitable projects. Members of the Foundation can be individuals or groups, but they must make a one-million-dollar donation. Anyone willing to commit such a sum then becomes a "Steward of St. Peter." The fund stands at around $250 million. A Chicago-born pope will have an obvious head start when it comes to communicating with these donors.

In the run-up to the 2025 conclave, members of the Papal Foundation and other conservative donors were in Rome. "This room could raise a billion to help the Church, so long as we have the right pope," an anonymous donor reportedly said. The Papal Foundation has, in the past at least, included members who supported President Trump. Their preferred candidate for pope was the Hungarian Cardinal Péter Erdö, who had been at odds with Francis on migration and on communion for divorced and remarried couples. Erdö also declined to criticize the anti-migrant policies of the party led by Hungary's president, Viktor Orbán. Erdö is a scholarly Church lawyer. Conservatives had hoped that that he would lay down the law on doctrine and provide a corrective to Francis's style and approach.

Cardinal Dolan of New York, who is favorable to Trump, leads the Papal Foundation. Others involved include Tim Busch, the founder of the Napa Institute, who, as I explained earlier, pushes an economic agenda that is at odds with the vision laid out by Pope Leo. Mr. Busch is a Trump supporter who has in the past donated to Rick Santorum, the politician and a Catholic. Santorum criticized Francis on climate change, saying he should leave science to the scientists. (As a father of seven, Santorum was also unhappy with a remark the late pope made during an in-flight press conference when he said that Catholics were not required to "breed like rabbits.")

The weakness of the Vatican's finances could potentially give an increased influence to donors. But what might those who donate want in return? The risk is that those who give money may, albeit subtly, seek to exert influence on appointments and Church initiatives. So Leo has to perform a balancing act. He needs to raise funds to deal with the Vatican's structural budget deficit, but that can't come at the cost of the papacy's freedom to speak boldly on social and political issues such as the environment, poverty, and inequality.

Francis cleans up the mess

Attracting an uptick in donations might be easier if the Vatican could first demonstrate that its own house is in order. The finances of the Holy See have in the past been a source of scandal. A small sovereign state, with little oversight, is an ideal place to hide illicit money. Famously, the Vatican was embroiled in the 1982 collapse of Banco Ambrosiano, Italy's largest private bank, following the discovery of enormous debts, much of them owed to the Vatican. Days after the collapse, Roberto Calvi, the bank's chairman (nicknamed "God's banker" because of his links to the Holy See), was found hanging beneath Blackfriars Bridge in London. At first it appeared as if he'd taken his own life, but decades later authorities determined that he'd probably been murdered. The bank's failure sparked a huge political and financial scandal. Calvi was reported to have set up offshore shell companies to help launder money for clients such as the Sicilian mafia. It was also rumored that he was in possession of information that threatened the interests of powerful figures. Calvi's family, who were appealing a conviction for currency violations at the time of his death, insist that foul play was involved. His son Carlo, who has worked as a banker in Canada, has said that his father was lured to London by the mafia to be murdered. When Ambrosiano's offshore deals went bad, the Vatican Bank, as the loan guarantor, was exposed. The Vatican Bank's then chairman was the US prelate Archbishop Paul Marcinkus, a priest of the archdiocese of Chicago. He was memorably quoted as saying, "You can't run the Church on Hail Marys." Although the Vatican denied any responsibility for Banco Ambrosiano's collapse, it paid a $250 million "good will gesture" out of moral responsibility.

Despite various attempts to clean things up, the Vatican's financial problems persisted. Even in 2010 and 2013 the Council of Europe's money-laundering watchdog revealed that the Vatican still had deficiencies in its financial controls and anti-money laundering measures. The Vatican simply didn't have a sufficient regulatory structure to freeze and investigate suspicious payments. The cardinals attending the 2013 conclave insisted that the next pope had to get a grip on the finances.

Soon after his election, Pope Francis moved swiftly to clean up the Vatican Bank—technically known as the Institute for the Works of Religion (IOR). He had considered closing down the IOR but instead decided to appoint new leadership and oversight. The major overhaul of the bank included combing through 30,000 accounts. The new management closed thousands of them, including two belonging to Pope Paul VI, who had died in 1978. One of the late pope's accounts held €125,310 and another $296,151. The Vatican financial system that Leo has inherited is in a much better state thanks to Francis.

The Vatican Bank is located in a fortress-like medieval tower where the ATMs offer an option of instructions in Latin, but it is catching up with the modern banking world. It now submits an annual report— in 2024 it made a profit of €32.8 million ($38 million)—and has stopped getting embroiled in scandals. Account holders are limited to those who work for the Vatican, ambassadors to the Holy See, and religious orders and other Church entities. Francis also overhauled the Vatican's financial regulatory system, toughening up checks and controls. In 2019 Francis appointed Carmelo Barbagallo as a watchdog to ensure transparency and supervise financial risks. Barbagallo had spent forty years in financial supervisory roles for the Bank of Italy. During the Francis pontificate the Holy See's banking practices improved significantly. By May 2024 the watchdog had given the IOR assessments of full or high compliance in thirty-five out of the thirty-nine categories.

The London property fiasco had demonstrated the Vatican's willingness to prosecute suspected wrongdoing. But there was another case in which Francis showed that he was determined to improve accountability and comply with international anti-money-laundering standards. In January 2021, Angelo Caloia, the president of the Vatican Bank from 1989 to 2009, was convicted by the Vatican court of embezzlement and money laundering. At the time, Caloia was the highest-ranking official of the Vatican Bank to be convicted of a financial crime. He and his associates were charged with selling properties owned by the bank for below-market values and pocketing millions in the process. Francis pursued the case vigorously. The Vatican court froze the defendants' Swiss bank accounts and ordered seizures of their assests.

The Argentine pontiff, during a meeting with clerics early on in his pontificate, reminisced about an elderly priest from Buenos Aires who was very careful with money. That priest, Francis told them, used to say: "If we don't know how to look after money, which you can see, how can we look after the souls of the faithful, which you can't see?" It was a mantra that guided Francis, and he used to caution frequently that the "Devil enters through the pockets," a warning not to prioritize money over the Church's mission.

Leo's predecessor was not afraid of putting noses out of joint in the Vatican. He ordered the streamlining and centralizing of the Vatican's investments, a move aimed at ending the practice of having different departments oversee their own pools of money. Francis's decision—following the London property debacle—that the Secretariat of State hand over the control of managing its assets to Apsa took a significant amount of power away from the Secretariat of State, which for years had managed donations and investments on behalf of the pope. Francis also ruled that the Vatican Bank should be the bank used by all Vatican bodies when it came to its investments, which in turn would be overseen by Apsa. This was to stop Vatican departments making poor investments in outside entities. Leo has, however, modified this ruling. He has said that while Apsa is still in charge, other financial institutions may be used "if more efficient and convenient," but he stressed collaboration and "co-reponsibility" when making any investment decisions.

Another of Francis's clean-up efforts was to bring in Cardinal George Pell as the first prefect of the Secretariat of the Economy, a structure Francis created. The secretariat reports to the Council of the Economy, which has oversight of all Vatican economic activities.

Pell was an Australian prelate, nicknamed "the ranger" by Francis for his efforts to bring order and transparency to the Vatican's economic problems. He had a no-nonsense, sometimes abrasive character, but also a keen political antenna and a dry sense of humor. On one occasion, I am told, he met with former British Prime Minister Boris Johnson, who was baptized a Catholic. When Mr. Johnson asked the cardinal to pray for him, Pell joked: "I wouldn't throw good money after bad." It's an anecdote revealing of the cardinal's economic thinking.

The Australian cardinal took up his role with gusto, bringing with him to Rome a trusted lay financial professional from Australia, Danny Casey, who was his former business manager in the archdiocese of Sydney. Soon after taking up his post, Pell made an announcement: he'd found that millions of euros were unaccounted for. To find the missing money, he would hire PricewaterhouseCoopers (PwC) to carry out a complete audit of all the Vatican's finances. But Pell was coming up against strong currents of internal resistance. When he signed the contract commissioning PwC's audit, he titled himself "Manager of the Holy See," which made some think that he was exceeding his authority. Among those most vociferous in resisting Pell's shake-up was Cardinal Becciu, then the papal chief of staff and the man essentially running the Vatican. Both men were formidable types. Pell was a 6-foot 4-inch former Australian rules football player. Becciu was a diminutive Sardinian who came from Pattada, a place known for making folding blade knives. The two became powerful adversaries.

In 2017 Becciu had a hand in the removal of the Vatican's first lay auditor-general, Libero Milone, who had previously held senior positions in Deloitte. Milone took legal action against the Holy See for unfair dismissal, claiming that he'd been ousted because he'd uncovered financial wrongdoing. The architect of his removal, he said, was Becciu. The cardinal, however, said that Milone been spying on senior members of the Roman Curia, including Becciu.

In the end, Pell's reforms were stymied. His overly combative style was part of the reason, but so was the fact that he was forced to return to Australia in 2017 to defend himself against allegations of child sexual abuse. Pell's supporters suggested that Becciu had supplied funds to influence the investigation against Pell. There was no evidence for this implausible claim, and Becciu strongly denied it. But it was illustrative of the fact that there was no love lost between these two.

Pell was convicted of five counts of child abuse and sent to a maximum-security prison. He languished there for more than 400 days before his sentence was overturned by Australia's highest court. The court ruled that there were reasonable doubts about the prosecution's case, which had largely relied on the evidence of a single accuser.

Balancing the Books

For years, Cardinal Pell had been at odds with Francis's vision for the Church, particularly when it came to offering communion to remarried divorcees and protecting the environment. In 2015, at a major Vatican synod on the family, Pell, along with twelve other cardinals, added his name to a private letter to Francis expressing serious concern that the synod was being manipulated into changing Catholic thinking on marriage, divorce, and homosexuality. When Pell returned to Rome after prison he became the the vanguard of the anti-Francis opposition, and closely aligned himself with those resisting Francis in the US. But in June 2023, he died suddenly following a hip operation.

After his death it emerged that Pell had been the author of an anonymous letter condemning Francis's pontificate as a "catastrophe" for not offering more forceful teachings on sexuality. He described the pope's synod reforms as a "toxic nightmare" in a posthumously published article in *The Spectator,* a British weekly magazine. Given the high position of trust and responsibility that Francis had given him, Pell's opposition was remarkable. In the anonymous letter criticizing the pope, Pell seemed to put aside his animosity toward Becciu, saying that it had been unjust to strip the Sardinian cardinal of his privileges before the Vatican had put him on trial.

Regardless of Pell's opposition to Francis, he did lay the foundations needed for future financial reforms. His establishment of the Secretariat for the Economy, an overarching finance body for the Vatican, was a major achievement. Today it is led by Maximinio Caballero Ledo, a Spanish financer who was formerly an executive at Baxter Healthcare, a US multinational based in Illinois. Francis paid tribute to Pell's "determination and wisdom." Although the PwC audit was canceled, the Holy See did go on to publish more transparent financial information and centralized its investments.

Leo has inherited a Vatican financial system that is virtually unrecognizable from twelve years earlier. It is now one where lay professionals hold leadership positions, where there is a legal framework of checks and balances, and where those in positions of authority—regardless of rank—have been prosecuted and convicted for wrongdoing.

Leo's priorities

Financial reforms remain a work in progress, and Leo has serious problems to fix. He is listening to advice. Following a recommendation from his council for the economy, he issued a ruling that reversed the decision by Francis and allowed the Holy See to use non-Vatican banks in the management of its assets. But he will need to be on his guard and keep an eye out for scandal. During the 2025 conclave, the Cardinal Becciu saga continued to cause problems. Five years earlier, Becciu had announced that he was suing the Italian news magazine *L'Espresso* after they had broken the story that prosecutors were investigating him. Becciu claimed €10 million ($11 million) in damages (to be given to charity) saying they had ruined his reputation and his chance of becoming pope. It was a breathtaking claim for a cardinal to make. Not only had it revealed his papal ambitions but he had essentially put a price-tag on the papacy. This went down very badly in the Vatican.

When Becciu's scandals surfaced, Pope Francis removed him from his positions in the Roman Curia and took away his "rights and privileges" as a cardinal. After Francis's death, however, Becciu indicated that he was intending to enter the Sistine Chapel to cast his vote in the conclave, telling a Sardinian newspaper that "there was no explicit will to exclude me." Becciu only backed down after he was shown two letters from Francis stating that he had been barred from the papal election. The first, dated September 2023 and signed "Francesco," was kept with one of the late pope's secretaries. The second was simply signed "F" by Francis in his hospital bed on March 2, 2025, when Cardinal Pietro Parolin, the Holy See Secretary of State, asked the pope to authorize a legal document blocking Becciu's participation. Francis reportedly told Parolin at the time, "You are already thinking about the conclave." The discovery of the letters prevented the potentially excruciating scenario of the doors of the Sistine Chapel shutting in the face of a cardinal trying to get in to vote.

Pope Leo met Cardinal Becciu on May 27, 2025. Some felt that Becciu's summary dismissal had been unfair on the man. Others point to flaws in the Vatican City State's justice process. During his long trial, Becciu looked broken. He cut a very different figure from the one who spent years as one of the most powerful figures in the Vatican. His case points to the challenges Leo faces in ensuring a system that holds people robustly and fairly to account.

It also points to the complexity of reforming the Vatican finances and the many different elements that need to be held together: investigations, due process, independence, and the demands of the Church for prudent and ethical investing.

The pope needs trusted people who can give him an accurate picture of the Vatican's financial situation. One of those is Cardinal Farrell, who not only runs the pension fund but has an impressive portfolio of other responsibilities. He's been appointed resident of the Vatican City State supreme court, president of the Holy See's Commission for Confidential Matters, and Committee for Investments, which aims at ensuring the ethical nature of investments. He also sits on the board of the Apsa property investment arm of the Vatican. He has regular meetings with Pope Leo, although at seventy-seven years old he will need to hand over responsibilities in the coming years.

One of the pope's priorities will be better communication about how Vatican finances work, and what money is spent on. Transparency is critical. "The Vatican has oftentimes given the wrong message, which certainly doesn't inspire people to say, 'Oh, I'd like to help you,'" he said in an interview. Too often, he said, it has left people thinking, "'I'll keep my money, because if you're not going to administer it properly, why should I give you more money?'"

Rather than relying on a small cadre of donors, the ideal scenario for Leo would be to establish an increased level of donations from the "People of God," the Catholics spread across the world, and other Christians, and those of good will who support the pope's mission, even in modest ways. If each Mass goer gave the equivalent of €5 once a year, then the Vatican's income problems would be solved.

Vatican City has no taxes. Employees' salaries are tax-free but tend to be lower than in the rest of Italy. Pay is based on a salary scale ranging from around €1,500 ($1,700) a month to €3,600 ($4,200) a month. Many employees work as gardeners, shop assistants, museum attendants, and cleaners. Some also work in the Vatican's supermarket, which offers cheaper food because it is tax free. The same is true for gasoline. Clergy in the lower ranks pay rent for their accommodation—often in rooms in Church-run properties—while the most senior officials receive a subsidy or rent-free housing. As part of his drive to cut costs, Francis moved to end the system whereby cardinals or top officials enjoy subsidized housing instead of paying a commercial rent. During the pandemic, the pope also cut the pay of cardinals, believed to be around €5,000 ($5,800) a month, by 10 per cent. The pope himself receives no salary, but all his costs are covered, and he has access to discretionary funds to support charitable initiatives. Francis also issued a hiring freeze in a bid to get costs under control. Those who retired tended not to be replaced.

Leo may, like Francis, continue to cut costs. In the long-term, he may aim for a zero deficit in the Vatican accounts, rather than profit. He has said that he's not losing sleep over the finances and is going to address the pensions blackhole. Cuts will only get Leo so far, however. At a certain point the only way to save a significant sum of money would be to shut down departments of the Church's central administration, which Leo is unlikely to do. Along with better communication to encourage donor confidence, the pope will also try get Vatican financial entities to work better together. He wants the Vatican Bank, Apsa, and the museums all to pull in the same direction, rather than jealously protect their own portfolios. For example, the Vatican's Dicastery for Evangelization (once known as the Propaganda Fide congregation) has large real-estate holdings and operates out of a palazzo near Rome's Spanish Steps. Its prefect was once so powerful that he was nicknamed "Papa Rosso" (Red Pope). Francis appointed the charismatic Cardinal Luis Antonio Tagle as the dicastery's prefect. He has a warm relationship with Pope Leo, and the pair have met several times since Leo's election.

Leo needs as complete and accurate a picture as possible of the Vatican's financial position, something that can be complex to ascertain in the siloed working culture in Rome. He is holding regular meetings with senior finance leaders to understand the state of play. Leo had released new regulations on employment and recruitment at the Vatican, effectively an HR handbook which covers pay, holidays, time off sick and other working practices. Francis hauled the Vatican's economic operations into the twenty-first century. He ended the murky scandals and put in place systems to investigate and prosecute misconduct. But if Leo wishes to raise the funds, he needs to share a transparent and detailed picture of where things stand. This is what Cardinal Pell had sought to do with his planned audit and his uncovering of hidden pots of money. During Francis's pontificate, the Holy See published its most-detailed-ever financial figures, including its first public consolidated financial statement and the first publicly released budget for Apsa. In Francis's final years, the Holy See stopped producing an annual budget statement, something that this pope is likely to remedy.

As a bishop in Peru, Leo was renowned for his practical approach. During crises, whether it was Covid, flooding, or the influx of migrants, Bishop Prevost found concrete ways to respond and help. He was known for his hands-on approach. As bishop, he led Chiclayo's charitable initiatives, known as "Caritas." He is a highly intelligent leader with a good head for figures. He understands what works and what won't when it comes to the money. It will be crucial for him to build a strong, well-trained team to tackle the underlying problems facing the Vatican's finances. Yet perhaps his greatest asset is that he's an American who can be trusted to get a grip on money management and give confidence to potential donors, and all Catholics, to support the mission of the pope, not only with their prayers but by dipping their hands into their pockets.

EPILOGUE

Gen Z Catholicism

On July 29, 2025, Pope Leo went over to meet a group of Catholic influencers inside St. Peter's Basilica. A choir was singing as the young people held their iPhones on selfie sticks or by hand, recording each moment. The Successor of St. Peter greeted some of them individually. Earlier that week Leo had addressed a group of influencers at a huge week-long summer youth gathering in Rome, part of the Catholic Church's jubilee celebrations. During this time, it was not unusual to see priests dressed in cassocks broadcasting live to followers on their phones. Nicola Camporiondo, a young theology student with a growing social media following, posted on Instagram his video interview with Cardinal Pietro Parolin, the Holy See Secretary of State, inside the Vatican's Apostolic Palace. Parolin spoke about the digital world as a "new frontier" to which the Church must move. It all felt like a new experience for Parolin. At one point the cardinal apologized for going on too long, remembering, perhaps, the need for short, bite-size replies.

For the Catholic Church, the digital world truly represents a "new continent." It is doing all it can to support a new wave of "digital missionaries"—Catholic social media influencers who explore questions of faith, prayer, and the meaning of life, and who are attracting large followings. Their presence in the basilica marked the opening of a new chapter for the Church. Leo XIV has become pope during a great change of era, one in which AI and the online world demand creativity and innovation from those seeking to communicate the Christian message. For Leo, technology is not something the Church should shy away from. "Faced with cultural changes throughout history, the Church has never remained passive," Leo told the influencers. "She has always sought to illuminate every age with the light and hope of Christ."

The numbers of Catholic influencers are evidence of Gen Z's growing interest in Catholicism, particularly in Europe, which is usually considered highly secular. In France, over the Easter of 2025, around 17,800 adults and adolescents were received into the Church—a record number, and a 45 per cent increase on the previous year. A 2024 survey in England and Wales showed a six-year rise in monthly Church attendance, with growth strongest among young adults and Catholicism especially popular among young men. In New York, priests are reporting a rise in the number of young people asking to become Catholics. Some are describing this as a "quiet revival."

I witnessed this phenomenon myself on the evening of August 2, 2025, when Leo arrived at Tor Vergata on the outskirts of Rome for a prayer meeting with around a million young people. He toured the grounds in his pope-mobile, waving, giving the thumbs up, and even catching a ball. His relative youth (and the benefits of regular gym workouts and tennis sessions) was evident: he carried a heavy wooden cross up dozens of steps to a raised platform. That evening, faced with a sea of young faces, Leo embraced the noisy enthusiasm, and then calmed everyone into quiet contemplation. You could have heard a pin drop as the pope led them first in silent prayer and then in eucharistic adoration—a devotional practice of praying in front of the consecrated host, which is believed to be the real presence of Jesus Christ. The evidence suggests that at least some of these young believers are looking for "full-fat Christianity"—a faith that makes demands on them and is no way watered down. This includes traditional Catholic devotions and periods of silence. As a contemplative himself, and one who has spent years following the Augustinian rhythm of daily silent prayer, Leo is ideally placed to respond to this spiritual hunger. His election has also seen a boom in interest in vocations to the Augustinians in the US, described by some as the "Leo effect". Around 400 young men have made inquiries to the order's east coast branch, while a similar number did so in the mid-west province, of which Leo was a member.

The following month, I saw young people flock to St. Peter's Square for the canonization of Carlo Acutis, the Catholic Church's first millennial saint. They had come from all over the world. Several fell to their knees during the liturgy presided over by Leo. It was his first canonization ceremony. Acutis was a London-born Italian teenager who had died of leukaemia in 2006 at the age of just fifteen. Since then he has aquired an extraordinary following. Nicknamed "God's influencer," Acutis was a computer whizz-kid who used his skills to spread awareness of the

Catholic faith, which included building a website that documented reports of miracles. Unlike the saints of old, Acutis is a highly relatable figure to young Catholics—he loved his PlayStation and made funny videos of his pets. He is frequently depicted in jeans and trainers. Acutis was canonized after the Church had investigated his life and found two miracles attributed to his intercession. The first concerned a young Brazilian boy, Matheus Vianna, whose medical condition meant that he was unable to eat properly; the second involved Valeria Valverde, a Costa Rican woman severely injured in a bicycle accident in Florence. Both were declared healed after prayers were said, asking for Acutis's help. Vatican commissions of medical experts ruled that there was no natural or scientific explanation for their recoveries. Acutis may be seen as a pioneer for the Church's engagement with the online world, someone who opened the door to the divine for young people and influencers. He has become a symbol for a younger generation's search for faith, even in a culture that is secular. Acutis did not grow up in an especially religious household. His faith was partly nurtured by a Polish nanny. His mother, Antonia Salzano, told me when I interviewed her for CNN that she had been "converted by her son."

Like Acutis, many of these Gen Z-ers who have developed an interest in Christianity have grown up outside of mainstream religion, in families where faith has not played a prominent part. In her book *Don't Forget We're Here Forever*, the journalist Lamorna Ash attempted to understand those grappling with the Christian faith in Britain today. She herself is a millennial, and began her research knowing very little about Christianity, having never read the Bible or attended a religious service. After the experience of writing the book, she now attends Quaker meetings, which take place in silence, and her local Anglican Church. She said that religious faith, and Christianity especially, appeals to young people at a time of financial precariousness and political uncertainty; it offers both a sense of community and the insights of a tradition that has been grappling with existential questions for centuries. "There is something about the particular structure and rituals within faith, it's just a different kind of architecture," she said. Technology and secularization cannot take away the spiritual dimension, and the search for something beyond the material. "We are all beings of longing, and that doesn't go away from generation to generation," she says.

For Leo, Gen Z's interest in Catholicism needs careful handling. "The danger is that a faith discovered online is limited to individual experiences," he told young people. While those experiences may be "reassuring," Leo said, the danger is that they become "disembodied" and not "lived alongside real-life situations."

In her research, Ash found that some young men are drawn to the Catholic Church by "a sense of order and certainty and history and being integrated into something larger," while its clear teachings on morality appeal to them, given the "blurriness" of morals in contemporary life.

A difficulty arises if the Church is seen as a refuge from the real world or, worse, is used as part of a culture war against certain issues (LGBTQ rights, the role of women, so-called woke culture, climate change, and so on). In the

Augustinian understanding, a person grows in faith as part of a community. Any political or liturgical preferences are put to one side. The temptation to push individual preferences is strong when it comes to the liturgy, and some Gen Z-ers—particularly in highly secularized societies—are drawn to the traditionalist liturgy. They like the Latin, the chanting, the incense, and the silence. As Leo has pointed out, however, the Mass reformed by the Second Vatican Council is still often said in Latin, and he has no problem with that. The reformed liturgy includes chant, incense, and silence. Traditionalism in the Church echoes broader trends in contemporary culture, such as the "tradwife" movement, where women embrace the role of homemaker, wife, and mother, drawing on 1950s or nineteenth-century ideals. The problem is not women wanting to be homemakers, or Latin in the liturgy, but the temptation to try to turn the clock back to an idealized golden age.

This is an area in which Leo's emphasis on listening will be crucial. Gen Z-ers' interest in traditionalism or the role of the Catholic Church in critiquing modernity is a threshold to a deeper conversation. The appeal of traditionalist liturgy may be a step on the journey, rather than the destination point. Leo will listen to a youger generation seeking the experience of authentic contemplation or "otherworldliness" in the liturgy, but he will encourage them to build on that experience and put their faith into action.

Gen Z's interest in Catholicism will allow Leo XIV's papacy to speak to the wider culture. When the Church engages the culture, whether by canonizing a millennial saint or welcoming gay Catholics to the Vatican, people take an interest. Across social media, different accounts are commenting on Leo's activities, taking note of his authenticity, and also seeing in him a lighter, more hopeful antidote to world events. He's a pope who understands the online world: he plays Wordle with his brother (and uses a different starter word each day), communicates with WhatsApp, and was even spotted using the Duolingo language app in the early hours of the morning. His love of sports, particularly baseball, helps him connect with people, whether he's holding a tennis racquet with Jannik Sinner or sporting the cap of his beloved Chicago White Sox. When passing in his popemobile he was even heard shouting, "They lost!" in response to someone who'd yelled, "Go Cubs!", the White Sox rivals.

Some of the "Leo appreciation" posts come from an account titled "L'Osservatore Bobberto" (a play on the pope's Christian name and the Vatican newspaper *l'Osservatore Romano*), or a caption that reads "Keep Calm and listen to Leo." An account called "Pope Crave" (a play on Pop Crave) has more than 100,000 followers. It began in 2024, posting about the movie *Conclave*, before moving on to content about Leo, Carlo Acutis, and Catholic stories such as the LGBTQ pilgrimage to the Vatican. Its content is full of memes; it blends light-hearted posts with news reporting. For some, it became a go-to account during the conclave period. *Conclave* had an enormous impact on the public's perception of the Vatican and, given the timing of its release so close to the death of Pope Francis, dramatically intensified interest in the conclave that elected Leo. This wave of public interest offers the American pope an opportunity to engage creatively with the "new continent" of the online world, one that is open to questions of faith, spirituality, and the Catholic-Christian tradition. On this point Leo likes to quote his spiritual father St. Augustine, who said: "Live well and the times will be good. We are the times."

Unique role of the papacy

Leo's opportunity to communicate the faith to a younger generation arises from the unique visibility of the papacy. No other church or religious leader can generate the same level of interest as the pope. As the social media fan accounts and AI deep fakes show, this level of interest is not going away. Although he is naturally shy, Leo is a world leader whose every move is now scrutinized. He can't pop out for a pizza with friends or take a drive in his car for a day out. The pope's words and appeals resonate, and his leadership extends beyond the institutional structures of the Catholic Church. His office gives him a moral voice on the world stage. This is understood not only at the levels of high diplomacy. Madonna, who was bought up a Catholic and was found to be a distant cousin of the pope, appealed to Leo, asking him to visit Gaza as he is "the only one of us who cannot be denied entry." She urged him to bring "light to the children of Gaza before it's too late." Then there are the world leaders and figures from business, sport, film, music, and the wider culture who are eager to meet him. In his repeated appeals to end wars, his defense of migrants, and his calls to protect the environment, Leo is excercising the soft power of the papacy.

He can also influence debate through his letters and official documents, whether the issue is poverty or AI, or through the work of communications, which he can personally hand to heads of state at the ends of meetings. Pope Francis's document on the environment, *Laudato si'*, resonated across the world. It inspired the creation of a global network of Catholic organizations that would take action on the environment. In some respects, it was more influential outside of the Catholic Church than inside. Francis's concept of integral ecology—that the future of humanity, the environment, and social justice are all connected—struck a chord everywhere. A Leo document on artificial intelligence, for example, could have a similar impact. It could offer a landmark ethical contribution to the development of a technology that is already making us question what it means to be human. The Vatican's convening power, its ability to bring the best thinkers together on virtually any topic, offers him further opportunities to shape and influence the debate.

Where Leo decides to travel in the world will be an important factor in how he exercises his soft power. Visits abroad offer a real opportunity for a pope to address a country's leadership and its Catholic community. Leo is a younger than his last two predecessors and is expected to travel widely. A visit home to the United States will be an extraordinary and unprecedented occasion, one in which the eyes of a nation will be on the Chicago-born pope, giving him a unique chance to spread a message of hope and reconciliation. Similarly, a trip to Leo's adopted home of Peru, the country that has deeply shaped him and influenced his papacy, is likely to generate off-the-charts levels of excitement.

But there are other visits that could also make waves, particularly in Asia. A trip to Vietnam is possible. In recent decades the Holy See has been working to establish full diplomatic relations with the country's communist regime. At the end of 2023, Pope Francis appointed the first resident papal ambassador to Vietnam. In the same year, Francis met President Vo Van Thuong, who invited the pope to visit. The Vatican foreign minister, Archbishop Paul Gallagher, made a trip there just before Francis died, which heightened hopes of a papal visit.

Pope Paul VI was deeply involved in trying to broker peace in the Vietnam War, making an historic appeal at the UN saying, "Never again war, never again war!" He sent a delegation to South Vietnam and met US Vice President Hubert Humprhey to encourage peace efforts. But no pope has ever visited Vietnam. A trip by the first American pontiff—given the US involvement in the Vietnam War—would be a remarkable symbol of the Church's efforts to overcome past divisions.

A visit to Vietnam would also continue the Catholic Church's shift away from Europe and toward Asia. Catholic communities in Asia are often in the minority but they punch above their weight when it comes to running schools and charitable organizations. They are also frequently involved in dialogue with other faiths. In September 2024, I saw the sheer dynamism of the region's churches during Pope Francis's trip to Indonesia, East Timor, Papua New Guinea, and Singapore. In East Timor, where the vast majority of people are Catholic, nearly half the population attended a Mass celebrated by Francis. I traveled with him on the papal plane, nicknamed "Shepherd One," and watched as the pope, then aged eighty-seven and wheelchair-bound, carried out the most ambitious visit of his papacy. Before the Mass in Dili, East Timor, the Esplanade of Taci Tolu, a large, open-air ceremonial site, was a sea of yellow and white umbrellas, the colors of the Vatican, as people sheltered from the heat while they waited for the pope. When he appeared, the welcome was ecstatic. In Vanimo, a remote and poverty-stricken part of Papua New Guinea, a joyful and exuberant crowd greeted Francis for the first ever papal visit to the city. It reminded me that the Church is often most alive in the most vulnerable and poorest parts of the globe. In Jakarta, Indonesia, relations between Catholics and Muslims are close. The city's cathedral and the important Istiqlal mosque, the largest in Southeast Asia, are connected by an underground "tunnel of friendship." At the mosque Pope Francis embraced the Grand Imam of Indonesia, Nasaruddin Umar. They were both dressed in white. Together they signed a joint declaration calling for peace, inter-religious harmony, and commitment to protecting the environment.

In recent years, there has been a rise in the number of Asian cardinals, and in the number of Asians chosen to lead religious orders. With a staggering 7 million members, the Vietnamese Catholic Church is the fifth largest in Asia, and it is flourishing. Large numbers of young Vietnamese are seeking to train for the priesthood or to join religious orders. Pope Leo's Augustinian order set up a community in Vietnam in 2019. Although still a communist-led country and constitutionally secular, Vietnam has had deep ties to the Catholic Church since Jesuit missionaries helped develop the modern Vietnamese alphabet in the seventeenth century.

South Korea is also on the list of countries that Leo is expected to visit. In August 2027 he will be in Seoul for the Catholic World Youth Day, an event that is likely to bring together hundreds of thousands of young people. The fact that South Korea was chosen to hold this major event is a sign of Church's rapid growth in the country. South Korean Catholics make up around 11 per cent of the population. A Korean cardinal, Lazarus You Heung-sik, leads the Vatican department for clergy; a former president of South Korea, Moon Jae-in, is a Catholic.

However, the most significant Asian visit that Leo could undertake would be to China. As prior general of the Augustinians, Leo visited China several times. The Augustinians have a presence in the country. But a visit to China could only happen if the Holy See and Beijing succeed in deepening their diplomatic ties, and that could take time.

The Vatican's diplomacy in Asia, and papal trips to the region, also reflect a deep shift in the world's political order, one in which China is now a superpower that rivals the US. The dizzying growth of the Church in Asia serves to underscore the fact that the papacy is no longer the chaplain to the West. Nor is the Catholic Church any longer a Eurocentric institution. As the most-traveled man to be elected as the Successor of St. Peter, Leo XIV understands this. His papacy will continue to support the diverse and universal contemporary Catholic Church, which has a presence in virtually every country in the world.

Leo is pioneering a particular leadership style. He's reluctant, as we've seen, to make dramatic headlines or push his personal opinions. Instead he seeks to build unity and consensus. His life to date has exposed him to the full spectrum of Catholic opinion. He trained for the priesthood in the progressive Catholic climate in Chicago, and he studied canon law in Rome before embarking for Peru as a missionary. He can see all sides of the argument. Added to this is the fact that he's led an international religious order and a diocese in Chiclayo, and he's served as prefect of one of the most important offices in the Vatican. If you were to draw up the ideal candidate profile for a pope, Robert Prevost's resumé would come about as close as you could get. Leo has a remarkable ability to hold the Church, with all its different viewpoints, together. He can make people with opposing views feel at peace and listened to. He mediates and calms; he does not inflame tensions. These may seem remarkable qualities in an age so marked by sometimes irreconcilable divisions. His style as pope is the antithesis of those politicians who sow division and stoke hatred to win power. For Leo, the Church's synodal process—characterized by deep listening before speaking—is the antidote to polarization. It makes him, as I have shown, the global counterweight to President Trump.

Leo is building on the legacy of his predecessor. He is firmly committed to the vision of the Second Vatican Council. As time goes on, and Leo's red lines, as it were, become clearer, he is likely to face opposition and hostility from the traditionalists who had hoped he would walk back Francis's reforms. At the same time, he's a pope who can't be pinned down to any side.

Leo's ability to lower the temperature in the Church, along with his expertise in applying canon law, could, in the long run, succeed in making deep and impactful reforms, far more so than those attempted by Francis, who so often came up against hostile internal resistance. That resistance came, overhwlemingly, from parts of the the English-speaking Catholic world. An American pope who embraces Francis's vision is uniquely placed to meet that resistance head on, and to begin the next chapter of the Church's reform and renewal.

Shaping the narrative

The Leo pontificate does face risks. His low-key style, his desire to see all sides of the argument, and his sometimes studious aversion to making news headlines, could be dangerous if it creates a perception of a papacy that has no clear narrative.

Rev. Antonio Spadaro, a senior official at the Vatican's culture and education office, worked closely with Pope Francis. He pointed out that part of President Trump's success is his uncanny ability to shape the narrative. Trump has shown that those in power today are able to "narrate" rather than demonstrate competence. "We need a counter-narrative," Rev. Spadaro wrote in *Commonweal*, a New York-based Catholic journal. "A new poetics of responsibility. Because today, in the grand theater of the world, those who cannot tell a story are doomed to silence."

These words could be taken as a constructive challenge to Leo: if a papacy cannot communicate a narrative that wins people to it, then it risks being defined by events. Francis, within hours of his election, established a clear narrative for his papacy: a poor Church for the poor led by an "outsider" pope. He paid his own hotel bill after the conclave, and he made his first trip outside of Rome to the Island of Lampedusa to stand in solidarity with migrants. He stated his mission from the outset, and continued to do so in his many interviews, visits abroad, and his powerful encyclical letters. Leo has taken the first year of his pontificate to listen deeply, analyze, figure out who he can trust. It's a wise strategy but, equally, he will soon need to communicate in even stronger terms what his papacy is all about. Much of this will involve judging the best way to get his message out, and how his appeals and initiatives can cut through to audiences and Catholics at the grassroots.

The other danger of not communicating a narrative is that outside events start doing it for you. A major Church scandal, a contentious internal debate—either of these could suddenly dominate the news and define the papacy. Francis faced plenty of problems throughout his pontificate, but the narrative he had established at the start held firm until the end. Leo has been compared to Paul VI, a pope whose reforms are often unfairly overlooked, in part because of the major controversy of his pontificate, which many felt came to define his papacy. Pope Paul VI's 1968 encyclical, *Humanae vitae*, prohibited the use of artificial contraception. The backlash against this caused a firestorm for the Vatican. Many lay Catholics, clergy and even bishops in Belgium, Germany, Austria, and Switzerland questioned the ruling. It was an episode that damaged papal authority. Paul VI was renowned for refusing to identify with any particular grouping in the Church. He would try to seek wisdom in the different sides of arguments. He was given the moniker the "Hamlet Pope," because of the way he anguished over different positions, and seemed inscrutable, hesitant, and equivocal.

The Leo papacy has had the perfect narrative beginning. He is the first American pope in the Catholic Church's 2,000-year history, and he was elected at a moment of great turbulence in the history of America, a time when many fear that the country's best days are behind it. He's someone who believes in the "Pax Americana," the long peace established by the United States after World War II, which President Trump is now threatening to unravel. He believes in nations collaborating, in dialogue between leaders, and in seeking peaceful solutions to the world's conflicts.

In many ways, Leo is a good example of a pre-Trump American. Robert Prevost was chosen by the cardinals partly because of his years in Peru, his international background, and the fact that his American identity had been somewhat diluted by his time abroad. But he was also chosen *because* he is an American: he can speak into the Trump moment and he will be heard. He embodies the very qualities people hold up to be the best of America, at a moment when it's often said that the American president is undermining them.

"Looked at another way, calling Robert Prevost the 'least American of the Americans' was the rest of the Church's way of saying that Robert Prevost is the most American of what the world used to think of, or idealize, as the best of America, and the best of American Catholicism," wrote David Gibson of Fordham University in the journal *American Catholic Studies*. "Many of the cardinals who voted for Cardinal Prevost seem to have been voting for an America that the rest of the world would like to see again. Perhaps the question that Leo's election ought to prompt is not how American he is, but how American we are."

It is still early days for Pope Leo. The mystery of how his papacy will manifest continues to unfold and reveal. There are many pitfalls and problems ahead. But at this perilous point in history, millions are looking to the first American pope with a great hope that he will guide the Church and the world toward a better future.

Acknowledgements

Writing a book about a recently elected pope is no easy task, given that any pontificate takes time to mature and develop. My hope, however, is that this book offers insights into Pope Leo XIV—his character, his influences, and what his pontificate might mean for both the Church and the wider world.

As a journalist covering the Vatican, I am constantly working to distil developments inside the Church into stories that are simple but never simplistic. When it comes to Pope Leo, the story can perhaps be summed up in three words: *First. American. Pope.* This book seeks to make sense of this truly historic moment.

No new pope begins with a blank sheet of paper. Pope Leo follows a long line of Successors of St. Peter, an office steeped in history. His election came after the extraordinary twelve-year pontificate of Pope Francis, which shook up the Catholic Church and opened new paths of reform. In these pages, I have sought to explain the most pressing challenges facing Leo, drawing on my experience covering the Francis era closely.

I am grateful to everyone who spoke to me for this book, particularly those who know Pope Leo—or Bob

Acknowledgements

Prevost, as he was previously known. Each person I interviewed, including those who spoke on background, helped me better understand Leo and what drives his ministry.

I would like to thank my publisher, Martin Redfern, for shepherding this book through to publication and for his perceptive insights in shaping its themes. I also owe a debt of gratitude to David John for his masterful and sensitive editing, and to Ellie Harris and Holly Purdham their all their work on the project.

My thanks also go to my colleagues at CNN, particularly Antonia Mortensen and Andrew Roy, and to the leadership of the network for backing me in writing the book. Joshua McElwee of Reuters, Gerry O'Connell and Elisabetta Piqué, Mark O'Connor, Rev. John Tabor and Christopher White have been generous friends and sounding boards throughout.

My journalism is, I hope, informed by some theological background, and I would like to thank Paul Murray at Durham University for his ongoing support and insight over the years.

This book would not have been possible without the love and patience of my family—my parents, Richard and Angela Lamb, who supported me throughout the writing, and my children, Joseph, Martha, and Tom, whose questions and curiosity kept me motivated.

Finally, to my wife, Isabel—steadfast in her support and encouragement, ensuring I could write the book and stay connected to the real world at the same time—my deepest thanks.

Bibliography

Allen, Elise Ann, *León XIV: Ciudadano del Mundo, Misionero del Siglo XXI / Pope Leo: Global Citizen of the World, Missionary of the 21st Century* (Penguin Random House, 2025)

Arendt, Hannah, *The Origins of Totalitarianism* (Penguin Modern Classics, 2017)

Ash, Lamorna, *Don't Forget We're Here Forever* (Bloomsbury, 2025)

Augustine, *Confessions*, trans. RS Pine-Coffin (Penguin Classics, 2002); *The City of God*, trans. Henry Bettenson (Penguin Classics, 2003)

Benedict, *The Rule of St. Benedict*, ed. and trans. Timothy Fry OSB (Liturgical Press, 1981), ch. 64

Benson, Robert Hugh, *Lord of the World* (Christian Classics, 2016)

Brother Lawrence, *The Practice of the Presence of God*, trans. by John J Delaney (Image Books, 1977)

Catechism of the Catholic Church (United States Catholic Conference of Bishops / Libreria Editrice Vaticana, 2019)

Code of Canon Law (Canon Law Society of America, 1983)

Cornwell, John, *Seminary Boy* (Crown Publishing Group, 2007)

Bibliography

Ivereigh, Austen, *The Great Reformer* (Allen & Unwin, 2014)

Laird, Martin, *Into Silent Land* (Darton, Longman and Todd, 2006)

Lamb, Christopher, *The Outsider* (Orbis Books, 2020)

Morris, William, Benedict, *Me and the Cardinals Three* (ATF Press, 2014)

Nuzzi, Gianluigi, *Via Crucis* (Chiarelettere, 2015)

O'Connell, Gerard, *The Election of Pope Francis: An Inside Account of the Conclave That Changed History* (Orbis Books, 2019)

Pelikan, Jaroslav, *The Vindication of Tradition* (Yale University Press, 1984)

Pepinster, Catherine, *The Keys and the Kingdom* (Bloomsbury T&T Clarke, 2017)

Prevost, Robert, *The Office and Authority of the Local Prior in the Order of Saint Augustin* (The Pontifical University of St Thomas (Angelicum), 1987)

Salinas, Pedro, *Mitad Monjes, Mitad Soldados* (Planeta Perù, 2015)

Sarah, Robert, *The Day Is Now Far Spent* (Ignatius Press, 2019)

Sarah, Robert, and Benedict XVI, *From the Depths of Our Hearts: Priesthood, Celibacy and the Crisis of the Catholic Church* (Ignatius Press, 2020)

Scaramuzzi, Iacopo, *Dio? In Fondo a Destra* (EMI, 2020)

Weigel, George, *The Next Pope: The Office of Peter and a Church in Mission* (Ignatius Press, 2020)

White, Christopher, *Pope Leo XIV: Inside the Conclave and the Dawn of a New Papacy* (Loyola Press, 2025)

Notes

PROLOGUE: THE CONCLAVE

posted an AI-generated image of himself dressed in the white cassock and miter of a pope: shared by the White House on May 3, 2025. https://x.com/WhiteHouse/status/1918502592335724809

"I'd like to be pope…": President Donald Trump talking to reporters as he left the White House, April 29, 2025. https://www.youtube.com/shorts/i4X9BR54nrw

"Not funny, sir": Pablo Virgilio David, Facebook post, May 3, 2025. https://www.facebook.com/pablovirgilio.david

"There could be an American pope …": interview with Cardinal Oswald Gracias, CNN, May 6, 2025. https://transcripts.cnn.com/show/ebo/date/2025-05-06/segment/01

"wasn't good … Who knows?": Cardinal Timothy Dolan, speaking outside the church of Nostra Signora di Guadalupe a Monte Mario, May 4, 2025. Philip Pullella, "New York Cardinal says Trump AI image 'wasn't good'", *Reuters*. https://www.reuters.com/world/us/new-york-cardinal-says-trump-ai-pope-image-wasnt-good-2025-05-04/

"We need a voice …": Cardinal Charles Maung Bo, email to author, April 28, 2025.

"The kingmakers …": discussion with author on background, May 2025.

"I think we can say this is white smoke …": Erin Burnett, CNN, May 8, 2025. https://transcripts.cnn.com/show/ip/date/2025-05-08/segment/01

Notes

"bruised, hurting and dirty ...": Pope Francis, *Evangelii gaudium*, November 24, 2013. https://www.vatican.va/content/francesco/en/apost_exhortations/documents/papa-francesco_esortazione-ap_20131124_evangelii-gaudium.html

"The first American pope has been elected! Cardinal Prevost!": author, live on CNN, May 8, 2025. https://youtu.be/1F0N55CDDqs?si=ydgS6ivjyaaTBhLO

"*La pace sia con tutti voi!*": Pope Leo XIV, speech from St Peter's Basilica, May 8, 2025. https://www.vaticannews.va/en/pope/news/2025-05/pope-leo-xvi-peace-be-with-you-first-words.html

INTRODUCTION

"Look, until America goes into political decline ...": attributed to Cardinal George, former Archbishop of Chicago (1997–2014), one of the most influential prelates in the Church of the United States in the latter part of the twentieth and early twenty-first centuries.

"I am sleeping well ...": Cardinal Prevost's message to Fr. Tony Banks OSA, shared with the author by Fr. Banks, October 2025.

denounced what he saw as the errors of "Americanism": Leo XIII's concerns were laid out in an apostolic letter, "*Testem benevolentiae nostrae*", addressed to Cardinal James Gibbons, Archbishop of Baltimore. https://www.vatican.va/content/leo-xiii/la/letters/documents/hf_l-xiii_let_18990122_testem-benevolentiae.html

including Golda Meir: in a statement after Pius XII's death, Meir, who was then Israeli foreign minister, praised the pontiff as a "great servant of peace," October 9, 1958. https://www.jta.org/archive/israel-government-u-s-jewry-join-in-world-grief-over-popes-death

"full, immediate and supreme power": *Code of Canon Law* (Canon Law Society of America, 1983), canon 332.1.

"presides in charity": the description of the Church of Rome by St Ignatius of Antioch (who died c.110) in his *Epistle to the*

Notes

Romans, which underlines the scope of the church in Rome's authority from the early years of Christianity.

"People in the Foreign Office ...": quoted in Catherine Pepinster, *The Keys and the Kingdom* (Bloomsbury T&T Clarke, 2017).

"Christendom no longer exists": Pope Francis, Christmas greetings to the Roman Curia, December 21, 2019. https://www.vatican.va/content/francesco/en/speeches/2019/december/documents/papa-francesco_20191221_curia-romana.html

a "preferential option for the poor": a principle of Catholic Social Teaching and a phrase believed to have first been used in 1968 by Rev. Pedro Arrupe, the superior general of the Society of Jesus (Jesuits) in a letter to the religious order.

"a church more closely resembling her Lord than worldly powers ...": Pope Leo XIV in his apostolic exhortation *Dilexi te*, signed October 4, 2025, released October 9, 2025. https://www.vatican.va/content/leo-xiv/en/apost_exhortations/documents/20251004-dilexi-te.html

did not block his appointment as auxiliary bishop in Kraków: Karol Wojtyla was appointed in 1958 by Pope Pius XII, becoming Poland's youngest bishop.

"revolution of conscience": George Weigel, "Aroused Consciences Changing History," georgeweigel.com, June 5, 2024. https://www.georgeweigel.com/aroused-consciences-changing-history/

"Let your Spirit descend and renew the face of the earth ...": Pope John Paul II, Holy Mass, Victory Square, Warsaw, June 2, 1979. https://www.vatican.va/content/john-paul-ii/en/homilies/1979/documents/hf_jp-ii_hom_19790602_polonia-varsavia.html

"I knew in a moment that everything had changed ...": Tom Fenton, a 34-year veteran of CBS News and respected foreign correspondent, on covering John Paul II's 1979 trip to Poland. https://youtu.be/F-oXXc5CfNw?si=L6LrjF05irkPP-fq

Francis had even called up Alitalia to book his own flights: Paul Vallely, "Pope Francis: Not so much a reformer as a revolutionary," *The Independent*, September 29, 2013. https://www.independent.co.uk/news/world/europe/pope-francis-not-so-much-a-reformer-as-a-revolutionary-8845052.html

Notes

signing a landmark agreement on inter-religious co-operation: this was the "Human Fraternity" document signed in Abu Dhabi by Pope Francis and the Grand Imam, Ahmad Al-Tayyeb, February 4, 2019. https://www.vatican.va/content/francesco/en/travels/2019/outside/documents/papa-francesco_20190204_documento-fratellanza-umana.html

From the south lawn of the White House: Pope Francis speech, September 23, 2015. https://www.vatican.va/content/francesco/en/speeches/2015/september/documents/papa-francesco_20150923_usa-benvenuto.html

he described President Trump's planned deportation of migrants as a 'disgrace': Pope Francis, interview with *Che Tempo Che Fa*, broadcast on Nove, owned by CNN's parent company Warner Bros. Discovery, January 19, 2025. https://edition.cnn.com/2025/01/19/world/pope-says-trump-immigrant-deportations-disgrace-intl-latam

another senior Vatican official, Cardinal Michael Czerny of Canada, was expressing his concern: Cardinal Czerny, interview with Nicole Winfield, *Associated Press*, February 10, 2025. https://apnews.com/article/vatican-us-usaid-pope-migration-6bf064630ff58022ab133f5375f5b5ef

the church's global charitable arm was warning: Caritas statement, February 10, 2025. https://www.caritas.org/2025/02/closure-of-usaid-foreign-aid-will-kill-millions/

told a reporter that the new American pope would "fight with Trump …": Cardinal Bo, interview with James Longman, ABC News, May 9, 2025. https://www.youtube.com/watch?v=P36ItJ849jk

One church source in Rome told me: "At least two cardinals I spoke to said electing a US pope was only possible because of Trump": discussion with author on background, June 2025.

Genealogical research has established that the pope has Creole roots: this was undertaken by Henry Louis Gates Jr, the Alphonse Fletcher University Professor and Director of the Hutchins Center for African & African American Research at Harvard University, and published in *The New York Times*,

Notes

June 11, 2025. https://www.nytimes.com/interactive/2025/06/11/magazine/pope-leo-xiv-ancestry-family-tree.html

Archbishop Paul Gallagher … described Leo's "family tree of many nations …": speaking at the US Embassy to the Holy See's July 4 celebration on June 30, 2025.

He made a decisive contribution to Catholic social thinking: found in Leo XIII's encyclical *Rerum novarum*, May 15, 1891. https://www.vatican.va/content/leo-xiii/en/encyclicals/documents/hf_l-xiii_enc_15051891_rerum-novarum.html

he praised the US Catholic community from which, more than a century later, his successor as Leo would emerge …: found in Leo XIII's encyclical *Longinqua oceani*, January 6, 1895. https://www.vatican.va/content/leo-xiii/en/encyclicals/documents/hf_l-xiii_enc_06011895_longinqua.html

The American pope says he chose the name Leo …: Pope Leo XIV, address to the College of Cardinals, May 10, 2025. https://www.vatican.va/content/leo-xiv/en/speeches/2025/may/documents/20250510-collegio-cardinalizio.html

1: LISTENING POPE

the Roman Curia, the church's central administration: the Curia assists in the management of the Holy See (the pope's leadership of the church globally) and the Catholic Church across the world. It is made up of departments, known as "dicasteries", which deal with different aspects of Church life, with each one led by a prefect and team of officials. The Roman Curia is distinct from the administration of Vatican City State, the sovereign territory. The Vatican is the physical headquarters for the Holy See.

"a small leaven of unity, communion and fraternity within the world": Pope Leo XIV, homily during Mass for the beginning of his pontificate, May 18, 2025. https://www.vatican.va/content/leo-xiv/en/homilies/2025/documents/20250518-inizio-pontificato.html

Notes

"Sometimes there's the presentation of the issues and then there's the real issue behind it": discussion with author on background, July, 2025.

"The Vatican scheduling system puts four audiences all at the same time ...": Pope Leo XIV, speaking to a meeting of the Italian American Foundation, June 4, 2025.

"*Sto imparando*": Leo's remarks at a meeting of media representatives attended by author, May 12, 2025.

One cardinal I spoke to said that Prevost's work ethic ... was one of the appealing aspects of his candidacy: discussion with author on background, July 2025.

"My priorities are Ukraine, Gaza, and Myanmar": discussion with author on background, September 2025.

wishing the Americans on board a "Happy Thanksgiving": "Pope Leo celebrates Thanksgiving with mid-flight pumpkin pie", CNN. https://edition.cnn.com/2025/11/27/world/video/pope-leo-celebrates-thanksgiving-on-plane-with-pie

Rev. Bernie Scianna, an Augustinian priest based in the United States, told me ...: interview in Rome, May 2025.

The author John Cornwell recounted his experiences of a minor seminary ...: John Cornwell, *Seminary Boy* (Crown Publishing Group, 2007).

John, one of his brothers, said that although it meant that Bob spent long periods away from home ...: Obed Lamy and Hallie Golden, "Leo XIV's brother recalls feeling of 'disbelief' over his sibling becoming pope", *Associated Press*, May 9, 2025. https://www.cleveland19.com/2025/05/09/leo-xivs-brother-recalls-feeling-disbelief-over-his-sibling-becoming-pope/?utm_source=chatgpt.com

The Augustinian order bases itself on the fifth-century rule of St. Augustine of Hippo: members of the Augustinian order make vows of poverty, chastity, and obedience. While the living out of poverty can vary in religious life, it means that a friar, monk, or religious sister will not amass personal wealth or even possess a personal bank account. All expenses are covered by the order.

his famous work, *Confessions*: St. Augustine, *Confessions* (Penguin Classics, 2002).

Notes

"You have made us for yourself, and our heart is restless until it rests in you": Pope Leo XIV, homily during Mass for the beginning of his pontificate, May 18, 2025. https://www.vatican.va/content/leo-xiv/en/homilies/2025/documents/20250518-inizio-pontificato.html

this form of contemplation: the practice of contemplation from an Augustinian perspective is explored in detail but in an accessible way by Martin Laird OSA, *Into Silent Land* (Darton, Longman and Todd, 2006).

Leo has cited a book: Brother Lawrence, *The Practice of the Presence of God*, trans. John J. Delaney (Image Books, 1977).

"I took a deep breath," he told reporters after his first foreign visit: Pope Leo XIV, press conference on board plane returning to Rome from Beirut, December 2, 2025. https://www.vaticannews.va/en/pope/news/2025-12/pope-leo-xiv-inflight-press-conference-turkiye-lebanon.html

"St. Augustine reminds us that before we speak, we must first listen …": Pope Leo XIV, video message, August 29, 2025. https://www.vatican.va/content/leo-xiv/en/messages/pont-messages/2025/documents/20250829-videomessaggio-santommaso-davillanova.pdf

"The rule emphasizes thirty plus times the [spiritual] movement 'within,' before you then go out in service; the two have to be mutual …": Rev. Tony Banks, interview with author, July 31, 2025.

"machismo and dictatorial attitudes": Pope Francis, interventions at the 18th General Congregation of the 16th Oordinary General Assembly of the Synod of Bishops, October 25, 2023. https://www.vatican.va/content/francesco/en/speeches/2023/october/documents/20231025-intervento-sinodo.html

in the form of a release of *"dubia"*: a series of questions were submitted to Pope Francis by four cardinals in November 2016, including US Cardinal Raymond Burke. The five questions sought a "Yes" or "No" reply from Francis. The late pope never responded. https://www.ncregister.com/news/four-cardinals-formally-ask-pope-for-clarity-on-amoris-laetitia

Notes

Viganò accused Francis of turning a blind eye to sexual misconduct: Archbishop Viganò released the dossier on August 25, 2018, during Pope Francis's visit to Ireland. https://s3.documentcloud.org/documents/4786599/Testimony-by-Archbishop-Carlo-Maria-Vigan%C3%B2.pdf

accusing Francis of supporting what he called the "climate fraud," and criticizing the late pope for promoting "an inclusive, immigrationist, eco-sustainable, and gay-friendly" Church: Archbishop Viganò, "J'Accuse", Exsurge Domine Foundation, June 28, 2024. https://exsurgedomine.it/240628-jaccuse-eng/

"I've got your note, let's do it!" before asking, "But are you going on vacation?": Phil Pullela, interview with author, April 2025.

"Oh, we pray for you," one of them said. "Especially when you speak off the cuff!": Christopher Lamb, *The Outsider* (Orbis Books, 2020).

it was revealed that he had used the derogatory slur "*frociaggine*" (faggotry): Christopher Lamb and Sharon Braithwaite, "Pope Francis apologizes for using a homophobic slur during a meeting with bishops," CNN, May 28, 2024. https://edition.cnn.com/2024/05/28/world/pope-francis-apologizes-reports-anti-gay-slur-intl

"In the end," one cardinal told me, "Francis found it increasingly difficult to effect reforms internally because he worked outside the system": discussion with author on background, May 2025.

In 1998, a network of powerful figures led by Esteban Caselli: Austen Ivereigh, *The Great Reformer* (Allen & Unwin, 2014).

In 2008, an adviser to Argentina's government even hatched an unsuccessful plot: Austen Ivereigh, "How the Pope's history with the Knights of Malta could be linked to the current row," *Crux*, January 14, 2017. https://cruxnow.com/vatican/2017/01/popes-history-knights-malta-linked-current-row

There followed an eighteen-month stand-off: Colleen Dulle, "Explainer: How Cardinal Fernández is changing the Vatican Doctrine Office", *America*, January 23, 2024. https://www.americamagazine.org/faith/2024/01/23/cardinal-fernandez-dicastery-doctrine-faith-247004/

"Ultimately he found those past experiences hard to shake off,"

Notes

one official told me: discussion with author on background, September 2025.

Culminating in 2022 with a new constitution for the administration: Pope Francis, "Praedicate Evangelium", March 19, 2022. https://www.vatican.va/content/francesco/en/apost_constitutions/documents/20220319-costituzione-ap-praedicate-evangelium.html

accusing the Roman Curia of a form of "spiritual Alzheimer's": Pope Francis, Christmas greetings to the Roman Curia, December 22, 2014. https://www.vatican.va/content/francesco/en/speeches/2014/december/documents/papa-francesco_20141222_curia-romana.html

One senior Vatican official told me that it was the most important intervention: discussion with author on background, September 2025.

"Popes pass, the Curia remains …": Pope Leo XIV, meeting with employees of the Holy See and the Vatican City State, May 24, 2025. https://www.vatican.va/content/leo-xiv/en/speeches/2025/may/documents/20250524-dipendenti-curia-scv.html

"Diversity is not the opposite of unity," Banks explains …: interview with author, July 31, 2025.

John even saying people would predict that his younger brother would one day become pope: both John and Louis Prevost have spoken about this, including in interviews for NBC Chicago (August 14, 2025) and a *Vatican News* documentary (November 10, 2025). https://www.youtube.com/watch?v=nYzssRwE7Gg

"Around age six, I was also an altar server in my parish. Before going to school—it was a parish school—we would attend 6:30 a.m. Mass…": Pope Leo XIV, dialogue with children, July 4, 2025. https://www.vaticannews.va/en/pope/news/2025-07/pope-leo-dialogues-with-children-build-bridges-from-early-age.html

the southside of Chicago was a place where "ethnicity, race, and class intersected": Margaret O'Brien Steinfels, "Nice Boy Up from the Parishes," *Commonweal*, June 4, 2025. https://www.commonwealmagazine.org/leo-xiv-chicago-catholicism-steinfels-prevost

Notes

"We had to learn Latin for Mass, but then it changed to English for me since I was born and raised in the US …": Pope Leo XIV, dialogue with children, July 4, 2025. https://www.vaticannews.va/en/pope/news/2025-07/pope-leo-dialogues-with-children-build-bridges-from-early-age.html

Vatican II called for the Church to share the "joys and the hopes, the griefs and the anxieties of the men of this age, especially those who are poor or in any way afflicted": *Gaudium et Spes*, "Pastoral Constitution on the Church in the modern world," December 7, 1965. https://www.vatican.va/archive/hist_councils/ii_vatican_council/documents/vat-ii_const_19651207_gaudium-et-spes_en.html

"We were studying now with laypeople, and with women," he told me …: Rev. Mark Francis CSV, interview with author, August 12, 2025.

"Pope Francis spoke a lot about the peripheries, but Leo is the first pope from the peripheries in one hundred years …": Andrea Tornielli, interview with author, September 15, 2025.

"I won't tell you the reason, but let's just say that when Cardinal Bergoglio and I met, we weren't always in agreement": Bishop Robert Prevost, meeting with bishops from Peru, March 14, 2023. https://www.youtube.com/watch?v=KNDnNPVBsns

One church source told me that it concerned the deployment …: discussion on background with source, July, 2025.

"Well, that's very good, and thank God I'll never be a bishop": Bishop Prevost, meeting with bishops from Peru, March 14, 2023. https://www.youtube.com/watch?v=KNDnNPVBsns

During that Mass, Francis spoke about the "restlessness" found in the writings of St. Augustine …: Pope Francis, homily during Mass for the beginning of the General Chapter of the Order of St. Augustine, August 28, 2013. https://www.vatican.va/content/francesco/en/homilies/2013/documents/papa-francesco_20130828_capitolo-sant-agostino.html

one cardinal had been overheard urging his fellow electors to vote for Ouellet because "Bergoglio is too old!": Gerard O'Connell, *The Election of Pope Francis: An Inside Account of the Conclave That Changed History* (Orbis Books, 2019).

Notes

he had given an interview to the Canadian broadcaster CBC: Cardinal Ouellet interview with Peter Mansbridge of CBC, March 4, 2013. https://www.cbc.ca/news/canada/quebec-papal-contender-ready-but-wary-of-media-spotlight-1.1358828

"If Francis had been able to vote in the conclave, he would have voted for Prevost," is how one Vatican official put it to me: discussion with author on background, September 2025.

Leo's appeal, in English, for an end to the "pandemic of arms" was reported around the world: Pope Leo XIV, Angelus, August 31, 2025. https://www.vatican.va/content/leo-xiv/en/angelus/2025/documents/20250831-angelus.html

Pope Francis's decision to send a North American Augustinian to that particular diocese in northern Peru was described to me as a "crisis appointment": discussion with author on background, September 2025.

According to Elise Ann Allen in her biography: Elise Ann Allen, *León XIV: Ciudadano del Mundo, Misionero del Siglo XXI / Pope Leo XIV: Global Citizen, Missionary of the 21st Century* (Penguin Random House, 2025).

"By the time he introduced changes to the way the diocese was run, he had the clergy of the diocese on his side," Jacinto wrote in a letter ...: Rev. José-Antonio Jacinto, "Leo's synodal path in Chiclayo," "Letters to the Editor," *The Tablet*, September 27, 2025.

Sister Nathalie Becquart ... told me that as bishop in Chiclayo Prevost was "committed to involving laypeople and women in leadership roles": email interview with author, October 1, 2025.

Leo quoted these words in his first public remarks: Pope Leo XIV, First blessing "Urbi et Orbi", May 8, 2025. https://www.vatican.va/content/leo-xiv/en/messages/urbi/documents/20250508-prima-benedizione-urbietorbi.html

He told Elise Ann Allen that at one point he was thinking "God, either make me better or take me, because this is awful": Elise Ann Allen's interview with Pope Leo XIV, July 2025.

McNabb was pioneering an inclusive model of the church ... which included the empowering of lay leaders: Austen Ivereigh made this point in his summary of Elise Ann Allen's biography in "Pope

Notes

Leo XIV—made in Peru," *The Tablet*, September 18, 2025. https://www.thetablet.co.uk/features/pope-leo-xiv-made-in-peru/

Leo has even admitted that if Peru played the United States: Pope Leo interview with Elise Ann Allen, July 2025.

Rev. Francis says that Leo's time in Peru has influenced him profoundly, particularly in "working with the poor, working with the people who are trying to get a voice in terms of society at large": Rev. Mark Francis CSV, interview with author, August 12, 2025.

At one point the bishop had sent people: contained in Austen Ivereigh's article reviewing Elise Anne Allen's biography of Leo in *The Tablet*, September 18, 2025. https://www.thetablet.co.uk/features/pope-leo-xiv-made-in-peru/

"Authority is service, and that service is rendered within a context of listening to what the Spirit is saying in His people …": Robert F. Prevost OSA, *The Office and Authority of the Local Prior in the Order of Saint Augustine* (The Pontifical University of St. Thomas (Angelicum), 1987). The thesis has been republished by Catholic University of America (October 2025), with a foreword by Thomas Joseph White OP, although the author had a copy before this date.

"We are truly seeing continuity …": Sister Nathalie Becquart, email interview with author, October 1, 2025.

"Traditionalism is the dead faith of the living, but tradition is the living faith of the dead": Jaroslav Pelikan, *The Vindication of Tradition* (Yale University Press, 1984).

According to his brother John, one of Leo's favorite ways to relax was to drive his car: John Prevost interview with Mary Ann Ahern, NBC Chicago, August 14, 2025, detailed by Zelda Caldwell, "14 things we learn about Pope Leo XIV from his brother's latest interview", *Catholic News Agency*, August 19, 2025. https://www.catholicnewsagency.com/news/266027/14-things-we-learn-about-pope-leo-xiv-from-his-brothers-latest-interview

One Church source told me that when he was Augustinian prior general he once drove from Rome to Holland to attend a meeting: discussion with author on background, September 2025.

Notes

2: SPIRITUAL COUNTERWEIGHT

President Donald Trump told reporters afterward that "we were a little bit surprised and very happy" about the election of the first American pope …: President Trump speaking to reporters at the White House, May 8, 2025.

Speaking at the end of July, Leo confessed that he had "not had direct conversations or met with the president": Pope Leo XIV, interview with Elise Ann Allen, July 2025. No meeting took place between President Trump and Pope Leo within six months of Leo's election. Neither the White House nor the Vatican reported on any phone calls taking place during this time either.

A person who thinks only about building walls, wherever they may be, and not building bridges, is not Christian: Pope Francis, in-flight press conference from Mexico to Rome, February 17, 2016. https://www.vatican.va/content/francesco/en/speeches/2016/february/documents/papa-francesco_20160217_messico-conferenza-stampa.html

Steve Bannon, a Catholic and an outspoken ally of Trump, described Leo's election as the "worst pick ever": Steve Bannon posted this on X with a picture of Leo on May 8, 2025.

Bannon had been deeply hostile to Francis's pontificate, describing the late pope as "beneath contempt …": Nicholas Farrell, "Steve Bannon goes to war with the Pope", *The Spectator*, December 7, 2018. https://thespectator.com/topic/steve-bannon-war-pope/?utm_source=chatgpt.com

reportedly advising Italy's former interior minister Matteo Salvini that the pope was the "enemy": Mark Townsend, "Steve Bannon told Italy's populist leader: Pope Francis is the enemy," *Guardian*, April 13, 2019. https://www.theguardian.com/world/2019/apr/13/steve-bannon-matteo-salvini-pope-francis-is-the-enemy

"He is very much in the line of Bergoglio" Bannon said after the election of Leo. "The Curia, the globalist Curia of the Bergoglio totally rigged this …": Viviana Mazza interview with Steve Bannon, "Bannon: 'The election of Prevost was

Notes

rigged, The Vatican needs money, there will be a battle over immigration,'" *Corriere delle Sera*, May 17, 2025. https://www.corriere.it/esteri/25_maggio_17/bannon-the-election-of-prevost-was-rigged-the-vatican-needs-money-there-will-be-a-battle-over-immigration-a69ea82d-de30-4a68-a2ff-074faee1exlk.shtml

"Pope Leo is in many respects the anti-Trump, but not in the sense that he is an active opponent or even a direct critic …": David Gibson, interview with author, September 30, 2025.

"The church cannot remain silent": Pope Leo XIV's meeting with Bishop Mark Seitz of El Paso, Texas and the Hope Border Institute in the Vatican, October 8, 2025.

The mistreatment of migrants, Leo says, is not the "legitimate exercise of national sovereignty" but a "grave crime": Pope Leo XIV, address to participants in the World Meeting of Popular Movements, October 23, 2025. https://www.vatican.va/content/leo-xiv/en/speeches/2025/october/documents/20251023-movimenti-popolari.html

"I don't have a lot of tolerance when I hear people say, 'Well, this is an alternate set of facts'": Pope Leo XIV, interview with Elise Ann Allen, July 2025.

"The ideal subject of totalitarian rule is not the convinced Nazi or the convinced Communist, but people for whom the distinction between fact and fiction and the distinction between true and false no longer exist": Hannah Arendt, *The Origins of Totalitarianism* (Penguin Modern Classics, 2017).

"I think it's the case that the cardinals were looking at America's dominance on the world stage, threats to democracy and threats to the church …": Dawn Eden Goldstein, interview with author, September 18, 2025.

Will.i.am, the front man for Black Eyed Peas, told me for CNN that to have a pope from Chicago is a "beautiful thing," given "all the things that are happening in America …": interview with the author, and see Christopher Lamb and Antonia Mortensen, "Vatican gathers world's big thinkers ahead of first-ever pop concert," CNN, September 13, 2025. https://edition.cnn.com/2025/09/13/europe/vatican-ai-summit-intl

Notes

One Church source told me that Louis' wife, is also a MAGA supporter: discussion with author on background, September 2025.

After his brother's election as pope, Louis conceded that he would probably "tone it down": Louis Prevost, interview with Piers Morgan, *Piers Morgan Uncensored*, May 12, 2025. https://www.youtube.com/watch?v=ML2M9icrrKw

"I really like his brother," Trump said of the pope. "His brother is a major, serious Trumper. You know that? He's MAGA all the way": President Trump, speaking to reporters, July 15, 2025. https://rollcall.com/factbase/trump/transcript/donald-trump-press-gaggle-before-marine-one-departure-july-15-2025/

Leo responded to these comments by saying simply, "That's fine ...": Pope Leo XIV, interview with Elise Anne Allen, July 2025.

a scary situation in which gang members had accosted them while they were riding bicycles: Louis Prevost has told this story in public a couple of times, including for a documentary produced by the Vatican Dicastery for Communication, "Leo from Chicago", 10 November, 2025. https://www.vaticannews.va/en/pope/news/2025-11/leo-from-chicago-the-documentary.html

"Then he switched to Spanish, and I thought, 'OK, quit showing off, you little jerk'": Louis Prevost, *Newsmax*, May 11, 2025. https://www.newsmax.com/newsmax-tv/pope-leo-louis-prevost-newsmax/2025/05/11/id/1210499/

a news story headlined: "Pope Leo looks to MAGA megadonors to shore up Church finances": Ben Munster, Hannah Roberts and Megan Messerly, *Politico*, June 28, 2025. https://www.politico.eu/article/pope-leo-maga-megadonors-church-finance-united-states-conservative/

"[Leo] would throw up if he saw that": discussion with author on background, July 2025.

"He's not a fan of the America number 1 chant," is how one cardinal put it to me: interview on background, September 2025.

Francis pointed out that Christ himself went through "the experience of having to take refuge in a society and a culture foreign to his own ...": Pope Francis, letter to the bishops of

Notes

the United States of America, February 10, 2025 (the letter was released on February 11; Francis was admitted to hospital on February 14). https://www.vatican.va/content/francesco/en/letters/2025/documents/20250210-lettera-vescovi-usa.html

Two church sources have confirmed to me that Cardinal Prevost played a crucial role in the drafting of that letter: discussion with author on background, September 2025.

As pope, Leo referred to this letter from Francis as "very significant" and said he was "very happy" that several bishops had agreed with it: Pope Leo XIV, interview with Elise Ann Allen, July 2025.

His decision to convert had been made "slowly and unevenly," he said, and was strongly influenced by the writings of St. Augustine: JD Vance, "How I Joined the Resistance," *The Lamp*, April 1, 2020. https://thelampmagazine.com/blog/how-i-joined-the-resistance

You love your family the most, then your neighbor, then your community, your fellow citizens and "then after that, prioritize the rest of the world": JD Vance, interview with Sean Hannity, *Fox News*, January 30, 2025. https://www.realclearpolitics.com/video/2025/01/30/vice_president_jd_vance_the_far_left_has_completely_inverted_the_christian_concept_that_you_love_your_neighbor.html

"Just google '*ordo amoris*'": JD Vance on X, January 30, 2025. https://x.com/JDVance/status/1885073046400012538?s=20

"Christian love is not a concentric expansion of interests …": Pope Francis, Letter of the Holy Father Francis to the Bishops of the United States of America, February 10, 2025. https://www.vatican.va/content/francesco/en/letters/2025/documents/20250210-lettera-vescovi-usa.html

"We are called to offer God's love to everyone …": Pope Leo XIV, homily during Mass for the beginning of his pontificate, May 18, 2025. https://www.vatican.va/content/leo-xiv/en/homilies/2025/documents/20250518-inizio-pontificato.html

"when we abandon free markets, the Church suffers": "The Man behind Catholic U's largest donation ever," *The Catholic World Report*, May 19, 2016. https://www.catholicworldreport.

Notes

com/2016/05/19/the-man-behind-catholic-us-largest-donation-ever/

described the Trump administration as the "most Christian he's ever seen": Tim Busch, "The Trump Administration: More Catholic Than You Know," *National Catholic Register*, March 6, 2025. https://www.ncregister.com/commentaries/trump-administration-catholic-christian-faith

He lamented the rise of "a wealthy elite, living in a bubble of comfort and luxury ...": Pope Leo XIV, apostolic exhortation *Dilexi te*, signed October 4, 2025, released October 9, 2025. https://www.vatican.va/content/leo-xiv/en/apost_exhortations/documents/20251004-dilexi-te.html

Napa sent out an email to everyone on its mailing list ...: the email was sent on October 9, 2025, at 5.44 p.m., and has been seen by the author.

Speaking at a Napa gathering in August 2025, Hanna asked: "what if—WHAT IF, the inequality is a feature of the common good, and not a bug?": Frank Hanna, "Christian Charity and the Demands of Economic Justice," Summer Conference speech, Napa Institute, August 28, 2025. https://napa-institute.org/christian-charity-and-the-demands-of-economic-justice/

Hanna was honored at a two-day $1,500-a-head event at the Metropolitan Club in New York: the "2025 Faith & Business Conference: The Promise and Perils of AI," October 14 and 15, 2025. https://napa-institute.org/event/faithandbusiness/

the company agreed to pay $114 million in restitution to consumers in settlement of charges ...: Mary Tomkins, "Sub-Prime Card Issuer Agrees to Settlement of $114 Million," *Finance Globe*, December 19, 2008. https://www.financeglobe.com/post/sub-prime-card-issuer-agrees-to-settlement-of-114-million/

the story of his conversion, which he laid out in *The Lamp* magazine, reveals someone who has made a sincere engagement with the Catholic faith: JD Vance, "How I Joined the Resistance", *The Lamp*, April 1, 2020. https://thelampmagazine.com/blog/how-i-joined-the-resistance

St. Augustine's famous work *The City of God*: St Augustine, *The City of God,* trans. Henry Bettenson (Penguin Classics, 2004).

Notes

Thiel, a financial backer of JD Vance, reportedly expressed in private lectures: Johana Bhuiyan, Dara Kerr, Nick Robins-Early, "Inside Tech billionaire Peter Thiel's off-the-record lectures about the antichrist", *Guardian*, October 10, 2025. https://www.theguardian.com/us-news/2025/oct/10/peter-thiel-lectures-antichrist

Paul Elie in *The New Yorker* observes, too, that Vance himself seems to have thrived through "mimetic rivalry": Paul Elie, "J.D. Vance's Radical Religion," July 24, 2024. https://www.newyorker.com/news/daily-comment/j-d-vances-radical-religion

spoke at a conference with the theme "Restoring a Nation: The Common Good in the American Tradition": Brian Fraga, "'New Right' academics argue for biblical lawmaking at Steubenville conference," *National Catholic Reporter*, October 17, 2022. https://www.ncronline.org/news/new-right-academics-argue-biblical-lawmaking-steubenville-conference

Chad Pecknold ... rejects what he calls a "liberal" reading of Augustine ...: CC Pecknold, "The Religious Nature of the City", in *Postliberal Order*, January 24, 2022. https://www.postliberalorder.com/p/the-religious-nature-of-the-city

Leo is "not out to rebuild Christendom" and "would not be in favour of an integralist understanding of City of God": Dawn Eden Goldstein, interview with author, September 18, 2025.

democracy is a valid form of government rooted in Catholic social teaching: *Gaudium et Spes*, "Pastoral Constitution on the Church in the modern world," December 7, 1965. Paragraph 75 states that "all citizens, therefore, should be mindful of the right and also the duty to use their free vote to further the common good." https://www.vatican.va/archive/hist_councils/ii_vatican_council/documents/vat-ii_const_19651207_gaudium-et-spes_en.html

he said it was evident "that democracy is not in good health in today's world," while repeatedly warning against polarization. "Ideologies are seductive ...": Pope Francis, speech in Trieste during the "50th Social Week of Italian Catholics," July 7, 2024. https://www.vatican.va/content/francesco/en/speeches/2024/july/documents/20240707-trieste.html

Notes

The late pope insisted that the cross must not be used as a "political symbol" or "a sign of religious status": Pope Francis, during the Byzantine Divine Liturgy of St. John Chrysostom, Prešov, Slovakia, September 14, 2021. https://www.vatican.va/content/francesco/en/homilies/2021/documents/20210914-omelia-presov.html

"polemics, narrow-mindedness, divisions and exclusivist attitudes": Pope Francis, speaking at the closing of the congress "La Religiosité Populaire en Méditerranée", Ajaccio, Corsica, December 15, 2024. https://www.vatican.va/content/francesco/en/speeches/2024/december/documents/20241215-ajaccio-congresso.html

"When I was flying in, I thought that we have created a good tradition ...": President Aleksandr Lukashenko, August 1, 2025. http://en.kremlin.ru/events/president/news/77637

Putin looked to Orthodoxy to "give depth and spirit to his power": Iacopo Scaramuzzi, *Dio? In Fondo a Destra* (EMI, 2020).

"He struck me as not an ideologue in any shape or form or [someone who is] influenced by right-wing thinking": Mark O'Connor, interview with the author, September 18, 2025.

"My own story is that of a citizen, the descendant of immigrants, who in turn chose to emigrate ...": Pope Leo XIV, audience with diplomats accredited to the Holy See, May 16, 2025. https://www.vatican.va/content/leo-xiv/en/speeches/2025/may/documents/20250516-corpo-diplomatico.html

Leo said he discussed the importance of respecting people, regardless of where they were born ...: Pope Leo, interview with Elise Ann Allen, July 2025.

Karoline Leavitt, the White House press secretary, later explained ...: "Karoline Leavitt Reveals Trump and Melania Have Invited Pope Leo XIV to White House", *Breitbart News*, May 19, 2025. https://www.youtube.com/watch?v=C6pMpifawA4

Vance has admitted ... "there's a lot I don't know" and that he tries "to be humble as best I can when talking about the faith": JD Vance, remarks by the vice president at the National Catholic Prayer Breakfast, February 28, 2025. https://www.presidency.

Notes

ucsb.edu/documents/remarks-the-vice-president-the-national-catholic-prayer-breakfast-0

"Leo handles JD Vance as a political leader who happens to be a Catholic …": Dawn Eden Goldstein, interview with author, September 18, 2025.

"JD Vance is wrong: Jesus doesn't ask us to rank our love for others": *National Catholic Reporter*, February 1, 2025. https://www.ncronline.org/opinion/guest-voices/jd-vance-wrong-jesus-doesnt-ask-us-rank-our-love-others

a tweet in 2018 from Cardinal Blase Cupich of Chicago condemning the separation of immigrant children from their parents: Cardinal Cupich tweet, "There is nothing remotely Christian, American, or morally defensible about a policy that takes children away from their parents and warehouses them in cages. This is being carried out in our name and the shame is on us all." June 20, 2018. https://x.com/CardinalBCupich/status/1009485529337991168?s=20

The article compared the suffering of migrants with that of Jesus Christ …: Bishop Evelio Menjivar-Ayala, "This Ordeal is The Passion," *Catholic Standard*, April 11, 2025. https://www.cathstan.org/voices/this-ordeal-is-the-passion

"I don't think he's going to be coming to the United States anytime soon, because of the political implications of a pope visiting …" Rev. Mark Francis CSV, interview with author, August 12, 2025.

It's important, too, given that the bishops lead the church of around 53 million in the US: Pew Research Center, "10 Facts about US Catholics", March 4, 2025. https://www.pewresearch.org/short-reads/2025/03/04/10-facts-about-us-catholics/

"Today, I stand as a leader of the Catholic Church thanks to these opportunities that allowed me to contribute to society …": Zac Davis, "A Catholic bishop and a Jewish candidate for NYC mayor go to immigration court," *America*, June 23, 2025. https://www.americamagazine.org/politics-society/2025/06/23/bishop-pham-immigration-san-diego-brad-lander-new-york-mayor-250989/

Notes

"a long period of prayer and discernment": The Diocese of Houma-Thibodaux, "Our Bishop", June 5, 2025. https://htdiocese.org/our-bishop

Cardinal Robert McElroy, the Archbishop of Washington, DC, spoke to me about Trump's immigration policies …: Christopher Lamb, "Exclusive: Trump's immigrant deportations are 'morally repugnant,' senior US Catholic leader says, CNN, July 3, 2025. https://edition.cnn.com/2025/07/03/americas/cardinal-robert-mcelroy-interview-intl

the extraordinary decision to dispense with the requirement that Catholics attend Mass on Sundays: decree, Diocese of San Bernardino, July 8, 2025. https://www.vaticannews.va/en/church/news/2025-07/california-bishop-san-bernardino-immigration-ice-usa.html

"the church stands with migrants … I will insist that you be treated with dignity …": Cardinal Blase Cupich, statement on Standing with Immigrants, October 21, 2025. https://www.youtube.com/watch?v=DIk9Cmy1IkE

Citing the Gospel of Matthew, he said: "Jesus says at the end of the world we are going to be asked, 'How did you receive the foreigner …'": Pope Leo XIV talking to reporters, November 4, 2025. https://www.vaticannews.va/en/pope/news/2025-11/pope-us-migrants-spiritual-rights-venezuela-gaza-work-rupnik.html

McElroy says that while Leo speaks about migration "in a universal context …": Christopher Lamb, "Exclusive: Trump's immigrant deportations are 'morally repugnant,' senior US Catholic leader says, CNN, July 3, 2025. https://edition.cnn.com/2025/07/03/americas/cardinal-robert-mcelroy-interview-intl

suggested that "canonical penalties" be imposed on any Catholics involved in separating children from their families at the US–Mexico border: Beth Dalbey, "Bishop: Excommunicate Catholics Involved In Immigration Policies," *Patch Media*, June 14, 2018. https://patch.com/arizona/tucson/bishop-excommunicate-catholics-involved-immigration-policies

In the archdiocese's seminary, for example, three prominent, long-serving professors had been hostile to Francis …: Mike

Notes

Lewis explained the background to the firing on the site he edits, *Where Peter Is*: "False orthodoxy and fired professors," July 27, 2025. https://wherepeteris.com/false-orthodoxy-and-fired-professors/

"What fuels so much of the resistance to Pope Francis in the United States?" Cardinal Prevost once asked ...: Christopher White, *Pope Leo XIV: Inside the Conclave and the Dawn of a New Papacy* (Loyola Press, 2025).

He told Dolan: "This is one more hurdle I hope we don't have to deal with ...": Michelle Caruso-Cabrera, "Pope's sharp words make a wealthy donor hesitate," CNBC, December 30, 2013 https://www.cnbc.com/2013/12/30/pope-francis-wealthy-catholic-donors-upset-at-popes-rhetoric-about-rich.html

I described the resistance to Francis in some circles as a phenomenon that had not been seen in centuries, if ever: Christopher Lamb, *The Outsider* (Orbis Books, 2020).

"We cannot insist only on issues related to abortion, gay marriage, and the use of contraceptive methods ...": Pope Francis, interview with Rev. Antonio Spadaro, September 21, 2013. https://www.vatican.va/content/francesco/en/speeches/2013/september/documents/papa-francesco_20130921_intervista-spadaro.html

Francis had a "temperamental and autocratic" personality whose "loose words" had "sowed confusion and conflict": Charles J. Chaput, "The Church After Francis," *First Things*, April 21, 2025. https://firstthings.com/the-church-after-francis/

While he praised the late pope's personal generosity and kindness, he said that Francis "was often a cause of disunity because of his style and temperament ...": "The courage to be candid' – Chaput on Francis, and what's next," *The Pillar*, April 29, 2025. https://www.pillarcatholic.com/p/the-courage-to-be-candid-chaput-on

the pope is the "visible source and foundation of the unity" between the bishops and the whole church: *Catechism of the Catholic Church*, revised edition with paragraph 2267 updated (United States Catholic Conference of Bishops / Libreria Editrice Vaticana, 2019), paragraph 882.

Notes

Pierre admitted that some priests and bishops "are terribly against Francis": Gerard O'Connell, "Cardinal Pierre on why the U.S. bishops are struggling to connect with Pope Francis," November 2, 2023. https://www.americamagazine.org/faith/2023/11/02/cardinal-christoph-pierre-interview-246416/

"In the United States the situation is not easy …": Rev. Antonio Spadaro, "The Water Has Been Agitated," report on Pope Francis's conversation with Jesuits in Portugal, *La Civiltà Cattolica*, August 28, 2023. https://www.laciviltacattolica.com/the-water-has-been-agitated/

although he has said he does not support Viganò's later views: Michael R Heinlein, "New USCCB president Coakley talks immigration, Vigano criticism, and lifting up saints," *Our Sunday Visitor*, November 12, 2025. https://www.osvnews.com/new-usccb-president-coakley-talks-immigration-vigano-criticism-and-lifting-up-saints/

"The fact that I am American…": Pope Leo interview with Elise Ann Allen, July 2025.

once joking that he called Trump more often than he called his mother: Christopher White, "Trump says he's 'best president in history of the Church' in call with Catholic leaders", *Crux*, April 26, 2020. https://cruxnow.com/church-in-the-usa/2020/04/trump-says-hes-best-president-in-history-of-the-church-in-call-with-catholic-leaders

the removal of Bishop Joseph Strickland of Texas: a statement on Strickland's removal (November 11, 2023) explained that "the continuation in office of Bishop Strickland was not feasible," and the bishop was removed after refusing to resign. https://archgh.org/news/cardinal-dinardos-public-statement-on-bishop-joseph-strickland

he forwarded to his fellow cardinals copies of a book: George Weigel, *The Next Pope: The Office of Peter and a Church in Mission* (Ignatius Press, 2020).

Some of them were left "speechless" by the decision to distribute this book, given the strict rules against campaigning for a papal candidate: Joshua J. McElwee, "Exclusive: Dolan sends book on 'The Next Pope' to cardinals around the world." *National*

Catholic Reporter, July 14, 2020. https://www.ncronline.org/news/exclusive-dolan-sends-book-next-pope-cardinals-around-world

On *Fox News*, the cardinal likened Kirk to a modern-day St. Paul: Cardinal Dolan on *Fox & Friends*, September 19, 2025. https://www.youtube.com/watch?v=fTDT4zUqql0

"I can't get over the idea of this Marxist who calls himself the head of your church being a representation of Christ our Lord": comments made on an episode of *The Charlie Kirk Show*, "Charlie and Michael Knowles Debate Religion at AmFest," January 2, 2025. https://thecharliekirkshow.com/podcasts/the-charlie-kirk-show/charlie-and-michael-knowles-debate-religion-at-amf

The sisters, while condemning Kirk's murder, said that Cardinal Dolan's comparison was ill-advised …: "Sisters of Charity of New York Respond to Cardinal Dolan's Remarks on Charlie Kirk," September 24, 2025. https://scny.org/sisters-of-charity-of-new-york-respond-to-cardinal-dolans-remarks-on-charlie-kirk/

O'Connell said the formulation of such a document by the bishops could "further polarize our people": Bishop Mark O'Connell, "From the Pastor," July 25, 2021. https://x.com/rfkram/status/1419302479712370695?s=20

And in 2018, Penny Mordaunt, then the UK's International Development Secretary …: Christopher Hope, "Minister tells Catholic Church: relax ban on contraception", *The Telegraph*, July 15, 2018. https://www.telegraph.co.uk/politics/2018/07/15/minister-tells-catholic-church-relax-ban-contraception/

He had previously been critical of Pope Francis, saying that Francis had created "confusion": Brian Burch, *Newsmax*, December 2023. https://www.instagram.com/reel/C1aWgHwvfvy/

what he described as a "pattern of vindictiveness": Brian Burch, interviewed in *The New York Times*, November 29, 2023. https://www.nytimes.com/2023/11/29/us/catholics-american-conservatives-pope.html

not an "American pope" but "a pope from America for the world": Ambassador Burch related what the pope had told him in a

Notes

speech at a reception held by the US Embassy to the Holy See on September 15, 2025.

the US embassy to the Holy See posted on X: US in Holy See X account, September 13, 2025. https://x.com/USinHolySee/status/1966871574197260465?s=20

"Chinese Catholics who for many years have lived some kind of oppression or difficulty in living their faith freely": Pope Leo XIV, interview with Elise Ann Allen, July 2025.

In September 2020, Secretary of State Mike Pompeo accused the Vatican of risking its "moral authority": Tweet from Mike Pompeo, September 19, 2020. https://x.com/SecPompeo/status/1307366983890018311?s=20 linking to his article "China's Catholics and the Church's Moral Witness", *First Things*, September 18, 2020. https://firstthings.com/chinas-catholics-and-the-churchs-moral-witness/

ruled that the death penalty was "inadmissible": Pope Francis amended 2267 of the *Catechism of the Catholic Church* on May 11, 2018. https://www.vatican.va/roman_curia/congregations/cfaith/documents/rc_con_cfaith_doc_20180801_catechismo-penadimorte_en.html

"THANK YOU for your courageous decision in signing into law the elimination of the death penalty": Rev. Robert Prevost, reported by Mawa Iqbal, *Chicago Sun Times*, June 23, 2025. https://chicago.suntimes.com/politics/2025/06/23/pope-prevost-thanked-quinn-ending-death-penalty

"inhuman" treatment of immigrants in the US, and added that it is "not really pro-life" to oppose abortion and support the death penalty: Pope Leo XIV's remarks to reporters, September 30, 2025. https://www.youtube.com/watch?v=FzLG-xEy4A0

one saying that his views are "disappointing" and "largely irrelevant": Phil Lawler, "The Pope's statement on the Durbin award: wrong, and irrelevant," *Catholic Culture*, September 30, 2025. https://www.catholicculture.org/commentary/popes-statement-on-durbin-award-wrong-and-irrelevant/

"Some popes are a blessing. Some popes are a penance": Jack Posobiec, posted on X, October 2, 2025. https://x.com/JackPosobiec/status/1973791542365311013?s=20

Notes

"pandemic of arms, large and small": Pope Leo XIV, Angelus, 31 August 2025. https://www.vatican.va/content/leo-xiv/en/angelus/2025/documents/20250831-angelus.html'

"It is the practice of the Holy See to grant requests for audiences addressed to the Pope by heads of state and government ...": statement from the Holy See Press Office, September 2, 2025.

The pope says that his most important task is ...: Pope Leo interview with Elise Ann Allen, July 2025.

3: UNIFYING THE CHURCH?

"He dresses like Benedict, speaks like Francis": discussion with author on background, September 2025.

a "scandal" to see young priests in Rome's ecclesiastical tailor shops trying on hats and elaborate robes: Pope Francis, intervention at the 18th General Congregation of the 16th Ordinary General Assembly of the Synod of Bishops, October 25, 2023. https://www.vatican.va/content/francesco/en/speeches/2023/october/documents/20231025-intervento-sinodo.html

stop wearing "grandma's lace": Pope Francis, address to the bishops and priests of the churches of Sicily, June 9, 2022. https://www.vatican.va/content/francesco/en/speeches/2022/june/documents/20220609-clero-sicilia.html

a good number of clergy were "unable to hear" what Francis said because they were "not mature enough to accept his rebukes": Robert Mickens, Union of Catholic Asia News, "Gentle, yet firm: Pope Leo and the church's clerical workforce," June 27, 2025. https://www.ucanews.com/news/gentle-yet-firm-pope-leo-and-the-churchs-clerical-workforce/109478

"They call it a head fake": discussion with author on background, July 2025.

"He is like a religious superior ...": discussion with author on background, September 2025.

"While great emphasis is placed upon the necessity of seeking consensus ...": Robert F. Prevost OSA, *The Office and*

Notes

Authority of the Local Prior in the Order of Saint Augustine (The Pontifical University of St. Thomas (Angelicum), 1987).

Prevost quoted Orsy when he wrote that "a discerning superior will find a balance...": Ladislas Orsy, "Government in Religious Life", *The Way,* Supplement, 6 (1966) 90-107.

There was Bishop Bill Morris: William Morris, *Benedict, Me and the Cardinals Three* (ATF Press, 2014)

Fr. Jacques Dupuis, placed under a two-and-half-year investigation: Gerald O'Collins, "A look back on Dupuis' skirmish with the Vatican," *National Catholic Reporter*, February 22, 2024. https://www.ncronline.org/news/people/look-back-dupuis-skirmish-vatican

praised her work as following the "style of God": Jim McDermott, "Pope Francis praises Sister Jeannine Gramick's 50 years of L.G.B.T. ministry in handwritten letter," *America*, January 7, 2022. https://www.americamagazine.org/faith/2022/01/07/sister-jeanine-gramick-letter-pope-francis-242157/

"remove this or that thing, which had been approved by a vote of the various groups ...": Rev. Antonio Spadaro, "What is the Church's Vocation? Pope Francis in conversation with the Maltese Jesuits," report on Pope Francis's conversation with Jesuits in Malta, *La Civiltà Cattolica,* April 15, 2022. https://www.laciviltacattolica.com/what-is-the-churchs-vocation-pope-francis-in-conversation-with-the-maltese-jesuits

According to a Mass listings site...: The "Latin Mass Directory", which gives details on where to find a Traditional Latin Mass. https://www.latinmassdir.org/

"incorporated elements from imperial and royal courts ...": Cardinal Blase Cupich, "Tradition vs. traditionalism," *Chicago Catholic*, September 3, 2025. https://www.chicagocatholic.com/cardinal-blase-j.-cupich-/-/article/2025/09/03/tradition-vs-traditionalism

"magnificent spiritual and cultural heritage" of the older rite: letter to *The Times,* July 2, 2024.

Francis's decision—which did not ban the older Mass outright but restricted it and left decisions in the hands of local bishops: the pope's ruling, *"Traditionis Custodes"* ("Guardians of

Notes

the Tradition"), was released on July 16, 2021; it abrogated Benedict XVI's earlier ruling in 2007, "*Summorum Pontificum*" ("Of the Supreme Pontiffs"). https://www.vatican.va/content/francesco/en/motu_proprio/documents/20210716-motu-proprio-traditionis-custodes.html

"failed to deliver on its vision for unity in the Church," and had created "rigid mutual mistrust": Mike Lewis, "French Bishops on TLM: 'Two worlds that do not meet,'" *Where Peter Is*, July 23, 2024. https://wherepeteris.com/french-bishops-on-tlm-two-worlds-that-do-not-meet/

a journalist sympathetic to the traditionalist case published a document written inside the Vatican: Diane Montagna, "Exclusive: Official Vatican Report Exposes Major Cracks in Foundation of *Traditionis Custodes*," Substack, July 1, 2025. https://dianemontagna.substack.com/p/exclusive-official-vatican-report

"You can say Mass in Latin right now. If it's the Vatican II rite, there's no problem": Pope Leo XIV, interview with Elise Ann Allen, July 2025.

a group of critics issued him with a "filial correction": published September 23, 2017. https://www.correctiofilialis.org/

some priests and scholars accused him of the "canonical delict of heresy": the letter was submitted during Easter Week, 2019, as an "open letter to the bishops of the Catholic Church". https://embed.documentcloud.org/documents/5983408-Open-Letter-to-the-Bishops-of-the-Catholic/

"I think that most of the faithful …": Mike Lewis, interview with author, September 22, 2025.

He once condemned *The Sound of Music* as "soul-rotting slush": Richard Williamson, November 2009. https://web.archive.org/web/20181106181939/https://leofec.com/bishop-williamson/222.html

removed some of Burke's privileges: the size of Cardinal Burke's apartment and those of other cardinals were revealed in documents published by Gianluigi Nuzzi in *Via Crucis* (Chiarelettere, 2015). More details on Pope Francis's removal of the cardinal's privileges are found in the author's report, "Pope

Notes

Francis on unprecedented attacks from American opponents," CNN, December 15, 2023. https://edition.cnn.com/2023/12/13/us/pope-francis-takes-on-unprecedented-attacks-from-american-opponents

A Vatican source, however, described granting permission for the Mass as an act of generosity on Leo's part: discussion with author on background, September 2025.

While still respecting hierarchy, the synodal vision, according to Leo, offers "a more humble church": Pope Leo XIV, homily during Mass for Jubilee of the Synodal Teams and Participatory Bodies, October 26, 2025. https://www.vatican.va/content/leo-xiv/en/homilies/2025/documents/20251026-giubileo-equipe-sinodali.html

He's also been unafraid to speak out against those "stubbornly" opposing the reforms of Vatican II: Christopher Lamb, "Stubborn opposition to Vatican II 'not Catholic' says cardinal," *The Tablet*, August 29, 2022.

"I wonder if a ritual that is over a thousand years old can be 'banned' ...": Giacomo Gambassi, "*Il cardinale Sarah e i suoi 80 anni: 'Guardo con fiducia a Leone XIV,'*" *Avvenire*, September 11, 2025. https://www.avvenire.it/chiesa/chiesa-italiana/il-cardinale-sarah-e-i-suoi-80-anni-guardo-con-fiducia-a-leone-xiv_94600

At a synod assembly in the Vatican, he denounced "Western homosexual and abortion ideologies and Islamic fanaticism": the cardinal said those ideologies are "what Nazi-fascism and communism were in the 20th century." Edward Pentin, "Cardinal Sarah: ISIS and Gender Ideology Are Like 'Apocalyptic Bests,'" *National Catholic Register*, October 12, 2015. https://www.ncregister.com/blog/cardinal-sarah-isis-and-gender-ideology-are-like-apocalyptic-beasts

In one of his books ... he warned that the West is opening itself to "new, barbaric civilizations": Robert Cardinal Sarah, *The Day Is Now Far Spent* (Ignatius Press, 2019).

He published a book—presented as jointly authored with Benedict XVI—defending the status quo on mandatory celibacy for priests: the book was titled *From the Depths of Our Hearts*:

Notes

Priesthood, Celibacy and the Crisis of the Catholic Church (Ignatius Press, 2020).

The decision to allow blessings, the cardinal later explained, had caused a "shockwave" in Africa …: the cardinal made his comments in an interview with French Catholic blog "Le Salon Beige", which were reported by the *National Catholic Register*, January 22, 2024. https://www.ncregister.com/cna/cardinal-explains-how-african-rejection-of-fiducia-supplicans-was-handled

"No blessing for homosexual couples in all Churches in Africa": statement released by the Symposium of Episcopal Conferences of Africa and Madagascar and signed by its president, Fridolin Cardinal Ambongo Besungu OFM Cap, January 11, 2024. https://secam.org/5924/

Fiducia supplicans **(Supplicating trust):** Francis's ruling was released on December 18, 2023. https://www.vatican.va/roman_curia/congregations/cfaith/documents/rc_ddf_doc_20231218_fiducia-supplicans_en.html

"deepen the concrete paths of a pastoral ministry of reconciliation and communion": from a statement signed by the Regional Episcopal Conference of North Africa, January 15, 2024. https://www.newwaysministry.org/2024/01/22/north-african-bishops-break-from-peers-affirm-lgbtq-blessings-and-more-news/

The Congolese cardinal described it as "a bad chapter" in Francis's pontificate: Paulina Guzik, "Pope Not There to 'Create Doubt' But to be 'Prophetic Voice' of Church, Congolese Cardinal says," OSV News, September 16, 2025. https://www.osvnews.com/pope-not-there-to-create-doubt-but-to-be-prophetic-voice-of-church-congolese-cardinal-says/

Sarah, meanwhile, said it is time to "clarify and perhaps reformulate …": Giacomo Gambassi, "*Il cardinale Sarah e i suoi 80 anni: 'Guardo con fiducia a Leone XIV,'*" *Avvenire*, September 11, 2025. https://www.avvenire.it/chiesa/chiesa-italiana/il-cardinale-sarah-e-i-suoi-80-anni-guardo-con-fiducia-a-leone-xiv_94600

He said that one delegate didn't want to sit next to him, one didn't want to use the word LGBTQ: Rev. James Martin SJ, interview with author, September 19, 2025.

Notes

Francis signaled a new approach when he famously said, "Who am I to judge?": Pope Francis, press conference on flight returning to Rome, July 28, 2013. https://www.vatican.va/content/francesco/en/speeches/2013/july/documents/papa-francesco_20130728_gmg-conferenza-stampa.html

his call for the decriminalization of homosexuality in the DRC and South Sudan: Pope Francis made this call both in an interview with Nicole Winfield of the *Associated Press*, January 25, 2023, and again in the press conference on the papal plane returning to Rome from South Sudan, February 5, 2023. https://www.vatican.va/content/francesco/en/speeches/2023/february/documents/20230205-voloritorno-sudsudan.html

"A Filial and Apprehensive Supplication to His Holiness Pope Leo XIV": this was delivered to the Vatican, September 15, 2025, and released publicly three days later. https://www.tfp.org/a-filial-and-apprehensive-supplication-to-his-holiness-pope-leo-xiv/

"esoteric character, its religious fanaticism, the cult of personality": Mike Lewis, "US Cardinal and Brazilian ideologues team up, attack synod," *Where Peter Is*, September 5, 2023. https://wherepeteris.com/us-cardinal-and-brazilian-ideologues-team-up-attack-synod/

"I would say there has been a development in the need for the church to open, and to be welcoming": documented by Catholic News Service, "Pope Leo on inclusion in the church," May 9, 2025. https://youtu.be/qsS5R6HHS-g?si=sZYom859-66gtJwY

"Go, celebrate the Mass with them!": reported by Rev, James Martin, Facebook post, September 6, 2025. https://www.facebook.com/FrJamesMartin/posts/incredible-bishop-francesco-savino-vice-president-of-the-italian-bishops-confere/1337043367781753/

a "big change" and something "he never would have imagined": Francis de Bernardo, interview with author for CNN, "A historic pilgrimage: Why LGBTQ Catholics hope Pope Leo will take up Francis' legacy," September 6, 2025, and "Vatican hosts first Catholic LGBTQ pilgrimage," September 8, 2025 (video). https://edition.cnn.com/2025/09/06/europe/lgbtq-catholics-pope-leo-pilgrimage-intl

Notes

The church's official principles: set out in the *Catechism of the Catholic Church*, revised edition with paragraph 2267 updated (United States Catholic Conference of Bishops / Libreria Editrice Vaticana, 2019), paragraphs 2357–59.

"We have to change attitudes before we can ever change doctrine": Pope Leo XIV, interview with Elise Ann Allen, July 2025.

it is notable that Leo has used the acronym LGBTQ in an interview …: Rev. James Martin SJ, interview with author, September 19, 2025.

described Leo's remarks on homosexuality as "extremely disappointing": Benedikt Heider and Lisa Maria Plesker, "Is the importance of sexual morality overstated?" KNA International, September 19, 2025.

Leo "is more Benedict than Francis …": Mary McAleese, "Pope Leo XIV—the first 100 days," *The Tablet*, August 6, 2025. https://www.thetablet.co.uk/features/pope-leo-xiv-the-first-100-days/

"He's very still, quiet, and reserved …": Rev. James Martin SJ, interview with author, September 19, 2025.

"I hate my opponent and I don't want the best for them": President Trump, Charlie Kirk memorial service, September 21, 2025.

"He's the one, he can bring unity to the US Church …": Rev. James Martin SJ, interview with author, September 19, 2025.

"the Church has no authority whatsoever to confer priestly ordination on women": Pope John Paul II, "Ordinatio Sacerdotalis" ("Priestly Ordination"), May 22, 1994. https://www.vatican.va/content/john-paul-ii/en/apost_letters/1994/documents/hf_jp-ii_apl_19940522_ordinatio-sacerdotalis.html

a "niche issue" that Catholics in the global north had become "obsessed" with: Bishop Anthony Randazzo, Vatican press conference, October 4, 2024. https://www.bbcatholic.org.au/news/latest-news/obsession-over-women-s-ordination-harmful-bishop-randazzo-says

A document produced by the synod gathering … describes it as an "open question": the synod final document says, "the question of women's access to diaconal ministry remains open," October

Notes

24, 2024. https://www.synod.va/content/dam/synod/news/2024-10-26_final-document/ENG---Documento-finale.pdf

"examine the theological background, history, and will wait to see what the Vatican study commissions come back with": Pope Leo XIV, interview with Elise Ann Allen, July 2025.

A Vatican commission reported to Leo saying it had voted against ordaining women as deacons: "Sintesi della Commissione di Studio sul Diaconato Femminile" December 4, 2025. https://press.vatican.va/content/salastampa/it/bollettino/pubblico/2025/12/04/0950/01725.html

Leo "speaks to the process," she said ...: Helena Jeppesen-Spuhler, interview with author, September 29, 2025.

Leo is up against some "entrenched negative attitudes toward women, all cultural and non-theological" ...: Phyllis Zagano, email interview with author, September 23, 2025.

they couldn't simply "reorganize things, change them and 'put them back together,'": Pope Francis, letter to the Church in Germany, June 29, 2019. https://www.vaticannews.va/en/pope/news/2019-06/pope-francis-letter-german-church-synodality.html

The pope has even described the process as an "antidote" to polarization: Pope Leo XIV, interview with Elise Ann Alen, July 2025.

"must so arrange everything that the strong have something to yearn for and the weak nothing to run from": St. Benedict, *The Rule of St. Benedict*, ed. and trans. Timothy Fry, OSB (Liturgical Press, 1981), ch. 64.

4: QUIET REFORMER

In March 2025, from his hospital bed, he signed off the next phase of the synod process which, he ruled, would culminate in an "ecclesial assembly" in Rome in 2028: Isabella Piro, "Pope approves convocation of post-synodal Ecclesial Assembly in 2028," *Vatican News*, March 15, 2025. https://www.vaticannews.va/en/pope/news/2025-03/pope-approves-convocation-of-l-ecclesial-assembly-in-2028.html

Notes

"He's the Pope Paul VI to [Pope] John XXIII": interview on background, September 2025.

"Once this lion roars, nobody is going to be able to convince him 'no, Holy Father, we don't do things like that'": Dawn Eden Goldstein, interview with author, September 18, 2025.

Francis gave a simple "no" in a CBS interview: Norah O'Donnell interview with Pope Francis, CBS, May 19 and 20, 2024. https://www.rev.com/transcripts/pope-francis-interview-with-norah-odonnell

When he was the bishop of Chiclayo, he said he held "diocesan assemblies" in a "synodal style" for seven of his nine years there ...: Cardinal Robert Prevost, Vatican press conference attended by author, October 25, 2023. https://www.youtube.com/watch?v=TQxkzHM14Xc

Responding to a Canadian bishop, he stressed the need for a synodal approach in light of the deteriorating relationship between the US and Canada ...: Pope Leo XIV, question and answer session, October 24, 2025. https://www.vatican.va/content/leo-xiv/it/speeches/2025/october/documents/20251024-equipe-sinodali.html

"we had an excellent dialogue with him": Sister Nathalie Becquart, email interview with author, October 1, 2025.

One Church source I spoke to described Brambilla as a highly capable leader who works closely with the clergy in her office: discussion with author on background, January 16, 2025.

One source said that the women who worked with Leo in the department all spoke positively of him because he treated them as trusted collaborators: discussion with author on background, September 2025.

"It was easy to approach him ...": Helena Jeppesen-Spuhler, interview with author, September 29, 2025.

the status of the gathering was "unclear": Simone Orendain, "This cardinal is questioning the 'canonical status' of the synod," *Our Sunday Visitor*, October 1, 2024. https://www.oursundayvisitor.com/cardinal-questions-canonical-status-of-synod-because-so-many-non-bishops-are-participating/

a "hostile takeover" of the Catholic Church: Cardinal Gerhard

Notes

Müller interview with Raymond Arroyo, EWTN, October 7, 2022. https://ewtn.co.uk/article-cardinal-muller-on-synod-on-synodality-a-hostile-takeover-of-the-church-of-jesus-christ-we-must-resist/

and a step toward "Protestantization": Riccardo Cascioli, "Muller: 'The Synod, a step towards Protestantisation,'" *Daily Compass*, November 2, 2023. https://newdailycompass.com/en/mueller-the-synod-a-step-towards-protestantisation

Francis responded to this "storm of chattering": Cindy Wooden, "Pope defends decision to give women, laymen voting rights at synod," *Catholic Review*, October 2, 2024. https://catholicreview.org/pope-defends-decision-to-give-women-laymen-voting-rights-at-synod/

"Sometimes bishops or priests might feel, 'synodality is going to take away my authority' …": Pope Leo XIV, interview with Elise Ann Allen, July 2025.

1983 *Code of Canon Law* says that laypeople are permitted to "co-operate" in the power of governance, rather than "share": *Code of Canon Law* (Canon Law Society of America, 1983), canon 129.1–2.

The decision to use the weaker, and more ambiguous word "co-operate" was taken after a commission had been set by John Paul II: this is authoritatively analyzed by Elizabeth McDonough OP in "Jurisdiction Exercised by Non-Ordained Members in Religious Institutes," *Canon Law Society of America Proceedings* 58 (1996): 292–307.

Leo has been codifying Francis' openings to women such as changing the law: Pope Leo, legal ruling, "On the composition and presidency of the Pontifical Commission for Vatican City State", November 21, 2025. https://www.vatican.va/content/leo-xiv/en/apost_letters/documents/20251119-il-governatorato.html

"A lot is possible without ordination": Helena Jeppesen-Spuhler, interview with author, September 29, 2025.

called for laymen and laywomen to be "given greater opportunities for participation …": Synod final document, October 24, 2024. https://www.synod.va/content/dam/synod/news/2024-10-26_final-document/ENG---Documento-finale.pdf

Notes

if these reforms are to move beyond a "pious wish": Tom Reese SJ, "Canon lawyers and theologians recommend ways to make synodality more concrete," *Religion News Service*, October 9, 2024. https://religionnews.com/2024/10/09/canon-lawyers-and-theologians-make-synodality-concrete/

In his doctoral thesis, written decades before the current debates: Robert F. Prevost OSA, *The Office and Authority of the Local Prior in the Order of Saint Augustine* (The Pontifical University of St. Thomas (Angelicum), 1987).

a legal ruling that allowed lay brothers to lead orders as religious superiors: Pope Francis's rescript was made public on May 18, 2022. https://www.vaticannews.va/en/pope/news/2022-05/pope-allows-non-clerics-to-be-major-superiors-in-certain-cases.html

Two years later, a Benedictine community, St. Anselm's in New Hampshire, elected their first brother as the community's abbot: Brother Isaac Murphy OSB was elected abbot on June 17, 2024. https://www.saintanselmabbey.org/about-us/abbot

"occupy spaces as preachers and officiants of sacraments": a proposed "general framework" for an Amazonian rite was released by the Ecclesial Conference of the Amazon on April 5, 2025. https://adn.celam.org/wp-content/uploads/2025/04/ESP-doc-marco-general-del-rito-amazonico-digital.pdf

In Germany, a new council is in the works for laypeople and bishops to sit together on an advisory and decision-making body: this proposal was put forward by *Der Synodale Weg* (The Synodal Path), September 10, 2022. https://www.synodalerweg.de/english/documents

"decision-making structures of Church governance": Fifth Plenary Council of Australia, "Witnessing to the Equal Dignity of Women and Men." July 4–9, 2022. https://plenarycouncil.catholic.org.au/wp-content/uploads/2022/07/FINAL-Decree-4-Witnessing-to-the-Equal-Dignity-of-Women-and-Men.pdf

the archdiocese of Los Angeles alone reaching an $880-million settlement in October 2024 ...: "Archdiocese of Los Angeles agrees to pay $880 million to victims of clergy sexual abuse," *Associated Press*, October 17, 2024. https://apnews.com/article/

los-angeles-archdiocese-clergy-sexual-abuse-bf23e8967410017c036f765bb83910f6

"Sexual abuse is above all also an abuse of power": MHG Study, "Sexual abuse of minors by Catholic priests, deacons and male members of orders in the domain of the German Bishops' Conference," September, 2018. https://www.dbk.de/fileadmin/redaktion/diverse_downloads/Dossiers_alt/dossiers_2018/MHG-eng-Endbericht-Zusammenfassung-14-08-2018.pdf

"an account of pastoral activity in various areas ... based on the implicit assumption ...": Synod final document, October 24, 2024. https://www.synod.va/content/dam/synod/news/2024-10-26_final-document/ENG---Documento-finale.pdf

the detailed, 449-page Vatican report into the abuse and misconduct perpetrated by the former archbishop of Washington, DC, Theodore McCarrick: "Report on the Holy See's Institutional Knowledge and Decision-Making Related to Former Cardinal Theodore Edgar McCarrick (1930 to 2017)," November 10, 2025. https://www.vatican.va/resources/resources_rapporto-card-mccarrick_20201110_en.pdf

a new framework for holding bishops and religious superiors accountable for their actions: Pope Francis, "*Vos Estis Lux Mundi*" ("You are the Light of the World"), June 1, 2019, updated April 30, 2023. https://www.vatican.va/content/francesco/en/motu_proprio/documents/papa-francesco-motu-proprio-20190507_vos-estis-lux-mundi.html

the difficulties of some countries: set out in an annual report from the Pontifical Commission for the Protection of Minors, "Building a Culture of Safeguarding," October 1, 2025. https://www.tutelaminorum.org/annual-report/

Rupnik was accused by dozens of nuns of "sexual, psychological, or spiritual" abuse: Nicole Winfield, "Woman who say she was abused spiritually and sexually by a once-famous Jesuit demands transparency," *Associated Press*, February 21, 2024. https://apnews.com/article/vatican-jesuit-abuse-rupnik-pope-a858293e17b8a24599f868ae70d37e0e

Zanchetta was later convicted in Argentina: "Argentinian Bishop sentenced to prison for sexual abuse despite pope's defense,"

Notes

Guardian, March 4, 2022. Zanchetta was released on parole in September 2025. https://www.theguardian.com/world/2022/mar/04/argentine-catholic-bishop-gustavo-zanchetta-sentenced-sexual-abuse-pope-francis

One abuse survivor I spoke to said that Leo's quiet personality is reassuring ...: Matthias Katsch, interview with author, October 22, 2025.

a book entitled *Half Monks, Half Soldiers*: Pedro Salinas, *Mitad Monjes, Mitad Soldados* (Planeta Perù, 2015).

an independent report was commissioned by the Sodalitium ...: Kathleen McChesney, Monica Applewhite, Ian Elliott, "Report on Abuses and Response in the Sodalitium Christianae Vitae", February 10, 2017. https://sodalicio.org/wp-content/uploads/2017/02/Informe-Abusos-English.pdf

CNN reported on the allegations: Stefano Pozzebon, Christopher Lamb, Caitlin Stephen Hu and David von Blohn, "How Pope Leo dealt with years of abuse allegations in a powerful Catholic society in Peru," CNN, May 18, 2025. https://edition.cnn.com/2025/05/18/americas/pope-leo-peru-sodalitium-intl-latam

senior Church officials prevented this from happening, which, according to Ugaz, caused Bishop Prevost "great frustration": interview with author for CNN article, May 18, 2025.

"As prefect of the dicastery, he was very efficient in evaluating the evidence and obtaining the resignation of Archbishop Eguren ": interview on background, May 15, 2025.

it emerged that Francis was dissolving the entire Sodalitium society: Christopher Lamb, "Pope Francis dissolves influential Peruvian Catholic group after investigation found 'sadistic' abuses,'" CNN, January 23, 2025. https://edition.cnn.com/2025/01/21/americas/pope-dissolves-peruvian-catholic-group-intl-latam

a statement asking for "forgiveness from the entire Church and society for the pain caused ...": "Suppression of the Sodalitum Christianae Vitae," April 14, 2025. https://sodalitium.org/statements/suppression-of-the-sodalitium-christianae-vitae/#gsc.tab=0

Leo had "helped to achieve something that hasn't been done in

Notes

Church history …": Matthias Katsch, interview with author, October 22, 2025.

"Wherever a journalist is silenced, the democratic soul of a country is weakened …": Christopher Lamb, "Pope Leo praises work of journalists in first public comments on clerical abuse scandal," June 21, 2025. https://edition.cnn.com/2025/06/21/europe/pope-leo-church-abuse-scandal-message-intl

A Vatican investigation found him to have committed "abuse in the exercise of the apostolate of journalism": details of the investigation and expulsion were released by Peru's bishops' conference, September 25, 2024. https://noticias.iglesia.org.pe/nota-de-prensa-de-la-conferencia-episcopal-peruana-3/

Bermúdez, known for a combative style on social media, retorted that …: Alejandro Bermúdez, post on X, September 28, 2024. https://x.com/albermudezr/status/1840122771629625771?s=20

Following the news of the expulsions, the archbishop of Denver, Samuel Aquila, said he was "shocked and saddened": Archdiocese of Denver, statement, September 25, 2024. https://www.denvercatholic.org/archdiocese-of-denver-statement-on-sodalitium-christianae-vitae-expulsions-1

"something is deeply wrong with Rome's latest treatment of the SCV (Sodalitium)": Francis X. Maier, "Rome, the SCV and Accountability," *First Things*, September 27, 2024. https://firstthings.com/rome-the-scv-and-accountability/

Bermudez posted on X, linking to an article titled: Riccardo Cascioli, "Prevost and Co, anyone involved in sexual abuse should not be pope", *Daily Compass*, May 6, 2025. https://x.com/albermudezr/status/1919868404753645732?s=20

On another occasion he mused …: Alejandro Bermudez on X, May 2, 2025. https://x.com/albermudezr/status/1918352942601843139?s=20

"continued questions over his handling of sexual abuse have also cast a cloud over his prospects": The College of Cardinals Report. https://collegeofcardinalsreport.com/cardinals/robert-francis-prevost/

"Why Prevost's papal prospects prompt pushback": JD Flynn, *The*

Notes

Pillar, May 5, 2025. https://www.pillarcatholic.com/p/why-prevosts-papal-prospects-prompt

One of the accused priests was seen publicly celebrating Mass while under investigation by the Church: Julie Turkewitz, Simon Romero, Mitra Taj, Elisabetta Povoledo, and Tomás Munita, "Judgments Are Sharply Divided on Pope Leo's Handling of Sex Abuse Cases," *The New York Times*, June 28, 2025. https://www.nytimes.com/2025/06/28/world/americas/pope-leo-catholic-church-sexual-abuse-peru-bishop-prevost.html

Leo himself has said there has been "a lot of manipulation": Pope Leo XIV, interview with Elise Ann Allen, July 2025.

A Vatican source close to the investigation of the Sodalitium told me …: interview on background, May 15, 2025.

Coronado told me that he has "no ties with the Sodalitium,": email to author, November 5, 2025.

"known and had friendly relations with members [of the Sodalitum] over the years,": Riccardo Coronado, letter to *Crux*, August 6, 2025 (shared with author).

he did so to "give them a voice and to hold the Church hierarchy accountable for alleged misdeeds": Coronado, letter to *Crux*, August 6, 2025 (shared with author).

"Prevost was not pope at the time; the conclave had not happened…": Coronado, email to *National Catholic Reporter*, September 29, 2025 (shared with author).

"My understanding from good sources in Peru…": Austen Ivereigh, interview with author, September 30, 2025.

"Coronado has accused the pope of…": Coronado, email to *National Catholic Reporter*, September 29, 2025 (shared with author).

He insisted to me that Leo was "afraid of the truth …": WhatsApp message with author, 6 November 6, 2025.

"If you would ask me if I believe that Prevost covered up": email to author, November 5, 2025.

"Nobody can claim that he is without fault in this world…": Rev. Hans Zollner, interview with author, September 30, 2025.

"I would like to put a question mark over the Pope's statement …": KNA International report of speech given by the bishop at

Notes

the Rhineland-Palatinate state parliament, September 25, 2025. https://www.swr.de/swraktuell/rheinland-pfalz/mainz/mainzer-bischof-kritisiert-papst-leo-wegen-aussagen-zu-sexuellem-missbrauch-100.html

Both Francis and Leo have recommended *Lord of the World*: Robert Hugh Benson, *Lord of the World* (Christian Classics, 2016).

He called for AI to be developed according to an "ethical criterion" and warned about its impact on the "intellectual and neurological development" of children: "Message of Pope Leo XIV to Participants in the Second Annual Conference on Artificial Intelligence, Ethics, and Corporate Governance," June 17, 2025. https://www.vatican.va/content/leo-xiv/en/messages/pont-messages/2025/documents/20250617-messaggio-ia.html

"we Christians have at times incorrectly interpreted the scriptures …": Pope Francis, *Laudato Si'*, May 24, 2015. https://www.vatican.va/content/francesco/en/encyclicals/documents/papa-francesco_20150524_enciclica-laudato-si.html

"If we lose sight of the value of humanity …": Pope Leo XIV, interview with Elise Ann Allen, July 2025,

The growth of conspiracy theories and misinformation is, he says, "very destructive, very destructive": Pope Leo XIV, interview with Elise Ann Allen, July 2025.

One source told me that Leo would like to address the ethics and purpose of communication at some point: discussion with author on background, July 2025.

5: BALANCING THE BOOKS

Toward the end of 2023, the Vatican found him guilty of embezzlement and "self-laundering": statement from the Vatican, "*Comunicato e Sentenza del Tribunale dello Stato della Città del Vaticano,*" December 16, 2023. https://press.vatican.va/content/salastampa/it/bollettino/pubblico/2023/12/16/0896/01954.html?

Notes

He has said that the Vatican case against him "rests on nothing": Christopher Lamb, "Vatican's 'trial of the century' sees cardinal given five-and-a-half-year jail sentence," CNN, December 18, 2023. https://edition.cnn.com/2023/12/16/world/vatican-trial-cardinal-verdict-intl-cmd

had "not been able to watch any tennis": comments made to the author and others as he arrived at court, July 5, 2025.

"You are making that up as you go along, aren't you?" Samek said to Peña Parra. "That last answer, I suggest to you, is a lie": I was present in court for the evidence. These remarks were also reported by various news outlets.

"You said that I was not honest. I accept that": Archbishop Peña Parra, giving evidence in court, July 4, 2025.

Justice Knowles, in his judgment, said that he accepted the "honesty of his [Peña Parra's] evidence at trial ...": Mr. Justice Robin Knowles, "Athena v Holy See" judgment, February 21, 2025. https://www.judiciary.uk/wp-content/uploads/2025/02/Athena-v-Holy-See-Judgment-210225-FINAL.pdf

"How did you manage that, Edgar?" Pope Francis is said to have remarked after the ruling. Peña Parra replied: "I don't know!": discussion with author on background, March 2025.

"Bad choices,": Pope Leo XIV, interview with Elise Ann Allen, July 2025.

The major problem, Lord Camoys told me, was that large investment portfolios were being overseen by clerics who were not trained in financial management or administration: in a series of interviews between the author and Lord Camoys, 2017–21.

It had great redevelopment potential and, the court was told, a supposed value of £275 million: "Athena v Holy See" judgment, February 21, 2025. https://www.judiciary.uk/wp-content/uploads/2025/02/Athena-v-Holy-See-Judgment-210225-FINAL.pdf

The £275 million figure, the Vatican said, had "no basis in reality": "Athena v Holy See", judgment, February 21, 2025. https://www.judiciary.uk/wp-content/uploads/2025/02/Athena-v-Holy-See-Judgment-210225-FINAL.pdf

Notes

while Mr. Mincione had been "ambitious and opportunistic" in seeking this payment it did not show "serious wrongdoing": "Athena v Holy See" judgment, February 21, 2025. https://www.judiciary.uk/wp-content/uploads/2025/02/Athena-v-Holy-See-Judgment-210225-FINAL.pdf

One Church source said that the Holy See faced paying £1 million ($1.2 million) each month in interest on the loan: discussion with author on background, March 2025.

the Vatican effectively purchasing an "empty box": Salvatore Cernuzio, "Vatican trial: Secretariat of State requests €177 million compensation for moral and reputational damages," *Vatican News*, September 29, 2023. https://www.vaticannews.va/en/vatican-city/news/2023-09/vatican-trial-secretariat-of-state-requests-177-million.html

"I would give Torzi nothing, and I would put him in jail several times": Christopher Lamb, "Pope's chief of staff gives evidence in landmark London property trial," CNN, July 5, 2025. https://edition.cnn.com/2024/07/05/europe/popes-chief-of-staff-london-property-trial-intl-latam

A legal source told me that the Vatican had little choice but to pay Torzi …: interview on background, July 2025.

with the captions "feeling at home" and "my paradise": Claire Giangravé, "Vatican prosecutors focus on role of 'Cardinal's Lady' in financial trial,'" *Religion News Service*, October 13, 2022. https://religionnews.com/2022/10/13/vatican-prosecutors-focus-on-role-of-cardinals-lady-in-financial-trial/

She denied wrongdoing: Ferruccio Pinotti, "*Cecilia, la consulente (senza laurea) con la passione per l'intelligence: 'I servizi segreti? Loro mi stimano,'*" *Corriere della Sera*, October 14, 2020. https://www.corriere.it/cronache/20_ottobre_14/cecilia-consulente-senza-laurea-la-passione-l-intelligence-servizi-segreti-loro-mi-stimano-b5ec541a-0ddb-11eb-9df8-9ad18fda6e17.shtml

"administrators are bound to fulfil their function with the diligence of a good householder …": *Code of Canon Law* (Canon Law Society of America, 1983), canon 1284.

According to a 2019 report: "*Memoria a sostegno*" (supporting statement), "To the Esteemed Court Vatican City State,"

Notes

attorneys for the Secretariat of State, October 4, 2023, shared with author.

In the London trial, Justice Knowles put his finger on some of the deeper problems ...: "Athena v Holy See" judgment, February 21, 2025. https://www.judiciary.uk/wp-content/uploads/2025/02/Athena-v-Holy-See-Judgment-210225-FINAL.pdf

According to figures from 2022: Secretariat for the Economy, "2022 Mission Budget: Presentation Holy See," January 28, 2022. https://www.obolodisanpietro.va/content/dam/obolodisanpietro/2022/bilancio-di-missione-2022/2022-Mission-Budget-Presentation-Holy-See.pdf

in 2015 the Catholic archdiocese of Cologne, Germany, revealed that it was worth €3.35 billion: Tom Heneghan, "German Catholic archdiocese reveals it's richer than Vatican," *Reuters*, February 19, 2015. https://www.reuters.com/article/world/german-catholic-archdiocese-reveals-its-richer-than-vatican-idUSKBN0LN1J8/

The Vatican accounts for 2024 showed a structural deficit of €44 million: Joshua McElwee, "Vatican Reports first budget surplus after years of deficits", *Reuters,* November 2025. https://www.reuters.com/world/vatican-reports-first-budget-surplus-after-years-deficits-2025-11-26/

Francis wrote to the College of Cardinals saying that there was a "serious prospective imbalance": Pope Francis, letter to "the College of Cardinals and to the Prefects and Heads of the Curial Institutions, the offices of the Roman Curia and the Institutions connected to the Holy See", November 21, 2024. https://press.vatican.va/content/salastampa/en/bollettino/pubblico/2024/11/21/241121d.html

In 2024, €58 million ($67 million) was raised in annual donations: Peter's Pence, "Annual Disclosure, 2024," June 2025. https://www.obolodisanpietro.va/en/rapporti-annuali/rapporto-annuale-2024.html

a decrease of 23 per cent between 2015 and 2019: Andrea Tornielli, "Fr. Guerrero: Peter's Pence supports the mission of the Church," *Vatican News*, June 25, 2021. https://www.

Notes

vaticannews.va/en/vatican-city/news/2021-06/guerrero-peters-pence-economy-holy-see-vatican.html

A priest who knew Bishop Prevost in Peru described his "mathematical" mentality ...: Regina Garcia Cano and Franklin Briceño, "Peruvians know him as the priest who went from 'Chicago to Chiclayo.' He is now Pope Leo XIV,'" *Associated Press*, May 9, 2025. https://apnews.com/article/peru-pope-leo-chiclayo-vatican-prevost-0f99859e5749decadade2d24ba7811dd

"Allow me to do some calculations with you ...": Pope Leo XIV, "Audience with Students participating in the Jubilee of the World of Education," October 30, 2025. https://press.vatican.va/content/salastampa/en/bollettino/pubblico/2025/10/30/251030d.html

Vatican (Apsa) has reported a €62.2 million ($72.3 million) profit for 2025, up by €16 million: Salvatore Cernuzio, "APSA budget shows increased profits, support for Holy See," *Vatican News*, July 28, 2025. https://www.vaticannews.va/en/vatican-city/news/2025-07/apsa-budget-shows-increased-profits-support-for-holy-see.html

"a form of social housing": remarks made by Bishop Nunzio Galantino, then president of Apsa, reported in *Vatican News*, October 22, 2019. https://www.vaticannews.va/en/vatican-city/news/2019-10/nunzio-galantino-apsa-vatican-not-at-risk-of-default.html

Almost $16 million was given in 2024: Peter's Pence, "Annual Disclosure, 2024," June 2025. https://www.obolodisanpietro.va/en/rapporti-annuali/rapporto-annuale-2024.html

The fund stands at $250 million: according to the Papal Foundation, as of 2023. https://www.thepapalfoundation.org/the-holy-fathers-calling/

"This room could raise a billion to help the Church, so long as we have the right pope": William Cash, "To understand Vatican politics, follow the US dollar," *The Times*, May 3, 2025. https://www.thetimes.com/article/9679eba1-7498-4b43-9ff4-d2133526f2c5

Their preferred candidate for pope was the Hungarian Cardinal Péter Erdö...: Alexander Faludy, "Conclave: is a Hungarian pope in the smoke?", *Balkan Insight*, March 11, 2025. https://balkaninsight.com/2025/03/11/conclave-is-a-hungarian-pope-in-the-smoke/

Santorum criticized Francis on climate change ...: interview with Philadelphia Talk Radio 1210 host Dom Giordano, June 1, 2015.

Santorum was also unhappy with a remark the late pope made: he told the radio talk show host Hugh Hewitt that "it's sometimes very difficult to listen to the Pope," January, 2015.

paid a $250 million "good will gesture" out of moral responsibility: "Vatican bank image hurt as JP Morgan closes account," *Reuters*, March 19, 2012. https://www.reuters.com/article/markets/vatican-bank-image-hurt-as-jp-morgan-closes-account-idUSL6E8EJ1F9/

including two belonging to Pope Paul VI, who had died in 1978. One of the late pope's accounts held €125,310 and another $296,151: Gianluigi Nuzzi, *Via Crucis* (Chiarelettere, 2015).

in 2024 it made a profit of €32.8 million: IOR press release, "IOR: Results at 31 December 2024 Approved," June 11, 2025. https://press.vatican.va/content/salastampa/en/info/2025/06/11/250611a.html

By May 2024 the watchdog had given the IOR assessments of full or high compliance in thirty-five out of the thirty-nine categories: Council of Europe Moneyval report, May 21, 2024. https://rm.coe.int/moneyval-2024-6-hs-vcs-5thround-1stenhfur/1680afcb11

convicted by the Vatican court of embezzlement and money laundering: Caloia was convicted on January 21, 2021; this conviction was then upheld a year later.

"If we don't know how to look after money ...": remarks reported by Gianluigi Nuzzi, *Via Crucis* (Chiarelettere, 2015).

Francis's decision ... that the Secretariat of State hand over the control of managing its assets to Apsa: legal ruling by Pope Francis, December 26, 2020. https://www.vatican.va/content/francesco/en/motu_proprio/documents/papa-francesco-motu-proprio-20201226_una-migliore-organizzazione.html

Notes

"if more efficient and convenient": legal ruling by Pope Leo XIV, September 29, 2025. https://www.vatican.va/content/leo-xiv/it/apost_letters/documents/20250929-coniuncta-cura.html

"I wouldn't throw good money after bad": from a conversation with someone present during the discussion.

he would hire PricewaterhouseCoopers (PwC) to carry out a complete audit: "Vatican appoints PricewaterhouseCoopers to audit accounts," BBC, December 5, 2015. https://www.bbc.co.uk/news/world-europe-35018430

an anonymous letter condemning Francis's pontificate: it was originally penned under the pseudonym "Demos" and circulated in 2022. https://www.cal-catholic.com/the-cardinal-pell-memo-in-full/

"toxic nightmare": Cardinal George Pell, "The Catholic Church must free itself from this toxic nightmare," *The Spectator*, January 11, 2023. https://www.spectator.co.uk/article/the-catholic-church-must-free-itself-from-this-toxic-nightmare/

Francis paid tribute to Pell's "determination and wisdom": Pope Francis, telegram of condolence, January 11, 2023. https://www.vaticannews.va/en/pope/news/2023-01/pope-telegram-cardinal-pell-death.html

Becciu claimed €10 million ($11 million) in damages (to be given to charity): Nicole Winfield, "Vatican Cardinal says ouster deprived him of possible papacy," *Associated Press*, November 19, 2020. https://apnews.com/article/international-news-lawsuits-london-pope-francis-da25455c97883063ad9b204bdbaf18b0

"there was no explicit will to exclude me": Paolo Matta, "Conclave, Cardinal Becciu's clarification: 'I will be there,'" *L'Unione Sarda* (English), April 22, 2025. https://www.unionesarda.it/en/conclave-becciu39-s-clarification-quot-i-will-be-therequot-k99fuwtr

The first, dated September 2023 and signed "Francesco," was kept with one of the late pope's secretaries ... "You are already thinking about the conclave": Francesco A. Grana, "*Le due lettere di Francesco: 'Becciu fuori dal Conclave*," Il Fatto Quotidiano, September 23, 2025. https://www.ilfattoquotidiano.

Notes

it/in-edicola/articoli/2025/09/23/le-due-lettere-di-francesco-becciu-fuori-dal-conclave/8135283/

"The Vatican has oftentimes given the wrong message, which certainly doesn't inspire people to say, 'Oh, I'd like to help you …'": Pope Leo XIV, interview with Elise Ann Allen, July 2025.

cut the pay of cardinals: legal ruling by Pope Francis, March 24, 2021. https://press.vatican.va/content/salastampa/it/bollettino/pubblico/2021/03/24/0180/00395.html

He's also released new regulations on employment in the Vatican: "Regolomento Generale della Curia Romana", November 24, 2025. https://press.vatican.va/content/salastampa/it/bollettino/pubblico/2025/11/24/0896/01618.html and "Regolamento del Personale della Curia Romana", November 24, 2025. https://press.vatican.va/content/salastampa/it/bollettino/pubblico/2025/11/24/0896/01619.html

EPILOGUE: GEN Z CATHOLICISM

Parolin spoke about the digital world as a "new frontier": conversation with Nicola Camporiondo, Instagram, August 2, 2025. https://www.instagram.com/nicola.camporiondo/?hl=en

"Faced with cultural changes throughout history, the Church has never remained passive": Pope Leo XIV, address to Catholic digital missionaries and influencers, July 29, 2025. https://www.vatican.va/content/leo-xiv/en/speeches/2025/july/documents/20250729-missionari-digitali.html

In France, over the Easter of 2025, around 17,800 adults and adolescents were received into the Church: according to an annual survey by the French Bishops' Conference, April, 2025. https://eglise.catholique.fr/approfondir-sa-foi/la-celebration-de-la-foi/les-sacrements/le-bapteme/baptemes-adultes/#adultes

A 2024 survey in England and Wales showed a six-year rise in monthly church attendance …: research carried out by the Bible Society, April 7, 2025. https://www.biblesociety.org.uk/research/quiet-revival

Notes

In New York, priests are reporting are rise in the numbers of young people ...: Kirsten Fleming, "New Yorkers turning to the church, number of Catholic converts soaring, according to priests", *New York Post,* November 16, 2025. https://nypost.com/2025/11/16/lifestyle/new-yorkers-turning-to-the-church-number-of-catholic-converts-soaring-priests-say/

His election has also seen a boom in interest in vocations: I was told of this interest by a senior Augustinian, and it is reported here by *The Augustinian*, magazine of the Province of St Thomas of Villanova, Fall 2025. https://augustinian.org/wp-content/uploads/2025/11/Aug_mag_fall2025_FINAL.pdf and Michelle Martin, "Pope's election increases interest in Augustinian vocations", *Chicago Catholic,* September 18, 2025 https://www.chicagocatholic.com/chicagoland/-/article/2025/09/18/pope-s-election-increases-interest-in-augustinian-vocations

His mother, Antonia Salzano, told me when I interviewed her for CNN that she had been "converted by her son": Christopher Lamb, "Carlo Acutis, nicknamed 'God's influencer,' becomes the first 'millennial' saint", CNN, September, 8, 2025. https://edition.cnn.com/2025/09/07/europe/millennial-saint-carlo-acutis-intl

the journalist Lamorna Ash attempted to understand those grappling with the Christian faith in Britain today: Lamorna Ash, *Don't Forget We're Here Forever* (Bloomsbury, 2025).

"There is something about the particular structure and rituals within faith, it's just a different kind of architecture ...": interview with author; and in Joseph Ataman and Christopher Lamb, "Faith is a hit among Gen Z. The Catholic Church may have influencers to thank," CNN, September 15, 2025. https://edition.cnn.com/2025/09/15/europe/faith-gen-z-catholic-church-influencers-intl-cmd

"While those experiences may be 'reassuring,' ...": Pope Leo XIV, address to members of the International Youth Advisory Body, October 31, 2025. https://www.vatican.va/content/leo-xiv/en/speeches/2025/october/documents/20251031-iyab.html

he plays Wordle with his brother: John Prevost has talked about playing Wordle with Pope Leo in interviews, including

283

Notes

with NBC News on May 8, 2025, and NBC Chicago, August 14, 2025. https://www.nbcchicago.com/news/local/does-pope-leo-still-play-wordle-with-his-brother-his-family-reveals-answer/3810335/

spotted using the Duolingo language app: users of the app spotted user @drprevost—the same as his now defunct X account—using the app for German and Italian studies. Activity logs indicated sessions at 3 a.m.

When passing in his popemobile he was even heard shouting, "They lost!": this occurred during the Wednesday General Audience, October 15, 2025.

"Live well and the times will be good. We are the times": St. Augustine, Discourse 80.8.

Madonna ... appealed to Leo: Madonna shared her plea with Pope Leo to visit Gaza on social media, August 11, 2025.

"Never again war, never again war!": Pope Paul VI, address to the United Nations, October 4, 1965. https://www.vatican.va/content/paul-vi/en/speeches/1965/documents/hf_p-vi_spe_19651004_united-nations.html

South Korean Catholics make up around 11 per cent of the population: Philip Connor, "6 Facts about South Korea's growing Christian population," Pew Research Center, August 12, 2014. https://www.pewresearch.org/short-reads/2014/08/12/6-facts-about-christianity-in-south-korea/

"We need a counter-narrative": Antonio Spadaro, "Trump & the Grand Theater of the World," *Commonweal*, August 14, 2025. https://www.commonwealmagazine.org/donald-trump-showrunner-spadaro-antonio-narrative

Pope Paul VI's 1968 encyclical: *Humanae vitae*, July 25, 1968. https://www.vatican.va/content/paul-vi/en/encyclicals/documents/hf_p-vi_enc_25071968_humanae-vitae.html

"Looked at another way, calling Robert Prevost the 'least American of the Americans' ...": David Gibson, "Why an American Pope?", *American Catholic Studies*, vol. 136, no.3 (Fall 2025): 1–9.

About the Author

Christopher Lamb is CNN's Vatican correspondent. He covered the funeral of Pope Francis and the conclave that elected Pope Leo XIV. He has been a journalist for two decades, starting as a reporter for the *Daily Telegraph* where he worked on the newspaper's diary column, a role that tasked him with breaking stories from the world of politics, showbusiness, royalty and the arts. As a Vatican reporter, he seeks to combine journalistic instincts with his understanding of theology and religion. Lamb studied theology at the University of Durham and worked for several years at *The Tablet*, a Catholic publication. His first book, *The Outsider*, lifted the lid on the resistance Pope Francis faced in his battle to reform the Catholic Church. He is based in CNN's Rome and London bureaux.

RAISING READERS
Books Build Bright Futures

Dear Reader,

We'd love your attention for one more page to tell you about the crisis in children's reading, and what we can all do.

Studies have shown that reading for fun is the **single biggest predictor of a child's future success** – more than family circumstance, parents' educational background or income. It improves academic results, mental health, wealth, communication skills and ambition.

The number of children reading for fun is in rapid decline. Young people have a lot of competition for their time, and a worryingly high number do not have a single book at home.

Our business works extensively with schools, libraries and literacy charities, but here are some ways we can all raise more readers:

- Reading to children for just 10 minutes a day makes a difference
- Don't give up if your children aren't regular readers – there will be books for them!
- Visit bookshops and libraries to get recommendations
- Encourage them to listen to audiobooks
- Support school libraries
- Give books as gifts

Thank you for reading.
www.JoinRaisingReaders.com